Plating

FOR GOLD

Plating for Gold

A DECADE OF DESSERTS FROM THE WORLD AND NATIONAL PASTRY TEAM CHAMPIONSHIPS

Tish Boyle

WILEY

JOHN WILEY & SONS, INC.

Photos © John Uher for competition years 2000–2005 and 2009–2010. Photos © Jeff Kaufman for 2006–2007, and © Jim Brown for 2008.

Published by John Wiley & Sons, Inc., Hoboken, New Jersey

Published simultaneously in Canada

For general information on our other products and services or for technical support, please contact our Customer Care Department within the United States at (800) 762-2974, outside the United States at (317) 572-3993 or fax (317) 572-4002.

Wiley publishes in a variety of print and electronic formats and by print-on-demand. Some material included with standard print versions of this book may not be included in e-books or in print-on-demand. If this book refers to media such as a CD or DVD that is not included in the version you purchased, you may download this material at http://booksupport.wiley.com. For more information about Wiley products, visit www.wiley.com.

Design by Vertigo Design NYC

Illustrations by Cheryl Grubbs

LIBRARY OF CONGRESS CATALOGING-IN-PUBLICATION DATA:

Boyle, Tish.
Plating for gold : a decade of desserts from the world and national pastry team championships / Tish Boyle.
p. cm.
Includes index.
ISBN 978-1-118-05984-5 (cloth); ISBN 978-1-118-28106-2 (ebk.); ISBN 978-1-118-28107-9 (ebk.); ISBN 978-1-118-28109-3 (ebk.)
1. Desserts. 2. Pastry. 3. Cookbooks. I. Boyle, Tish II. Title.
TX773.B694 2012
2011032552

Printed in China

10 9 8 7 6 5 4 3 2 1

To all the talented pastry chefs who were brave enough
to put their reputations on the line and compete in the
World and National Pastry Team Championships

CONTENTS

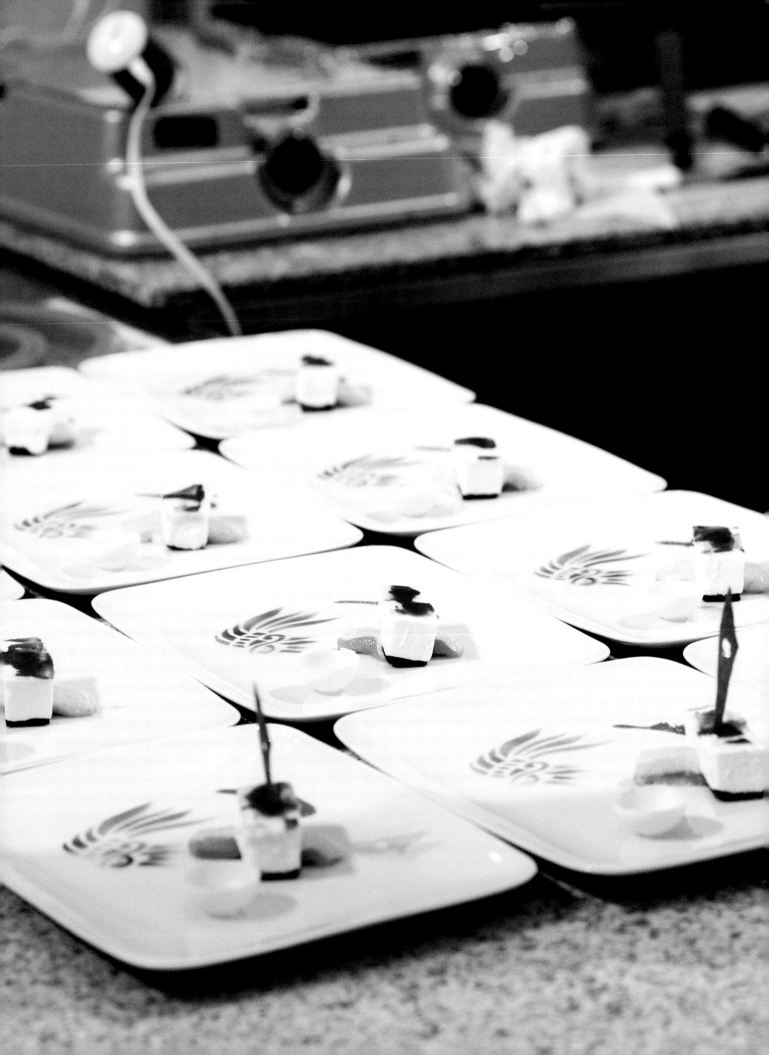

INTRODUCTION

A PLATED DESSERT IS THE MEASURE OF A PASTRY CHEF. THE ARRANGING OF DESSERT COMPONENTS ON A PLATE—A SLICE OF CAKE, A QUENELLE OF SORBET, A TWIRL OF TUILE—IS AN ART FORM, AND ONE THAT REQUIRES A COMBINATION OF TECHNICAL SKILL, A SENSE OF TIMING, AND AN EYE FOR DESIGN.

Pastry chefs assemble plated desserts every day at restaurants around the world, where, informally at least, they are judged by diners. Here, on home turf, the chef is not under much pressure and is motivated by the opportunity to gain recognition from critics and the restaurant's clientele. But put a formal spin on this ritual by having a group of top pastry chefs as the judges analyzing every step of the process and scrutinizing every detail of the finished product, and then you have a pastry competition. This is real pressure, and it's the type of pressure that challenges competitors to step out of their comfort zone, learn new tricks, and exceed their reach.

This book focuses on America's most prestigious pastry competition, the Pastry Team Championships—World and National—along with fifty recipes for plated desserts from the top teams that have competed over the years. These team competitions bring together the most talented pastry chefs in the world in a three-day whirlwind of sweat, skill, and high drama, with big money and pastry bragging rights as the ultimate prize.

The championships were started in 1999 by Michael Schneider, the co-owner of a company that publishes *Dessert Professional*, a pastry magazine for professionals. Having worked with pastry chefs for many years, Schneider came to consider them more as artists than craftsmen. Instead of paint or clay, however, these artists use flour, sugar, eggs, and butter as their medium. Schneider's idea for the championships was inspired by the Coupe du Monde de la Pâtisserie, a global pastry competition that was founded in 1989 by Pastry Chef Gabriel Paillasson M.O.F. The "Coupe," as it's known, takes place every two years in Lyon, France, and brings together the world's finest dessert experts in a highly demanding head-to-head competition. In the Coupe, each participating country is represented by a team of three, and each team has ten hours in which to prepare a daunting menu that includes a plated dessert, three chocolate desserts, three frozen fruit desserts, an ice sculpture, a chocolate sculpture, and a pulled sugar showpiece. Technical, artistic, and performance skills are put to the test, and each team is under considerable pressure, with the honor of their home country at stake. As one might expect, countries that compete successfully in Olympic sports are usually represented at this event, including the United States, France, Switzerland, Japan, and Italy, to name a few.

For his competition, Schneider decided to take the idea of the Coupe du Monde to a new level, to create a pastry championship that was, unquestionably, the most challenging in the world. He opted to alternate national and world competitions, with the national challenges held in odd-numbered years and the world competitions in even years. Whichever team won the national event would represent the U.S. at the world event the following year. The first competition took place in Beaver Creek, Colorado, in 1999. From the beginning, competitors—even seasoned Coupe veterans—found the new championship to be a grueling test of will and skill. In this competition's format, each team has thirteen hours over the course of two days to present the following items:

— A plated dessert

— An entremets (cake)

— An entremets glacé (frozen bombe)

— Three types of bonbons

— Three types of *petites gâteaux* (small cakes)

— A sugar showpiece

— A chocolate showpiece

— An amenity piece composed of chocolate and sugar, on which to present the bonbons

Scoring is based on a point system, with 40 percent of the total score determined by taste, 30 percent by showpieces, and 30 percent by how cleanly and efficiently each team works. Each team has two judges representing them. At the end of the thirteen hours, when the final whistle blows and all work stops, each team has a half hour to transport their work, which can include huge sugar and chocolate showpieces, from their kitchen to the presentation table. This can be a stressful maneuver, a time when disaster can strike and dreams can shatter. At the 2003 National Pastry Team Championship, for example, Pastry Chef Chris Hanmer created one of the most magnificent sugar pieces anyone had ever seen. Just as Hanmer was about to place his six-foot-tall, *Phantom of the Opera*–inspired piece on the presentation table, he accidently dipped it forward a tiny bit. He realized this and compensated by tilting it back. When he did this, the piece moved in a whiplike motion and suddenly exploded into tiny bits of pulled sugar. At the end, Hanmer stood there holding the base of the piece, the only thing that was intact. None of the shattered pieces of sugar around him was bigger than a silver dollar. Hanmer, head down, simply swept up the mess and returned to his kitchen without saying a word. A producer from the

Food Network, which was filming the event, was not quite so stoic—she broke down in a flood of tears.

There are other challenges inherent in this event. "One big difference between the Coupe du Monde and the Pastry Team Championships," notes Schneider, "is that at the Coupe, the use of molds by the chefs to create their elaborate showpieces is accepted. So if a team wants to bring a mold in the shape of a six-foot scorpion, no problem. I can't emphasize enough how much this means in the heat of the competition. Having a mold at hand to create intricate shapes that are part of a showpiece is a huge labor- and time-saver. When you have to form an animal or object without a mold, things can get pretty hairy." In the Pastry Team Championships, the use of complex molds is strictly forbidden. The only molds that are allowed are ones for simple geometric shapes—it is unrealistic, explains Schneider, to expect chefs to create a perfect sphere or cube.

Other rules also create problems for competitors. Each team is required to submit a detailed recipe of each dessert they are presenting, including all ingredients and amounts. If the judges can't taste an ingredient listed in a team's recipe, it's considered to be a violation, which usually results in a large scoring deduction. One year, for example, the Swiss team made a plated dessert that was supposed to contain lavender. But none of the judges tasted any lavender, and the team received an enormous deduction. Afterwards, they tried to argue their case—they only used a scant amount, they said, because lavender can be overpowering—but to no avail. If the team used such a small amount that a panel of chefs with highly refined palates could not detect it, then what was the point of using any at all?

Another year, the Italian team was the focus of a scoring controversy. They presented a plated dessert that was enveloped in a veil of vapor. To create the vapor, a small piece of dry ice was concealed in a covered container on the plate. During the judging of the dessert, the head judge, who was Swiss, warned another judge to "be careful when tasting this—dry ice is poisonous, you know." In the end, the Italian team lost out to Switzerland for third place by one point. The Italian Team, who had heard about the "poisonous" remark, complained about the possibility of the remark having a negative effect on their score. Had one of the judges who was tasting Team Italy's plated dessert given one less point to them because of the comment, it would have affected the outcome of the competition. In the end, though the final scores stood, Schneider agreed that the remark was contentious and did not ask the Swiss judge to return as head judge of the competition.

With a total prize purse of $50,000 and an opportunity to be called one of the world's finest pastry chefs, it's not hard to see why the World Pastry Team Championship attracts so many competitors. But the competition itself is no easy feat. Some teams will prepare for up to eighteen months in advance, meeting weekly or more for long practice sessions. To get ready for the 2010 event, Team Japan actually staged mock competitions, creating all required elements, including showpieces, as if it were the real championship. They did this *fifteen times* before the actual event. With this work ethic and preparation, it is no surprise that Team Japan captured gold at the 2010 competition.

Michael Schneider sees the pastry industry as a whole as the benefactor of these competitions. "In a funny sort of way I think the National and World Pastry Championships do more for the dessert industry than any other event. They inspire pastry chefs to try new techniques and reach levels that they might not have attempted otherwise. And because the events are televised, pastry chefs have gained recognition and respect for what they do." This recognition translates into career advancement and prestige that is worth more than any one-time financial reward. Of course the money's nice, too.

RECOMMENDED EQUIPMENT

IT MATTERS LITTLE HOW MUCH EQUIPMENT WE USE; IT MATTERS MUCH THAT WE BE MASTERS OF ALL WE DO USE.   —*Sam Abell*

A pastry chef competing at competition level needs to use the best equipment available. Though each team will have their own specific list of equipment required for their showpieces and desserts, following is a list of basic equipment that most teams use during the course of a competition.

Basic Equipment

CAKE DECORATING TURNTABLE: Turntables are useful for applying frosting to cakes and entremets.

HOTEL PANS: These stainless steel pans are available in various sizes and are useful for baking custards and preparations in a water bath, or chilling down mousses and other fillings quickly.

SAUCEPANS AND SAUTÉ PANS: A good selection of assorted saucepans and sauté pans are necessary for a number of tasks in the pastry kitchen. Choose heavy-bottomed, high-quality pans for your collection.

STAINLESS STEEL BOWLS: You should have a variety of sizes, from small to large.

TIMER: A good timer, preferably with the ability for multiple time settings, can spell the difference between success and disaster during a competition.

Bakeware

CAKE PANS: These pans are now available in a variety of materials, including silicone, tinned steel, and aluminum.

CAKE RINGS: These stainless steel rings are available in a variety of diameters and heights and are used for molding cakes and individual desserts.

COOLING RACKS: Made of chrome-plated steel wire, these racks are used for cooling baked goods and glazing cakes and confections.

FLEXIBLE SILICONE MOLDS: Made of silicone-coated fiberglass, these molds come in a huge variety of sizes and shapes. They can be used for baking as well as molding chocolate and frozen desserts.

SHEET PANS: These rimmed rectangular, aluminum baking pans come in quarter, half, and full sizes. Make sure that yours are not warped before the event.

SILICONE BAKING MATS: Used for lining sheet pans, these handy mats can withstand oven temperatures up to 500°F (260°C). Available in full- or half-sheet pan sizes.

TART AND TARTLET PANS: Made of tinned steel, these pans have fluted sides and usually have removable bottoms. Available in a variety of sizes in round, rectangular, and square shapes.

TUILE TEMPLATES: Many pastry chefs make their own tuile templates from large plastic lids, but you can also purchase high-quality templates made from high-density polyethylene in a huge variety of shapes.

Scaling and Measuring Tools

DIGITAL SCALES: Since pastry is all about precision, having a good scale is important. Sensitive scales that can measure small amounts generally have a small capacity, so you might want to have one scale for small amounts and another for larger ones.

MEASURING CUPS AND SPOONS: You should have a variety of liquid and dry measuring cups on hand and a few sets of measuring spoons to measure small ingredient amounts that might be too small to register on your scale.

THERMOMETERS: You will need a good digital instant-read thermometer that is able to read a wide range of temperatures, and you may need, depending on your preference, a digital probe thermometer and a deep-fat or candy thermometer for other tasks. A laser thermometer is an infrared thermometer that measures the electromagnetic radiation coming from the surface of a sauce, or whatever it's aimed at.

Small Tools

CAKE COMBS: Made from plastic or metal, these tools have serrated edges and are used for making decorative designs on cakes, pastries, and chocolate.

DOUGH DOCKER: A roller with spikes, a docker is used to prick doughs like puff pastry, which prevents them from rising too much during baking.

GRATERS: A box grater is useful for some grating and slicing tasks, while a citrus zester can be used to remove small amounts of zest from citrus fruit. A rasp (or microplane grater) is a more efficient tool for zesting citrus fruit, and can also be used for finely grating chocolate.

KNIVES: A variety of high-quality knives are crucial to pastry work. You will need an assortment that includes a chef's knife, utility knife, paring knife, and cake, bread, and slicing knives.

IMMERSION BLENDER: Also known as a hand or stick blender, this tool functions as an inverted blender. The advantage is that you can use this tool directly in a saucepan or pot.

LADLES: Available in a variety of sizes, ladles are useful for portioning sauces and other liquids.

MANDOLINE: This utensil is used to uniformly slice or julienne fruit and vegetables. A mandoline will also cut paper-thin slices for making fruit chip garnishes.

PARCHMENT PAPER TRIANGLES: These precut triangles can quickly be turned into small parchment paper cones, or cornets, for delicate piping jobs.

PASTRY BAGS: These cone-shaped bags come in assorted sizes and are available in nylon, cloth, or plastic. Disposable plastic pastry bags are most convenient to use in a competition.

PASTRY BRUSHES: Available in several sizes, with plastic or wooden handles and natural, nylon, or silicone bristles, these are used for jobs such as applying egg wash or glaze, prepping cake pans, and decorating *macarons*.

PASTRY CUTTERS: Sold individually or in sets, pastry or cookie cutters are available in an endless variety of shapes and sizes.

PASTRY TIPS: Made of nickel-plated metal, pastry or piping tips come in a large variety of shapes and sizes. Generally, the higher the number on the tip, the larger its opening.

PEELERS, CORERS, AND REAMERS: You will need a swivel-bladed peeler (make sure that the blade is sharp) for peeling fruit, a manual apple corer for coring fruit, and a lemon reamer made of wood, metal, or plastic for juicing citrus fruit.

PLASTIC SQUEEZE BOTTLES: These bottles are primarily used for decorating plates with sauce.

ROLLING PINS: Available in an array of sizes, rolling pins are usually made of wood, but are also available in marble, plastic, and porcelain.

SCOOPS: Used for portioning dough and scooping ice cream, sorbet, and mousses, spring-operated scoops are an essential tool. Choose the appropriate shapes and sizes for your needs during the competition. Melon ballers (also known as Parisienne scoops) are available in round and oval shapes and are essential for forming small, perfect rounds or ovals of fruit or other ingredients.

SIEVES: A fine-mesh sieve is useful for sifting dry ingredients, while a chinois is ideal for straining sauces and fillings.

SPATULAS AND SCRAPERS: You should have an assortment of rubber and silicone, high temperature–resistant spatulas for tasks such as scraping batters, stirring sauces, and folding ingredients together. A plastic bowl scraper is useful for scraping out every bit of batter from a bowl. Regular and offset metal spatulas in an assortment of sizes are essential for tasks such as applying and smoothing frosting, leveling batter, and transferring cake slices.

WHISKS: An assortment of small and large whisks is needed for tasks such as emulsifying sauces and ganache, or incorporating air into a batter.

Tools for Chocolate Work

CHOCOLATE MOLDS: Rigid polycarbonate plastic molds yield excellent results and are easier to care for than tin molds.

CHOCOLATE CUTTERS: Made of tinned steel or fiberglass and plastic composite, chocolate cutters have sharp edges and are available in a variety of sizes and shapes.

CARAMEL BARS: These metal bars are used for framing ganache and caramel to a specific thickness and dimension.

DIPPING TOOLS: These come in a variety of shapes, and are used for dipping ganache, fruit, nuts, or confections in chocolate or fondant.

FONDANT FUNNEL: This metal or plastic funnel is used for filling chocolates and portioning sauces.

GUITAR: This stainless steel cutter is used to cut precise pieces of ganache, caramel, and gelées.

HEAT GUN: Like a blow-dryer without the air, a heat gun can be used to keep chocolate in temper.

TEMPERING MACHINE: This machine automatically melts and then tempers chocolate, alternately heating and cooling while constantly moving the chocolate. The machine then maintains the tempered chocolate at the correct temperature.

TRANSFER SHEETS: Acetate sheets with cocoa butter designs on them, transfer sheets are used to create imprinted designs on chocolate.

Tools for Sugar Work

AIRBRUSH: This tool is used to spray food coloring onto pulled sugar and pastillage pieces (as well as a number of other confections).

DESICCANT: Desiccants prevent sugar garnishes from deteriorating from exposure to moisture. Common desiccants are silica gel and quicklime.

SUGAR LAMP: This lamp has a weighted base with an infrared heat bulb and is used for keeping pulled sugar pliable.

BLOWN SUGAR PUMP: A rubber squeeze ball attached to an aluminum tube, this device is used to pump air into sugar to create a balloon, which can then be shaped.

Equipment That Is Usually Provided at the Competition

FIVE-QUART ELECTRIC STAND MIXER: Also known as a vertical or planetary mixer, this mixer has a stationary bowl with an orbiting mixing attachment. It comes with three standard attachments—a paddle, whisk, and dough hook.

INDUCTION COOKTOP: In an induction cooktop, heat is generated directly in the pot or pan, as opposed to being generated in the stovetop by electrical coils or burning gas. To be used on an induction cooker, a cooking vessel must be made of a special ferromagnetic metal.

FOOD PROCESSOR: This machine has a motorized base with a plastic work bowl fitted on a stem on top of it. It uses a variety of blades and attachments to rapidly grind, purée, knead, or slice food.

CONVECTION OVEN: In this oven, fans force air to circulate around food, cooking it evenly and quickly. They are generally ideal for baked goods.

MICROWAVE OVEN: This oven uses microwave radiation to heat polarized molecules in food, which cooks or reheats food quickly.

CHOCOLATE WARMER: This machine melts chocolate and keeps it in a liquid state.

BAKER'S RACKS: Also known as speed racks, these are vertical aluminum structures that can hold a number of sheet pans. They are ideal for storing baked goods or chocolates.

BATCH ICE CREAM FREEZER: This machine churns a specific amount of ice cream or sorbet base at one time. Its capacity is larger than that of a home ice cream maker, but not as large as that of a commercial continuous freezer.

Packing Your Equipment

The teams with big budgets ship their equipment in big crates via a trucking company. They make the crate the same dimensions as the competition kitchen and assemble their equipment in the crate as it will be positioned in the kitchen. This way they can easily transfer everything from the crate to their kitchen. These teams also have furniture built to store sheet pans and other equipment. The furniture slides under kitchen counters and enables them to efficiently store *mise en place* so that it's out of the way as they work.

INGREDIENTS

IN THE ABSTRACT ART OF COOKING, INGREDIENTS TRUMP

APPLIANCES... —*Bob Blumer*

Using the best-quality ingredients possible is crucial for competing in pastry at a high level, where every detail counts and may make the difference between winning and losing. The following is information on choosing, handling, and storing ingredients that you'll most likely be using during the competition.

Flours

ALL-PURPOSE FLOUR is a blend of hard (high-gluten) and soft (low-gluten) wheats, which produces a flour of medium strength with a protein content of 8 to 12 percent. There are two kinds of all-purpose flour.

BLEACHED ALL-PURPOSE FLOUR contains bleaching agents, which whiten the flour and make it easier to blend with ingredients with higher percentages of fat and sugar. A bleached flour produces a slightly more tender cake.

UNBLEACHED ALL-PURPOSE FLOUR is creamier in color, slightly heavier, and will yield a firmer crumb.

BREAD FLOUR is an unbleached, hard-wheat flour that gives more structure to baked goods. It has a gluten content of 11 to 13 percent.

CAKE FLOUR is made from soft winter wheats, and contains less gluten than all-purpose flour, about 6 to 10 percent. It is more refined than all-purpose flour. Cakes made with this flour will have a delicate grain and texture.

PASTRY FLOUR has a protein content ranging from 8 to 10 percent and can be used for pie dough, muffins, and pastries.

SEMOLINA is a durum wheat flour that is coarsely ground and yellow in color. Its protein content ranges from 12 to 14 percent.

WHOLE WHEAT FLOUR, milled from the whole wheat kernel, is sometimes used in combination with other flours, and will provide a nutty flavor and a coarse texture to baked goods.

STORING AND MEASURING FLOUR

Flour should be stored in airtight containers in a cool, dry place. Store whole wheat flour in an airtight container in the refrigerator. All-purpose and cake flours should be used within 15 months of purchase; whole wheat flour should be used within 6 to 8 months. Flours can be frozen; this might extend their life to up to two years. Double-seal the flour in plastic containers and/or resealable bags before freezing. Always measure flour by weight.

Sweeteners

GRANULATED SUGAR is pure refined sucrose derived from sugarcane or sugar beets. With small, even crystals, it is the most common form of sweetener used by the pastry chef.

SUPERFINE GRANULATED SUGAR, also known as caster sugar, has very fine crystals that allow it to dissolve quickly. It is sometimes used in cake batters and meringues. Because it is used frequently in the preparation of cocktails, it is also known as bar sugar. It can be substituted for granulated sugar in equal amounts in recipes.

PEARL SUGAR has large, pearl-shaped crystals and is used for decorating baked goods.

CONFECTIONERS' SUGAR, also called powdered sugar, is granulated sugar that has been processed commercially to a fine powder. Although a small amount of cornstarch is added to prevent clumping (up to 3 percent by weight), it should be sifted before use. Confectioners' sugar is available in different grades, according to fineness (10-X sugar is finer than 6-X sugar).

BROWN SUGAR is granulated sugar with molasses added. There are two basic types: light and dark. Light brown sugar has a more delicate flavor and lighter color than its darker counterpart, which contains more molasses (dark brown sugar has about 6.5 percent molasses while light brown sugar contains about 3.5 percent). Because it has a tendency to dry out and become rock-hard, brown sugar should be stored tightly wrapped in a plastic bag inside an airtight container.

DEMERARA SUGAR is an unrefined sugar with a large grain, blond color, and creamy molasses flavor.

MUSCOVADO SUGAR is a dark cane sugar with a fine, moist texture and a lingering, musky molasses flavor.

TURBINADO SUGAR is a coarse-textured, pale blond, raw sugar with a delicate molasses flavor.

SANDING SUGAR is fine granulated sugar, which is available in a variety of textures and colors. It is ideal for decorating cakes and other pastries after baking.

ISOMALT is a white, crystalline substance that is a sugar substitute. It is made from sucrose and is used in diabetic baking. It is also used extensively for pulled sugar because it absorbs very little water and does not break down when heated.

CORN SYRUP is a thick, sweet syrup made from cornstarch processed with enzymes or acids. It contains 15 to 20 percent glucose, other sugars, water, and flavorings. There are two types: light and dark. In general, the light and dark varieties can be used interchangeably. The dark has a richer flavor, reminiscent of brown sugar.

GLUCOSE SYRUP, like corn syrup, is made through the conversion of starch into sugar. Glucose syrup is 42 DE (dextrose equivalence) corn syrup and is used in sauces, confections, and pulled sugar.

MOLASSES, a by-product of the sugar-refining process, is a thick, brownish black syrup with a distinctive, hearty flavor. It comes in three forms: unsulphured, sulphured, and blackstrap. Unsulphured has a relatively mild flavor, while sulphured molasses has a more pronounced flavor and darker color. Blackstrap molasses has the strongest flavor and darkest color of the three.

GOLDEN SYRUP, also known as refiner's syrup, is a thick, delicious, golden syrup that is a by-product of the sugar-refining process. It can be used interchangeably with light corn syrup.

HONEY is a golden syrup with a slightly higher sweetening power than sugar and a distinct flavor. Its flavor varies depending on the flowers the bees fed on, and it can range from pale and mild to dark amber and robust.

MAPLE SYRUP is made from the concentrated sap of the sugar maple tree. It is available in different grades, ranging from Grade AA, which is thin in texture and mild in flavor, to Grade C, which is thick and robust.

INVERT SYRUP, also known as inverted syrup or Trimoline, is derived from sucrose that has been split into glucose and fructose, and is manufactured by adding an acid to sucrose. Products made with invert syrup, such as sorbet, are less prone to crystallization than those made with standard sugar.

Sugar Syrup Stages

Precise temperatures vary in sugar conversion tables. Below are the basic stages you will need for the recipes in this book.

215° TO 230°F (102° TO 110°C) · **THREAD STAGE.** When you dip a metal spoon into the syrup, a thin thread drips from its edge.

234° TO 240°F (112° TO 115°C) · **SOFT BALL STAGE.** When you drip a small amount of the syrup into a bowl of ice water, you will be able to form a very soft, malleable ball, which may not hold its shape. This syrup is used for French-style buttercreams.

244° TO 248°F (116° TO 120°C) · **FIRM BALL STAGE.** When you drip a small amount of the syrup into a bowl of ice water, you will be able to form a firm, flexible ball that holds its shape.

250° TO 265°F (122° TO 130°C) · **HARD BALL STAGE.** When you drip a small amount of the syrup into a bowl of ice water, you will be able to form a hard ball that is slightly malleable.

270° TO 290°F (132° TO 144°C) · **SOFT CRACK STAGE.** When you drip a small amount of syrup into a bowl of ice water, a string of syrup will form; it will crack when broken, but is still pliable.

300° TO 310°F (150° TO 155°C) · **HARD CRACK STAGE.** When you drip a small amount of syrup into a bowl of ice water, a brittle string of syrup will form; it will crack when broken and is not at all pliable.

320° TO 338°F (160° TO 170°C) · **LIGHT CARAMEL STAGE.** The color of the syrup changes from gold to light amber brown.

338° TO 356°F (170° TO 180°C) · **MEDIUM CARAMEL STAGE.** The color of the syrup changes from light amber to medium amber brown.

356° TO 374°F (180° TO 190°C) · **DARK CARAMEL STAGE.** The color of the syrup changes from medium amber to dark amber brown and begins to smoke.

Thickeners and Gelling Agents

GELATIN is made from the bones, skin, and connective tissue of animals, and is available in sheet or granulated form. It is used in many pastry components as a gelling agent, stabilizer, thickener, and foaming agent. Sheet gelatin is available in different bloom strengths or grades.

PECTIN is a gelling agent extracted from citrus fruits or apple skins. It is commonly used as a thickener for jams and jellies, but is also used for a variety of confections and sauces. Pectin is available in powdered or liquid form.

AGAR AGAR is a gelling agent derived from the cell walls of sea vegetables. It has very strong gelling properties and is used as a gelatin substitute.

POTATO STARCH, also known as potato flour, is made from potatoes that are cooked, dried, and ground into a fine powder. It is a very refined starch that, when cooked, yields good clarity and binding strength.

CORNSTARCH, made from ground corn, is primarily used as a thickening agent in sauces and custards, though it is also used with flour to produce a tender crumb in cakes and other baked goods. Cornstarch is also used as an anticaking agent in confectioners' sugar.

TAPIOCA is a starch derived from the root of the cassava (or manioc) plant and is used worldwide as a thickening agent. It is available as flour, flakes, granules, and pearls.

Dairy Products

MILK is sold today homogenized and pasteurized, and it is labeled according to its milk-fat content.

> **WHOLE MILK** contains at least 3 percent milk fat.

> **REDUCED-FAT MILK** contains 2 percent milk fat.

> **LOW-FAT MILK** contains 1 percent milk fat.

> **FAT-FREE MILK** contains less than 0.1 percent milk fat.

> **NONFAT DRY MILK** is made by removing the water from defatted milk.

> **EVAPORATED MILK** is whole or fat-free milk that is heated in a vacuum to remove about 60 percent of its water content.

> **SWEETENED CONDENSED MILK** is evaporated milk with added sugar, which yields a very thick, sweet product that is sold in cans.

> **BUTTERMILK** was originally the by-product of churning milk into butter, but is now usually made by adding a bacterial strain to nonfat milk. Buttermilk has a thick texture and slightly sour flavor.

> **YOGURT** is a cultured milk product that is made from whole, low-fat, or nonfat milk and is available plain or flavored. Greek yogurt is yogurt that has been strained to remove the whey, giving it a very thick consistency.

CREAM contains at least 18 percent milk fat and, like milk, is also homogenized and pasteurized. It is sometimes ultrapasteurized to extend its shelf life. Many pastry chefs prefer cream that has not been ultrapasteurized because it reaches a greater volume when whipped.

> **HEAVY** or **WHIPPING CREAM** must contain at least 35 percent milk fat.

> **LIGHT CREAM** contains between 16 and 32 percent milk fat.

> **SOUR CREAM** is cultured cream that contains 16 to 22 percent fat.

> **CRÈME FRAÎCHE** is made by adding a bacterial culture to cream that has about 28 percent butterfat. It has a higher fat content and is less thick than sour cream.

Eggs

Eggs bring richness and moisture to baked goods, as well as structure. Egg yolks, rich in fat, are generally used in baking as a thickener and binder, but they also make cakes tender. Egg whites, high in protein, are often whipped and used to add volume and air to cakes and other baked goods.

Eggs are graded for quality and freshness as AA, A, or B. Grade AA is best for baking; it has a thick white and strong yolk. Eggs should be stored in the coldest part of the refrigerator, in their original carton, with the more pointed end down. Because of the potential threat of salmonella poisoning, keep eggs refrigerated until shortly before using them. Bring the eggs to room temperature by setting them in a bowl of very warm water for 10 to 15 minutes (dry the shells before cracking the eggs). Do not use eggs with cracked shells.

Pasteurized eggs are available as whole eggs, yolks, or whites, and in refrigerated or frozen liquid form. They are also available in dried or powdered form.

Fats

Fats make baked goods rich and tender and provide aeration to help leaven batter or dough. They also add flavor and moisture, act as emulsifiers, and lubricate the gluten in flour. There are several types of fat, each with its own properties that result in particular flavors and textures.

BUTTER has great creaming abilities and flavor that make it the most important fat for baking. It is produced in salted and unsalted forms. Always use unsalted butter in baking, as it permits you to control the salt content in a recipe. Butter can be stored, wrapped in plastic, in the freezer for up to 6 months.

By law, American butter must contain at least 80 percent butterfat. Some pastry chefs use butter with a higher butterfat content—up to 86 percent—and some of the recipes in this book specify this higher-fat butter.

SOLID VEGETABLE SHORTENING is 100 percent fat and contains no water or minerals. It is soft and has the ability to surround air bubbles well, providing good aeration in batters. Since it is flavorless, shortening should be used in combination with butter.

VEGETABLE OIL is used in many cakes, notably the chiffon cake, and makes for a very tender crumb.

Chocolate

To store chocolate, wrap it first in plastic wrap, then in heavy-duty aluminum foil, and place it in an airtight container. Ideally, chocolate should be stored in a cool, dry place with a consistent temperature of around 65°F (18°C). White chocolate must be stored away from light because of the milk solids it contains. Light will accelerate its oxidation, so that the chocolate may turn rancid overnight. Store it, well wrapped, in a dark place. Properly stored, unsweetened and dark chocolate may keep for as long as 2 years. Milk chocolate will keep for 1 year and white chocolate for 7 or 8 months.

CACAO NIBS are edible, crunchy bits of roasted cacao bean. They can add taste and texture to a variety of baked goods and confections.

COCOA BUTTER, the natural fat of the cacao bean, is responsible for the incomparable mouthfeel of chocolate. It is frequently used by the pastry chef, along with equal parts of chocolate, for spraying the exterior of desserts to give them a velvet finish.

COCOA POWDER is the result of a hydraulic press operation in which virtually all of the cocoa butter is separated from pure chocolate liquor. The cake that results is then ground into fine powder. To produce alkalized (or Dutch-process) cocoa powder, an alkali such as potassium carbonate is added to the powder in order to neutralize the astringent qualities of the cacao beans.

UNSWEETENED CHOCOLATE, also known as baking chocolate, consists of pure chocolate liquor (ground cacao nibs) and lecithin (a stabilizer). It has a cocoa butter content of at least 50 percent.

BITTERSWEET and **SEMISWEET CHOCOLATE** must contain at least 35 percent chocolate liquor. These dark chocolates are manufactured with a variety of cacao beans and with different amounts of added ingredients, including extra cocoa butter, sugar, lecithin, and vanilla, so their taste profiles and characteristics vary considerably from brand to brand. While bittersweet chocolate generally contains less sugar than semisweet chocolate, there is no standard technical distinction between the two.

COUVERTURE is a term that applies to professional-quality coating chocolate with a high percentage of cocoa butter—from 32 to 39 percent. This extra cocoa butter makes it easier to work with the chocolate in melted form, and it can be used to form a thinner shell for enrobing chocolates and confections.

MILK CHOCOLATE must contain at least 10 percent chocolate liquor plus a minimum of 3.7 percent milk fat and 12 percent milk solids. Manufacturers also add sugar, cocoa butter, lecithin, and vanilla.

GIANDUJA is a blending of pulverized hazelnuts and milk chocolate that is very popular in Italy.

WHITE CHOCOLATE is composed of cocoa butter, butterfat, sugar, milk solids, lecithin, and flavorings.

Leaveners

BAKING POWDER is composed of baking soda, cream of tartar, and cornstarch. When combined with a liquid, it releases carbon dioxide. Always use double-acting baking powder, the most common type, which releases some carbon dioxide when it is combined with a liquid and the rest when exposed to oven heat. Baking powder has a shelf life of about a year, after which it loses its strength. To test it, sprinkle some over hot water. If it fizzes, it is still active.

BAKING SODA is sodium bicarbonate, which produces carbon dioxide bubbles when combined with an acid such as buttermilk or yogurt. It has an almost indefinite shelf life if stored in a dry place.

ACTIVE DRY YEAST is composed of dehydrated, dormant yeast cell granules. It must be proofed or rehydrated to become active before using.

RAPID RISE YEAST is dehydrated yeast granules that become extremely active once rehydrated, and then die quickly.

INSTANT DRY YEAST is a yeast product that can be used without rehydration, and will cause dough to ferment through all phases of production.

FRESH YEAST is sold as a compressed, moist, firm block. It is highly perishable and should be stored in the refrigerator.

Salt

TABLE SALT is available with or without added iodine. It has small, dense grains and is most commonly available to diners in salt shakers around the world. Table salt does not adhere easily to food and it does not dissolve easily in liquid, which is why it is not popular with chefs.

KOSHER SALT has a much larger grain size than table salt, dissolves more easily in liquid, and adheres well to food.

SEA SALT is derived from the evaporation of seawater. It has a flaky texture that allows it to adhere well to food, and it dissolves easily in liquid. Because it contains various minerals that are present in the waters from which it comes, sea salt has a more complex flavor than table salt. It also varies in flavor, depending on its origin.

FLEUR DE SEL, "flower of the salt" in French, is a type of sea salt that is hand harvested by workers who collect only the top layer, the best part of the salt, before it sinks to the bottom of the pans. Because it is so labor-intensive to collect, fleur de sel is one of the most expensive sea salts. It is frequently paired with dark chocolate and caramel in desserts and confections.

Spices

ALLSPICE is the dried berry of the *Pimenta dioica* plant. The small berries are brown and resemble peppercorns. The flavor of allspice is similar to a combination of cinnamon, nutmeg, and cloves.

CARDAMOM comes from a plant in the ginger family. It has a distinctive aroma that is both spicy and sweet, and is available in whole pods or ground.

CINNAMON is the dried inner bark of evergreen trees from the genus *Cinnamomum*. Its flavor is hot and aromatic, and it is available in whole sticks or ground.

CLOVES are the dried flower buds of a tropical evergreen tree. They have a strong aromatic flavor, and are available whole or ground.

GINGER in its fresh form is the subterranean plant stem of the aromatic rhizome ginger. It has a strong, slightly hot flavor, and is available fresh, dried, crystallized, or ground.

NUTMEG, though it resembles a nut, is actually the egg-shaped seed of the nutmeg tree. It has a delicate, slightly sweet flavor, and is always used grated. It is available whole or ground, but is best grated fresh.

VANILLA comes from the pod of the orchid flower. It is possibly the most important flavor of the pastry world because of its delicate, perfume like flavor. It is available in whole beans, and as an extract, powder, and paste.

Nuts and Seeds

ALMONDS are the seeds of the almond tree, which are encased in a pale tan, woody hull. They are available whole, in the shell or shelled, blanched or raw, sliced, slivered, or as almond flour or paste.

ANISE SEEDS are small, grayish seeds with an intense licorice flavor.

CARAWAY SEEDS are small, brown, crescent-shaped seeds with a distinctive flavor. They are usually used in rye bread.

CASHEWS are kidney-shaped nuts that are buttery and slightly sweet. They are grown throughout the world, but especially in India. Because they have a high fat content (48 percent), they can turn rancid quickly and should be stored in an airtight container in the refrigerator.

CHESTNUTS have glossy brown shells encasing a soft, roundish nut. They are available whole, in the shell or shelled, canned (in syrup or water), candied, frozen, vacuum-packed, or as a purée.

HAZELNUTS, also known as filberts, are grown in Spain, France, and Turkey, but production is now also thriving in the U.S. in the states of Washington and Oregon. They are sweet and rich and pair beautifully with chocolate. Hazelnut paste, with or without added sugar, is a common ingredient used in pastry.

MACADAMIA NUTS, rich and buttery, are grown primarily in Hawaii. Macadamias are expensive because they are labor-intensive to cultivate and process, and because they are relatively scarce—a 100-pound harvest yields a mere 15 pounds of edible nuts. They are available salted or unsalted.

PEANUTS are grown throughout the southern United States. Though there are several varieties, the most common ones are the Virginia and Spanish peanuts. Store shelled peanuts in an airtight container in the refrigerator for up to 3 months, or in the freezer for up to 6 months.

PECANS are sweet, rich nuts. The pecan is a member of the hickory family. The best pecans are from Georgia and Texas; their peak season is fall. Be careful how you store pecans, as they will turn rancid quickly. They can be refrigerated for up to 3 months or frozen for up to 6 months.

PISTACHIOS are sweet nuts that originated in Turkey and are now grown in central Asia, the Near East, the Mediterranean, and California (a latecomer, as the first decent crop was not harvested there until 1978). Shelled, they will keep for 3 months in the refrigerator, or up to 6 months frozen. Unshelled, they can be refrigerated for 6 months or frozen for a year.

POPPY SEEDS are tiny, round, blue gray seeds with a nutty, slightly musty flavor. They are available whole or as a paste.

PUMPKIN SEEDS are flat, oval, green-colored seeds that are sold whole in the shell or shelled.

SESAME SEEDS are small, flat, oval seeds that can be either cream-colored, tan, or black. They have a rich, nutty flavor and are oily. They are sold whole, hulled or unhulled, and as a paste, known as tahini.

WALNUTS are grown in temperate areas throughout the world. American black walnuts have the richest flavor, which is faintly buttery and woodsy. The English, or Persian, variety is most common, and comes in three sizes: large, medium, and baby. Walnuts in the shell should not have any cracks or holes; out of the shell, walnuts should look healthy, not shriveled. They can be stored in a cool, dry place for several months, in the refrigerator, tightly covered, for 6 months, or in the freezer, well wrapped, for up to a year.

Fruit Purées and Concentrates

FRUIT PURÉES are made from puréed raw fruit and sometimes added sugar (up to 10 percent), which acts as a preservative. Some delicate fruits also require the addition of ascorbic and citric acid to preserve them. Fruit purées offer chefs the luxury of having the flavor of a variety of perfectly ripe fruits available to them at any time of the year.

FRUIT CONCENTRATES are obtained by evaporating part of the water from fresh fruit juices in a vacuum at a low temperature. They offer a highly concentrated flavor, and are suitable for a variety of pastry preparations, from sauces to custards and mousse fillings.

Fruits

POME FRUITS

APPLES, the pomaceous fruit of the apple tree, are one of the most widely cultivated fruits, and extremely popular in the pastry kitchen. There are hundreds of varieties of apples grown throughout the United States. Apples that are popular for baking include Granny Smith, Red and Golden Delicious, McIntosh, and Rome Beauty. Other good choices include Northern Spy, Jonathan, Fuji, Braeburn, and Gala varieties.

PEARS, the fruit of the pear tree, are available in hundreds of varieties in the United States and thousands worldwide. Popular baking varieties include Bartlett, Bosc, Comice, d'Anjou, and Seckel.

BERRIES

BLACKBERRIES, also known as bramble berries, are a deep purple black color with a sweet-tart flavor.

BLUEBERRIES are small and round, with a blue purple color and a flared crown shape at one end. They have a mild, sweet flavor; smaller berries tend to be sweeter than larger ones.

CLOUDBERRIES are similar in shape to raspberries and blackberries, but they are amber in color with a distinctive tart flavor.

RASPBERRIES are small, red berries that have a distinctive sweet-tart flavor. Though less common, they are also available in white, golden, or black varieties.

RED CURRANTS are crimson-colored round berries with a very tart flavor. Because they are so tart, they are an ideal foil for sweet components in plated desserts.

STRAWBERRIES are heart-shaped red berries with tiny seeds on their exterior. Their sweet flavor and pretty appearance make them one of the most popular berries in the pastry world. Generally, the smaller the strawberry, the sweeter the taste. **FRAISES DES BOIS,** also known as wild or woodland strawberries, are small strawberries that are prized for their intensely sweet flavor.

GOOSEBERRIES are round, smooth-skinned berries surrounded by a papery husk. They are generally green, but can also be white, golden, red, or purple.

STONE FRUITS

APRICOTS resemble small peaches, though they are not as juicy and their color is yellow orange. They have a thin skin covered with a light fuzz and a sweet interior with a hard stone in the center.

CHERRIES can be found in many varieties, from the yellow-colored Royal Ann to the light red Queen Anne to the blackish red Bing. Textures range from soft and juicy to firm and crisp, and flavors run from sweet to sour. Cherries are available fresh, canned, dried, candied, or frozen.

NECTARINES look very similar to peaches in shape and color, but their skin is smooth.

PEACHES have a thin, yellow-orange-rose skin that is covered with a light fuzz. They come in many different varieties, and their sweet, juicy flesh ranges from white to yellow to red.

PLUMS have a sweet and very juicy flesh with a tart, shiny, smooth skin. They come in many varieties and range in color from light yellow to dark purple.

PLUOTS are a cross between a plum and an apricot. They have a smooth, purple exterior that resembles a plum. Their flesh is sweet, very juicy, and intensely flavored.

MELONS

CANTALOUPES are round melons with a tan and dark green variegated rind. Their flesh is firm, orange, juicy, and fragrant.

CHARENTAIS MELONS are an exceptional variety of cantaloupe. They are sweetly perfumed, with a succulent orange flesh surrounding a core of inedible seeds.

HONEYDEW MELONS have a cream-colored rind with a pale green flesh that has a sweet, delicate flavor.

WATERMELONS are large, oval melons that can weigh up to 30 pounds. They have a light and dark green striped rind and, as their name suggests, a very juicy interior. There are many different varieties of watermelon available; the most common kind has a deep pink color and is studded with black seeds, though other varieties may be white, yellow, or pink, with or without seeds.

CITRUS FRUITS

BERGAMOT ORANGE, also known as sour orange, is the size and shape of an orange, with lemon yellow skin. Its juice is astringent, so the fruit is not eaten raw. The juice is used for sauces and in marmalade, and the peel is frequently candied.

BLOOD ORANGES look similar to ordinary oranges, but they are slightly smaller and have a crimson-colored flesh. They range from tart to sweet, depending on the variety.

BUDDHA'S HAND is a bright yellow citron with lobes that resemble a human hand. It is also known for its pleasant fragrance.

CITRONS range in size from medium to very large, and vary in shape, though they are usually oblong. Their skin is very thick and bumpy, and they are hard to peel. The flesh is firm, and slightly dry, with lots of seeds in it. Candied citron peel is very popular in baking, and is a key component of fruitcake.

CLEMENTINES are a cross between the sour orange and the Mediterranean mandarin. They have a deep orange color, and their flesh has notes of apricot.

GRAPEFRUITS come in two types: white fleshed and pigmented. White grapefruits have a yellow skin with a green blush, and their flesh is pale yellow. Seedless varieties are available. Pink grapefruits have yellow skin with a pink blush, and their flesh is pink. Red grapefruits have a reddish blush and a deep red flesh.

KUMQUATS are the smallest citrus fruit; they measure about 1½ inches in diameter and are either round or oval in shape. They have a thin, edible skin and a juicy, tart flesh.

LEMONS have a deep yellow skin and very tart flesh with seeds.

LIMES have darkish green, smooth skin and flesh that is tart and without seeds.

KEY LIMES are smaller and more acidic than common limes and have light green yellow skin and seeded flesh.

MEYER LEMONS are not true lemons; they are a cross between a lemon and an orange. Their skin is yellow, and they are rounder than a true lemon. Their flesh is light orange yellow and sweeter than a lemon's.

ORANGES are divided into four types: eating, juice, bitter, and mandarin. Eating oranges, such as the navel, are generally large and easy to peel and segment. Juice oranges are smooth-skinned, sweet, plump, and juicy; they are difficult to peel. Bitter oranges are used to make marmalade, and mandarin oranges, which include tangerines and clementines, are seedless and have thin skins that are easy to peel.

POMELOS are one of the largest of the citrus fruits; they range from large grapefruit to melon-sized. They have very thick, yellow to pink skins, and their flesh varies in color from yellow to pink to red. Most varieties are sweet, juicy, and slightly acidic.

TANGERINES are a variety of mandarin orange; they are smaller and less tart than oranges.

SUBTROPICAL FRUITS

ASIAN PEARS, also known as Chinese, sand, or apple pears, are round, rather than pear-shaped, with a speckled yellow or green skin. Their flesh is crisp and juicy with the texture of an apple and a sweetness similar to a pear.

CHERIMOYA, also known as the custard apple, is a cone-shaped fruit with a thick, shingled, pale green rind. Its flesh is creamy white and studded with large, black, inedible seeds. Its flavor is sweet, with notes of banana, vanilla, and mango.

DATES are the fruit of the date palm. They have a thin, papery skin and a very sweet, sticky flesh. Fresh dates are yellow, golden brown, or black, but they are usually available semidried and are brown.

FIGS are thin-skinned and either round or pear-shaped. Depending on the variety (of which there are over 600), they range from pale greenish yellow to purple, with a flesh that ranges from white to red. When ripe they have a soft, juicy texture and a sweet, musky flavor.

GRAPES are smooth-skinned, small orbs that grow in bunches. They range in color from pale green to deep purple and in flavor from sour to sweet. **CONCORD GRAPES** are dark blue or purple with a light-colored bloom which can be rubbed off. They are prized by pastry chefs for their highly aromatic, sweet flavor.

GUAVA can be either round or oval shaped, and has an edible skin that is white, yellow, green, or pink. The flesh can be white, yellow, or pink. Different varieties have different flavors, and may taste like strawberry, pineapple, or lemon.

LYCHEE or **LITCHI** have a rough, leathery pink or red shell, encasing a sweet, juicy white flesh. Its flavor is similar to grapes.

PERSIMMONS have a smooth, orange skin and a custard-textured flesh that has a sweet and tangy flavor similar to a cross between banana and mango.

POMEGRANATE has a reddish brown shell with a pink flesh that contains a multitude of edible crimson seeds that are sweet-tart.

PRICKLY PEAR, also known as cactus pear, is the fruit of the desert cactus and contains a large number of crunchy, edible seeds. The skin and flesh can range from orange to red to purple and its flavor is similar to kiwi, though not as acidic.

UNIQ FRUIT, also known as **UGLI FRUIT,** is a hybrid of the grapefruit, tangerine, and sour orange. Its orange yellow flesh has a sweet-tart flavor similar to a combination of orange and grapefruit.

TROPICAL FRUITS

These fruits, all of which are intolerant to frost, are too numerous to name. Below is a listing of the most popular tropical fruits used in the pastry kitchen.

COCONUT is the fruit of the palm tree. The coconut has a woody brown outer shell covered with fibers and a creamy white, rich interior. Used extensively in the pastry kitchen, coconut is sold as a whole nut, or flaked or shredded (sweetened or unsweetened), frozen, or desiccated. Other coconut products include coconut milk, cream of coconut, and coconut oil.

BANANAS are a highly versatile fruit, and are available in a variety of sizes and colors, including yellow, purple, and red. Their flesh is soft and sweet, and can be used in a variety of pastry preparations.

CARAMBOLAS, also known as star fruit, have a unique shape and, when sliced, they look like a perfect star. They have a golden, waxy skin that is edible, and their flesh is sweet and succulent.

DURIANS are the fruit of an evergreen tree and are covered with a green, semihard shell with small spines on it. The shell of many varieties has a very strong fetid odor, which discourages vendors from selling this fruit in the United States. The flesh of the durian is rich, yellow, and sweet, with a desirable custardlike consistency.

FINGER BANANAS look like miniature versions of the standard banana, though they are sweeter with a more concentrated flavor.

GUANABANAS, also known as soursops, are the heart-shaped fruit of an evergreen tree, with a thin, spiny, green skin. Its delicious white flesh is pulpy, aromatic, and slightly acidic. Its seeds are toxic.

KIWIS, also known as Chinese gooseberry, are egg-shaped fruit with brown skin covered with tiny hairs. The flesh of the fruit is bright green and succulent with edible black seeds. The flavor of kiwi is sweet, slightly tart, and reminiscent of strawberry and banana.

MANGOES come in many different varieties. Generally, they have a thin skin that ranges in color from red to yellow to orange to purple. The flesh of the mango is firm and sweet with a bright yellow color that surrounds a large, oval pit in the center.

MANGOSTEENS have a thick, purple brown hard shell that encases a waxy white flesh that is divided into segments. Their flavor is sweet and delicate.

PAPAYAS are pear-shaped and grow in clusters on a herbaceous tree. When unripe they are hard and green, but turn golden or rose when ripe. Their flesh is an orange rose color, smooth, and aromatic. At its center is a large cluster of edible black seeds.

PASSION FRUIT are round or slightly oval, with a tough, bumpy skin that ranges from yellow to red to dark purple. Its flesh is composed of yellowish green seeds and pulp that have a sweet-tart floral flavor.

PINEAPPLES grow on a cactuslike plant and have a rough, bumpy skin that is a greenish yellow when ripe. Its flesh is yellow and juicy with a tangy, sweet flavor.

PLANTAINS, also known as cooking bananas, are physically similar to bananas, but are larger and wider with a thicker skin. Their flesh is starchier and less sweet than bananas, with a texture similar to squash. They are not eaten raw.

RAMBUTANS have a spiny red shell covering a sweet, white flesh with a single seed. Its flavor is mild and refreshing.

Extracts

Extracts are used extensively by pastry chefs to add flavor to a variety of dessert components, from cakes to sauces to mousses. They are alcohol-based, and can lose their potency over time or when exposed to heat, light, or air. Store extracts tightly capped in dark glass jars, away from light and heat.

Liqueurs

Liqueurs are alcoholic beverages that are flavored with fruit, herbs, flowers, or spices and combined with sugar. They generally have a lower alcohol content than spirits. Because they are sweet, liqueurs are commonly used in the pastry kitchen.

PLATING FOR POINTS

GOOD DESIGN IS THE MOST IMPORTANT WAY TO DIFFERENTIATE OURSELVES FROM OUR COMPETITORS. —*Yun Jong Yong*

A PLATED DESSERT WILL SHOW EXACTLY WHAT KIND OF PASTRY CHEF YOU ARE. —*Francisco Migoya*

A GREAT PLATED DESSERT IS AN UNDENIABLE SENSE OF PLEASURE. —*En-Ming Hsu*

The Flavor Factor

What makes a plated dessert worthy of a gold medal? Pastry chefs may debate the finer points of this question, but there is little doubt as to what the most important factor is in creating an exceptional plated dessert: *flavor*. Whether it's a simple slice of pie served in a diner or an intricate, multicomponent dessert crafted for a competition, flavor is what makes a dessert memorable. Flashy presentations may draw admiring "oohs" and "aahs," but it's the taste of a dessert that remains embedded in our memory banks. Sébastien Canonne, co-founder of the French Pastry School at City Colleges of Chicago, sums it up by saying, "It's all about taste. Nothing else comes first." This concept is borne out by the fact that 40 percent of each team's score in the National and World Pastry Team Competitions is based on taste, also known as *dégustation*.

There are different schools of thought regarding how flavors should be combined in plated desserts, but most top pastry chefs recommend limiting the number of main flavors to three. Robert Ellinger, pastry chef–owner of Baked to Perfection in Port Washington, New York, served as the head judge during the 2010 World Pastry Team Championship. He has what he refers to as a "three flavor rule." Otherwise, he says, "you get the 'fruit salad effect,' and then you don't know what the hell you're tasting—there's just too much going on there."

En-Ming Hsu, a pastry chef consultant based in Las Vegas, has been a team member, coach, and head judge at the World Pastry Team Championships. She also cautions against using too many flavors in a dessert, particularly in an international competition. "Some teams become excited by the competition and become excessively flavorful," she notes. "They choose many flavors because they want to impress the jury. It's better to find two or three primary flavors that are understood and then complement them with one or two interesting flavors. Judges may taste as many as twelve desserts in one sitting. It's impossible for their palates not to become confused. The clearer the flavors are in the dessert, the more successful it will be—judges like to know what they are eating. It's always important to consider the flavor profile carefully, particularly for an international panel of judges."

Stephen Durfee, who runs the Baking and Pastry Arts Program at the Culinary Institute of America at Greystone, has a similar view on the danger of using too many flavors in a dessert. "I do think that you can overwhelm a person's palate pretty quickly by offering them too many things at once, so I think that's good advice," he explains. "I know this happens to me at school—I'll have eighteen people in a class each doing a menu, and I'll have to sit and try fifty-four desserts in a four-hour period. And after the fourth or fifth one, you're just like, 'Whoa!' So I know what it's like to be in that position to have to taste so many different flavors."

Francisco Migoya, an associate professor at the Culinary Institute of America in Hyde Park, also has strong views about the use of too many flavors. He advises, "Do not use more than three 'frontal' flavors, since the human brain cannot handle more than that." Frontal flavors, he explains, are clear flavors that are almost immediately identifiable. Examples include passion fruit, chocolate, strawberry, and lime. "More than three just becomes a jumbled mass of unidentifiable flavors," says Migoya. "You may add some 'background' flavors in addition to the frontal flavors, but for the sole purpose of enhancing the frontal flavors." Background flavors, he notes, "help push other flavors forward and round them out without taking over completely." Vanilla, caramel, and coconut are common examples of background flavors.

After the decision of how many flavors to feature is the equally important choice of *which* flavors to combine. In part, this decision should be based on the ingredients that are available at the competition site. Over the years, some teams designed their plated desserts without considering whether the featured ingredients could be easily procured in the area where the competition was held. Finding incredible produce in the Napa Valley, for example, is much easier than finding it in Phoenix in July, as Stephen Durfee discovered at the 2005 NPTC. "In Napa, you just go to the farmers' market and you come home with the best strawberry in the world, and you serve it, but you can't do that in Phoenix. So we went out to a store to get some strawberries the day before the competition, and that's tough to do. Nowadays, if I were doing a fruit dessert, I would rely more on a fruit purée, because you never know what the quality of fruit is going to be in the area."

Teams that have had success with their plated desserts tend to stick to the most popular flavors, which Robert Ellinger refers to as the "Five Cs": chocolate, caramel, coffee, cream cheese, and citrus (and other fruits). Innovation for innovation's sake is generally not a good idea, and will probably not impress the judges. Team Spain, led by master pastry innovator Albert Adrià, found this out during the

2002 WPTC in Las Vegas when it finished outside of the top six teams. Their plated dessert was a Berry Membrillo with Rose and Goat's Milk. A *membrillo* is a classic Chilean dessert, but it most likely did not have much resonance with the judges, none of whom were Chilean. And though the combination of floral rose and tangy goat's milk works, it probably didn't remind the judges of memorable desserts from their childhoods. That year Team Spain also featured an unusual chocolate bonbon featuring a filling made with Fisherman's Friend throat lozenges. That's right, cough drops. Innovative choice? Yes! Smart choice? No!

Francisco Migoya has firm views on the subject of innovation. "We are always so concerned about being unique and different that often we forget about the basic and straightforward flavors our profession is based on," he points out. "I am much more impressed by a pastry chef who can properly execute a flawless ganache than a pastry chef who can execute a flawless foam. Foam is easy, proper ganache is not."

Many chefs who have either judged or participated in the competitions cite the importance of knowing—or making an educated guess about—the judges' tastes before determining what flavors to showcase. When Robert Ellinger is preparing for a competition, this is the first thing he thinks about. "I find out who the judges are and what they like and dislike. You can have the best plated dessert, but if it has pineapple in it, and you put it in front of somebody who doesn't like pineapple, you're probably not going to do very well. We're all human beings. It's just not going to make my score go up if I give them something they don't like."

Sometimes the problem can't be foreseen at all. At the NPTC in 2005, Stephen Durfee made a meringue cake paired with chocolate, honey, and apricot. As a child, he used to eat toasted rye bread with butter and apricot jam, and loved that particular combination of flavors. So he decided to add caraway seeds to the meringue in his cake, to mimic the flavor of the rye bread. After the judging, one of the judges, Stanton Ho, came up to him to complain that he still had a caraway seed stuck between his teeth, and he couldn't get rid of the taste of it. "I guess I didn't grind up the caraway seeds as much as I should've," admits Durfee. "I think I know flavors pretty well, I think that's my strongest suit, but it certainly didn't serve me well that day. It might come down to in the midst of the competition making a mistake, or having someone just flat-out disagree with your idea of what flavors go together. It was something that I didn't even really think was a gamble. In that environment, you want to save your creativity for techniques that are really going to impress a judge and not with flavors."

Looks Count

After flavor, the second most important element in the design of a great plated dessert is presentation. Simple, clean designs tend to work best. "Judges," according to En-Ming Hsu, "like to see desserts that appear simple, but are technically difficult. Simple desserts are more challenging because every detail counts and flaws become more apparent. In order to appear appetizing, the dessert presentation must look effortless and harmonious with each component fitting together and contributing to the presentation and taste. Judges are greatly influenced by the first impression."

Every detail counts in the presentation of a plated dessert, down to the choice of the plate. Some teams use simple, white plates that will keep the focus on the dessert. Others use plates that have been custom designed and made to their specifications for their dessert. Gimmicks, however, may invite trouble. At the 2008 WPTC, Team USA caused a stir by using a specially crafted plate that some viewed as a gimmick. "You moved the spoon and the sauce trickled down a niche in the plate," said Robert Ellinger. "There were rumors that they spent up to $1,500 per plate, but I don't know if that's true. I don't know what those plates cost. It was actually a pretty incredible design by a group of brilliant pastry chefs, but it was a gimmick. Now they've changed the rules so that you can't go crazy with the plates anymore, which is probably a good thing."

En-Ming Hsu's advice regarding plate choice is to keep it simple. "The plate is the frame that holds the dessert together. A custom-made plate will make a

statement. If it creates a cutting-edge presentation, it may create some controversy at the same time. Sometimes it's best not to give judges something to talk about. A team can't go wrong with a simple, round, white, bone porcelain plate. If they design their dessert to fit the plate, it will be a classic, understated presentation."

Others see the use of custom plates as an unfair advantage for teams that have more resources than cash-strapped teams. As Stephen Durfee, who was at the 2010 WPTC, puts it, "It's really not fair when one team is so much better funded than another and can afford to do something like that. If I had been a judge, I would've been so blown away by that plate that Team USA had—it was so clever and so fun and whimsical. But, at the same time, I would've felt bad for another team that obviously didn't have the same resources. It's not a level playing field if you are able to bring in your own plate design. It's different than everyone just having a white plate and seeing what you can do with that."

As for the overall look of the dessert, En-Ming Hsu advises that "the presentation be approachable." In other words, don't go for anything that looks too complex. Kathryn Gordon, chef-instructor at the Institute of Culinary Education in New York, has more specific advice on plating: "Looking at the plate from a three-dimensional perspective, your eye should be able to flow across the components, and therefore, appreciate them first as a whole, and then more individually, if you look that closely." She adds, "There should be movement on the plate, not a static weighing down of color or dark components, but the curve upwards of a tuile, or the connection between two components with a chocolate or caramel stick, or the flow of coulis with a brushstroke. The viewer's eye should never be *caught* on the plate—the proximity of the food creates a sculpture that should be appealing visually, and attract the eye of the diner before being eaten." She also suggests that the main component of the dessert should never be centered, but should either be placed at 8 o'clock or 10 o'clock, looking at the plate as the face of a clock. Generally, sauce, ice cream or sorbet, and main garnishes should radiate off the main component without a lot of separation. This allows the plate to have a balance of white space on the plate and not look too busy or confusing.

Contrast Can Be Good—or Bad

Another important element in designing a plated dessert is contrast. This is achieved by juxtaposing different textures and temperatures of components in the dessert, which delivers interest and pleasant surprise to the diner. "I can remember a dessert I had at Arzak in San Sebastian over a decade ago," recalls Francisco Migoya. "It consisted of a simple sphere of pumpkin ice cream inside a warm chocolate pudding. The ice cream was unexpected. How could this ice cream stay frozen inside the hot chocolate pudding? I would learn the method later, but at the moment I was baffled and mystified and humbled by the simple genius of these two components that seemingly shouldn't coexist peacefully, and yet they did. In retrospect, it is an easy dessert to pull off, but the fact is that at that moment I had never heard or known of such a thing. If you can pull that off, your dessert will be memorable, and even more so if the flavors are there."

But Chef Migoya warns against using contrast haphazardly. "Contrast for the sake of contrast in anything—flavor, texture, temperature, color—can be absurd, and most chefs and sophisticated diners will be able to see right through that. However, when it is done correctly, it can be what makes the dessert successful, because it shows that there is a profound thought process behind the plate."

Some chefs advise against using too many colors on the plate. Gilles Renusson, professor and pastry chef at Grand Rapids Community College in Michigan, and a regular attendee at the World and National Pastry Team Championships, has strong views about using artificial colors to create color contrast. "Recently I saw in a competition components of a plated dessert that had been sprayed with color in order to add some contrast. It was hideous. It's just like all these bright-colored *macarons* that keep on popping up all over. And then we wonder why the rate of cancer is so high in this country?" Regarding temperature, however, he is in favor of strong contrasts. "I remember the first time I ate baked Alaska. What a wonderful shock it was!" He advises, however, that pastry chefs use common sense here, too. "Be realistic; you would not want to put a scoop of frozen ice cream on top of a soufflé, for example. It would deflate the soufflé instantly and the iced element would melt."

For En-Ming Hsu, contrasts in a dessert can create interest and "help make the dessert exciting to eat." She advises, "The contrast should relate to the style of dessert. If a dessert is styled to be simple, it may become confusing if too many contrasting colors are used. If there are too many textures involved, it can become confusing to eat as well. It's better to not create confusion and cause the jury to have to think too much about what they are eating."

Presenting a plated dessert with contrasting temperatures can present major challenges during a competition, but if a team can pull it off, it can work to their advantage. In En-Ming Hsu's opinion, "Temperatures are very difficult to control in a competition setting because there is usually so much going on at one time. Competition kitchens can be quite chaotic, even for the most organized team. For a dessert requiring warm and frozen components, it requires detailed planning and precision to coordinate proper service." She also emphasizes the importance of serving the dessert at the correct temperature. "In a competition, the smallest details count. If a dessert is served too warm or too cold, the judges sense it right away. Judges with more sensitive palates will quickly detect if a dessert is too sweet, too sour, or not sweet enough, simply because the temperature is off." Chef Hsu says that this can sometime be attributed to misuse of the blast freezer, a freezer that cools food to a low temperature very quickly. "One of the best pieces of equipment is the blast freezer. Teams gain so much time and have the ability to increase their production when it is used. However, it can be their downfall if the blast freezer is incorrectly used. Many times, beautiful desserts with the potential to win do not score well because they are served frozen. A dessert that is meant to be served at room temperature could easily be served partially frozen in the center, or worse, completely frozen if the freezing time is misjudged."

Francisco Migoya points out the challenges of executing a plated dessert with contrasting temperatures: "[It] can be a smash hit, but again, it depends on the nature of the plate. Consider that there is a possibility that the judge who will be tasting the dessert may not be doing so immediately after you have plated it. As the clock ticks, the dessert dies. Perhaps a table-side addition of a hot or cold or frozen ingredient to the plated dessert can ensure that temperature contrast."

For Kathryn Gordon, the use of contrasting textures is a primary necessity in the success of a plated dessert. "When I was growing up, I remember my mother making mousse for dinner parties. Back then, nobody seemed to think twice about the fact that it was just one texture, and superrich—like eating a slab of cheesecake. Now, I can't imagine a competition chef just plating with just one texture. We eat with our eyes first, but then the mouth takes over and it reacts to textures."

The Final Flourish

Some pastry chefs may not regard garnish as an integral part of their design for a plated dessert, but it is generally foolish not to do so. Competition judges pay close attention to garnishes, which can make the difference between a good and a great plated dessert. "A garnish is the essential finishing touch for a plated dessert. Without it, the plate looks incomplete," reflects En-Ming Hsu. She also advises competitors to keep the garnish simple. "Garnishes look best when they are light and delicate. Judges like to see garnishes that are created with an interesting or unusual technique. It is most likely the technique that they will remember and use themselves in the future."

Garnishes should also work within the context of the dessert. "They must," explains Francisco Migoya, "make sense with the dish. I often see chocolate décor being used for the sake of decorating a plate or to give it height, but none of the other components of the dish have anything to do with chocolate." He criticizes the use of pulled sugar garnishes for a different reason—they are seldom executed well.

"Stay away from pulled sugar if you don't feel that you can make the pieces thin enough to be easily broken with a fork and eaten without causing dental damage. Thin and delicate is the way to go with pulled sugar."

Robert Ellinger also discourages the use of elaborate garnishes. "You don't want to have to dismantle the dessert to eat it," he points out. "People who construct their plated desserts with elaborate garnishes are taking a gun and shooting themselves in the foot. Even a really elegant swirl of sugar is a wasted element because you're not going to eat it. If it's something you can't eat, it shouldn't be on the plate. During the judging you'll see garnishes like that get left on the plates as they're cleared. It's a wasted opportunity, because you had a chance to give the judges a great-looking garnish that they could eat, and you didn't do it. The garnishes that always impress me are the ones that you can eat. Even if it's a lowly mint leaf that you've candied—it's something I can eat, and that's what we're looking for. I know that every time I get a plated dessert that I need to dismantle before I eat it, I will deduct points as a judge."

On the subject of garnishes, Stephen Durfee says, "I don't add something just for the heck of it. I don't use a mint leaf unless the dish has mint as an integral part of the flavor profile. To me, that's a sign of laziness or poor imagination. The garnish," he adds, "is important for the opportunity it presents to add contrast to the dessert, especially with texture. That's why, so many years later, I still find a simple tuile-type cookie to be a great garnish."

Molecular Gastronomy: *Oui ou Non?*

In the past few years, many top pastry chefs have embraced the techniques of molecular gastronomy, a cutting-edge style of cooking that takes advantage of innovations in scientific discipline. But the use of these techniques in pastry competitions tends to be limited. A few brave souls may use a technique like "spherification"—shaping liquid into caviarlike spheres—in their plated desserts, but on the whole, the prevailing theory is that it's just too much of a risk when being judged by those who favor classic French techniques. Francisco Migoya sums it up this way: "Often the judges are 'old school' and could potentially be unfamiliar with these techniques. The last thing you want to do is scare a judge or incite his contempt. A good génoise is always better than a not-so-good foam. Also, molecular gastronomy is still too new and too closely associated with a small group of chefs—Adrià, Blumenthal, Achatz, Dufresne—and it may seem like you are ripping them off. Eventually the items that are considered part of molecular gastronomy may become commonplace. Hey, at one point, crème anglaise was invented by someone and then it was adapted by many others, to the point where now many pastry chefs have no idea who invented crème anglaise and no one has real ownership over its invention."

Stephen Durfee concurs. "In this competition, I would lean towards making things that are more classic. And I think that a classic, executed perfectly, is always going to be better than something that is innovative and not executed perfectly." Robert Ellinger was surprised at the lack of cutting-edge techniques at the most recent competition. "I noticed no spherification or other techniques from molecular gastronomy. In fact, I don't think I've ever seen it being used in this competition, which is surprising."

It Takes a Team

While competitors tend to focus primarily on recipes and techniques in preparing for the World and National Team Pastry Championships, it is important to remember that 30 percent of the final score is for how cleanly and efficiently each team works. Working together as a well-oiled team is crucial for success. Stephen Durfee, who competed at the 2005 and 2007 NPTCs, says that before he competes he writes "a pretty specific schedule of the order that we do things in, and as you practice and refine it, you shave away time." One day a friend, Pascal Janvier, owner of Fleur de Cocoa patisserie in Los Gatos, California, came to watch Durfee and his team practice and offered him his opinion. "He said, 'You know, Stephen, you work so fast and you

do so many things, that you look like you're out of control. You need to give some jobs to other people.' Someone else said, 'You look like a hummingbird—you're twice as fast as everybody else, and you do so many things, but in the end it comes across as if you don't know what you're doing because you look frantic.'" Durfee's frantic pace in the kitchen during practice was a result of a workload that was not divided efficiently among the members of his team. By giving his teammates a few of his tasks, Durfee was able to work at a more reasonable pace and appear more in control of his environment.

As En-Ming Hsu puts it, "Even if it's the most creative and flavorful dessert, it won't win if it is unable to be completed or served on time. . . . . Judges like to see a team challenge itself and make good use of time. If the team members work together, communicate, and share responsibility, it shows good team effort." A team's ability to work well together allows them to create more complex and challenging desserts. "The team needs to be well prepared and have control over their timing," explains Hsu. "Depending on the rules, the team may only have a few hours to prepare their plated dessert. They have to ensure that their program is feasible. If they maximize their time and make good use of their tools and equipment, they can push the boundaries and be impressive. However, if timing becomes a challenge, it's better for the team to stay simple and focus effort on enhancing the best-quality products available."

There's enough pressure built into the competition without a team adding extra stress by being disorganized and incommunicative. As Robert Ellinger puts it, "Some teams look great on paper, but can't handle the pressure when they get in the kitchen. They're just not prepared. It's like building a beautiful airplane. And then you put it in the air and the wings fall off because of the stress and pressure." His best advice for teams is to practice, practice, practice. "There are a lot of guys that I know who should've done really well, but didn't, because they didn't practice the stress element of the competition. The only way to win a competition is to practice. That's how you get all the kinks out. Otherwise, you might as well stay home."

PLATED DESSERT FLAVOR PAIRING GUIDE

THE FOLLOWING IS A LIST OF COMMON DESSERT FLAVORS

AND SOME OF THE FLAVORS THAT COMPLEMENT THEM, AS

RECOMMENDED BY PASTRY CHEFS.

ALLSPICE
apple
banana
carrot
cinnamon
cloves
coriander
currant
ginger
mace
nutmeg
nuts
pear
pineapple
pumpkin
sweet potato

ALMOND
apple
apricot
banana
blackberry
brandy
butter
butterscotch
caramel
cherry
chocolate (dark,
  milk, or white)
coconut
coffee
cranberry
cream cheese
currant
fig
goat cheese
honey
orange
peach
pear
plum
ricotta cheese
rum

spices
vanilla

ANISE
allspice
almond
apple
cardamom
carrot
chestnut
cinnamon
cloves
coffee
fennel
fig
fruit
ginger
goat cheese
lemon
melon
nutmeg
orange
peach
pear
pineapple
plum
prune
pumpkin
quince
raisin
ricotta cheese
rhubarb
star anise
strawberry
sweet potato
tea
vanilla

APPLE
allspice
almond
apricot
Armagnac

bacon
black pepper
blackberry
bourbon
brandy
brown sugar
butter
butterscotch
Calvados
caramel
cardamom
cheddar cheese
cherries
chestnut
cinnamon
cloves
Cognac
cranberry
crème fraîche
currant
dates
ginger
goat cheese
hazelnut
honey
lavender
lemon
lychee (or litchi)
mango
maple
molasses
nutmeg
nuts
orange
pear
pecan
pine nut
pineapple
pistachio
plum
pomegranate
prune
pumpkin

quince
raisin
raspberry
rhubarb
rosemary
rum
sour cream
star anise
sweet potato
tamarind
vanilla
walnut

APRICOT
almond
black pepper
brandy
butter
caramel
cardamom
cherry
cinnamon
coconut
coffee
Cognac
cranberry
cream cheese
ginger
hazelnut
honey
lemon
maple
mascarpone
nectarine
nutmeg
orange
peach
pecan
pine nut
pineapple
pistachio
plum
raisin

raspberry
ricotta cheese
rum
sour cream
strawberry
vanilla
walnut
white chocolate
yogurt

ASIAN PEAR
allspice
almond
apple
black pepper
black tea
blackberry
blueberry
bourbon
brandy
brown butter
butterscotch
caramel
cardamom
cashew
cinnamon
clove
fig
ginger
hazelnut
honey
macadamia
maple
mascarpone
nutmeg
pecan
pistachio
prune
raisin
raspberry
rum
vanilla

BALSAMIC VINEGAR
apricot
brown butter
cherry
honey
raspberry
strawberry

BANANA AND RED BANANA
allspice
almond
apricot
Armagnac
black pepper
blackberry
blueberry
brandy
Brazil nut
brown butter
brown sugar
buttermilk
butterscotch
caramel
cardamom
cashew
cherry
chocolate (dark, milk, or white)
cinnamon
clove
coconut
coffee
Cognac
cream cheese
crème fraîche
date
fig
ginger
guava
hazelnut
honey
lemon
lemongrass
lime
macadamia
mango
maple
molasses
nutmeg
orange
papaya
passion fruit
peanut
pecan
pineapple
pistachio
pomegranate
raisin
raspberry
rum
sesame
sour cream
strawberry
sweet potato
tamarind
vanilla
walnut
yogurt

BASIL
apple
apricot
black pepper
blueberry
chocolate (white)
cinnamon
coconut
ginger
goat cheese
grapefruit
honey
lemon
lime
mint
nectarine
orange
peach
pine nut
pineapple
raspberry
ricotta cheese
strawberry
vanilla

BAY LEAF
allspice
apple
caramel
chestnut
chocolate (dark)
date
fig
lemon
nectarine
peach
pear
plum
prune
pumpkin
quince
strawberry
vanilla

BLACK OLIVE
almond
basil
Cognac
goat cheese
lemon
orange
pine nut

BLACK PEPPER
almond
apple
apricot
banana
basil
cardamom
cherry
chestnut
cinnamon
clove
coconut
fig
ginger
grapefruit
lemon
lime
mango
melon
orange
papaya
peach
pineapple
plantain
pumpkin
raspberry
strawberry
sweet potato

BLACKBERRY
almond
apple
apricot
banana
black pepper
blueberry
brandy
brown sugar
buttermilk
caramel
Champagne
chocolate (dark or white)
cinnamon
cloves
cornmeal
cream cheese
crème fraîche
ginger
goat cheese
hazelnut
honey
lemon
lime
mango
mascarpone
melon
mint
nectarine
orange
peach

plum
Port
raspberry
sour cream
strawberry
vanilla

BLOOD ORANGE
allspice
almond
cardamom
chocolate (dark or white)
cinnamon
clove
fig
ginger
honey
pistachio
pomegranate

BLUEBERRY
allspice
almond
apple
banana
black pepper
blackberry
brandy
buttermilk
chocolate (white)
cinnamon
clove
cornmeal
cream cheese
crème fraîche
ginger
honey
lemon
lime
mango
maple
mascarpone
melon
mint
molasses
nectarine
nutmeg
orange
peach
pear
pecan
pine nuts
pineapple
raspberry
rhubarb
ricotta cheese
rum
sour cream
strawberry
vanilla

walnut
yogurt

BUTTERSCOTCH
almond
chocolate (dark)
coconut
coffee
cream cheese
lemon
rum
vanilla

CANTALOUPE
basil
black pepper
fennel
ginger
grapefruit
lemon
lemongrass
lime
mint
raspberry
star anise
tarragon

CARAMEL
almond
apple
apricot
banana
bourbon
cherry
chocolate (dark, milk, or white)
cinnamon
coffee
cream cheese
lemon
lime
macadamia
mango
nutmeg
passion fruit
peach
peanut
pear
pecan
plum
raisin
rhubarb
rum
sesame
vanilla

CARDAMOM

anise
apple
apricot
banana
black pepper
black tea
blueberry
carrot
chocolate (dark,
   milk, or white)
cinnamon
clove
coffee
date
ginger
grapefruit
honey
lemon
lime
nectarine
orange
peach
pear
pistachio
plum
raspberry
strawberry
sweet potato
vanilla
walnut

CARROT

allspice
almond
black pepper
brandy
brown butter
brown sugar
cinnamon
crème fraîche
fennel
ginger
hazelnut
honey
lemon
lime
maple
molasses
nutmeg
orange
pecan
raisin
rum
star anise
tamarind
walnut

CASHEW

almond
apricot
banana
brown butter
brown sugar
caramel
cinnamon
chocolate (dark,
   milk, or white)
cinnamon
coconut
coffee
cream cheese
date
ginger
grapefruit
guava
honey
lemon
macadamia
mango
mint
nutmeg
papaya
passion fruit
persimmon
pineapple
rum
vanilla

CHAMPAGNE

blackberry
cherry
cranberry
lemon
lime
melon
mint
nectarine
peach
raspberry
strawberry

CHERRY

allspice
almond
apricot
Armagnac
black pepper
bourbon
brandy
buttermilk
caramel
chocolate (dark,
   milk, or white)
cinnamon
clove
coconut
coffee
cream cheese

crème fraîche
fennel
fig
ginger
hazelnut
honey
lemon
lime
mascarpone
melon
nectarine
orange
peach
pecan
pistachio
plum
Port
quince
raspberry
red wine
ricotta cheese
rose
rum
sour cream
vanilla
walnut
yogurt

CHESTNUT

apple
Armagnac
black pepper
brandy
caramel
cardamom
chocolate (dark,
   milk, or white)
cinnamon
cloves
coffee
crème fraîche
fennel
fig
ginger
honey
lemon
maple
Marsala
mascarpone
nutmeg
orange
pear
prune
raisin
raspberry
ricotta cheese
rum
vanilla

CHOCOLATE, DARK

allspice
almond
anise
apricot
Armagnac
banana
basil
black pepper
black tea
bourbon
brandy
butterscotch
caramel
cardamom
cashew
cherry
chocolate (dark,
   milk, or white)
cinnamon
clove
coconut
coffee
Cognac
cream cheese
crème fraîche
currant (dried and
   red)
date
fig
ginger
green tea
hazelnut
honey
lavender
lemon
macadamia
maple
mascarpone
mint
orange
passion fruit
peanut
pear
pecan
prune
raisin
raspberry
ricotta cheese
rum
sour cream
strawberry
vanilla
walnut

CHOCOLATE, MILK

almond
apricot
caramel
cherry
chestnut
cinnamon
coconut
coffee
ginger
hazelnut
honey
lavender
orange
peanut
pear
pecan
raspberry
rum
walnut

CHOCOLATE, WHITE

almond
apricot
banana
basil
blackberry
blueberry
caramel
cashew
cherry
chocolate (dark,
   milk, or white)
cinnamon
coconut
Concord grape
cranberry
date
fig
ginger
hazelnut
lemon
lime
macadamia
mango
mint
orange
papaya
passion fruit
persimmon
pistachio
pomegranate
prune
raspberry
red currant
rum
strawberry
vanilla

CILANTRO
apricot
basil
blackberry
blueberry
cardamom
carrot
cherry
coconut
corn
fig
ginger
lemon
lemongrass
lime
mint
nectarine
orange
peach
plum
raspberry
strawberry

CINNAMON
apple
apricot
banana
black tea
blackberry
blueberry
caramel
cardamom
cherry
chocolate (dark, milk, or white)
clove
coffee
cream cheese
fig
ginger
honey
lemon
mango
maple
nectarine
nutmeg
orange
peach
pear
pecan
plum
pumpkin
red wine
star anise
tamarind
vanilla
yogurt

CLOVE
allspice
almond
apple
apricot
banana
black tea
cardamom
carrot
cinnamon
coffee
date
fennel
ginger
honey
lemon
lime
nectarine
orange
peach
pear
pine nut
pineapple
plum
pumpkin
red wine
star anise
tamarind
vanilla
walnut

COCONUT
allspice
almond
apricot
banana
basil
blackberry
caramel
cashew
cherry
chocolate (dark, milk, or white)
cilantro
cinnamon
clove
date
fig
ginger
grapefruit
green tea
honey
kumquat
lemon
lemongrass
lime
lychee (or litchi)
macadamia
mango
maple
mascarpone

mint
nutmeg
orange
papaya
passion fruit
peanut
pineapple
pistachio
plantain
rum
sesame
vanilla

COFFEE
almond
anise
banana
bourbon
brandy
caramel
cardamom
cherry
chocolate (dark, milk, or white)
cinnamon
clove
coconut
Cognac
date
fennel
fig
hazelnut
honey
lemon
lime
macadamia
maple
nutmeg
orange
pear
pecan
prune
raisin
ricotta cheese
rum
star anise
vanilla

COGNAC
apple
chocolate (dark, milk, or white)
prune
raisin
vanilla

CORN
allspice
basil
blackberry
blueberry
buttermilk
carrot
caramel
cilantro
fennel
ginger
lemon
lime
maple
mascarpone
nutmeg
raspberry
star anise
vanilla

CRANBERRY
allspice
almond
apple
apricot
brown sugar
chocolate (dark, milk, or white)
cinnamon
clove
cream cheese
ginger
goat cheese
hazelnut
honey
lemon
lime
maple
orange
peach
pear
pistachio
pumpkin
raisin
quince
star anise
tangerine
vanilla
walnut

CRÈME FRAÎCHE
apple
brown sugar
caramel
cherry
nectarine
peach
raspberry
strawberry

CUCUMBER
allspice
buttermilk
coconut
cream cheese
crème fraîche
lemon
lime
melon
mint
pineapple
sour cream

CURRANT
chocolate (dark, milk, or white)
lemon
lime
orange
Port
raspberries
red wine
strawberries

CURRY
allspice
cardamom
cashew
cinnamon
clove
coconut
crème fraîche
fennel
lime
ginger
lemongrass
star anise
tamarind

DATE
almond
apple
apricot
Armagnac
banana
brandy
brown sugar
buttermilk
caramel
cherry
chocolate (dark, milk, or white)
cinnamon
coconut
coffee
cranberry
cream cheese
crème fraîche
currant
fig
ginger

hazelnut
honey
lemon
lime
macadamia
maple
mascarpone
orange
pecan
pistachio
prune
quince
raisin
rum
vanilla
walnut

ELDERBERRY
apricot
cream cheese
fig
honey
lemon
nectarine
raspberry
peach
plum
strawberry
red wine

FENNEL
almond
anise
apple
crème fraîche
ginger
honey
lemon
lime
mint
orange
pear
pecan
star anise

FIG
almond
anise
black pepper
caramel
goat cheese
chocolate (dark,
    milk, or white)
cinnamon
coconut
crème fraîche
ginger
honey
lavender
lemon
mint

molasses
orange
peach
pear
pecan
Port
praline
quince
raspberry
red wine
sour cream
strawberry
thyme
vanilla
walnut

GINGER
allspice
almond
anise
apple
apricot
banana
black tea
caramel
cardamom
carrot
cashew
chocolate (dark,
    milk, or white)
cinnamon
clove
coconut
cranberry
fennel
fig
grape
grapefruit
hazelnut
honey
kumquat
lavender
lemon
lemongrass
lime
lychee (or litchi)
macadamia
mango
maple
melon
mint
nectarine
orange
papaya
passion fruit
peach
peanut
pear
persimmon
pineapple
plum

prune
pumpkin
quince
raisin
raspberry
rhubarb
rum
star anise
strawberry
tamarind
vanilla

GOAT CHEESE
almond
apple
apricot
black pepper
blackberry
cherry
cinnamon
cranberry
date
fennel
fig
grape
honey
lemon
mint
nutmeg
orange
pear
pecan
pine nut
pistachio
Port
raspberry
rum
star anise
strawberry
vanilla
walnut

GOOSEBERRY
chocolate (white)
hazelnut
honey
raspberry
strawberry
white chocolate

GRAPE
almond
apple
chocolate (white)
fennel
goat cheese
hazelnut
mint
pear
pecan
pistachio

raspberry
strawberry

GRAPEFRUIT
banana
caramel
cashew
coconut
ginger
hazelnut
honey
lemon
lime
macadamia
melon
mint
orange
papaya
pecan
pineapple
pomegranate
Port
raspberry
rum
star anise
strawberry
tarragon
vanilla
walnut
yogurt

GUAVA
banana
cashew
chocolate (white)
coconut
cream cheese
ginger
honey
huckleberry
lemon
lime
macadamia
mascarpone
orange
passion fruit
pineapple
raisin
rum
strawberry
vanilla

HAZELNUT
almond
apple
apricot
banana
buttermilk
caramel
cherry
chestnut

chocolate (dark,
    milk, or white)
cinnamon
coffee
Cognac
cranberry
cream cheese
date
fig
ginger
goat cheese
grape
grapefruit
honey
lemon
mango
maple
mascarpone
mint
nectarine
orange
peach
pear
pecan
persimmon
plum
prune
pumpkin
raisin
raspberry
red wine
rum
strawberry
walnut
white chocolate

HONEY
almond
apple
apricot
banana
buttermilk
chocolate (dark,
    milk, or white)
chestnut
cinnamon
coconut
coffee
Cognac
date
fig
ginger
goat cheese
grape
grapefruit
guava
hazelnut
kiwi
kumquat
lavender
lemon

lime
lychee (or litchi)
mascarpone
melon
mint
nectarine
orange
papaya
peach
pear
pecan
persimmon
pineapple
pine nut
pistachio
plum
pomegranate
prune
pumpkin
quince
raspberry
red currant

KIWI
apple
banana
cherry

coconut
honey
lemon
lime
mango
orange
passion fruit
strawberry

KUMQUAT
blackberry
cherry
chocolate (dark,
  milk, or white)
cinnamon
coffee
persimmon
plum
raspberry
strawberry

LAVENDER
almond
apple
black tea
blackberry
blueberry
cherry
fig
ginger
honey
lemon
mint
orange

peach
pistachio
plum
raspberry
rhubarb
strawberry
vanilla
walnut

LEMON
apple
apricot
banana
basil
blackberry
black pepper
blueberry
buttermilk
caramel
cardamom
cherry
chestnut
chocolate (dark,
  milk, or white)
cinnamon
coconut
coffee
cranberry
cream cheese
date
fig
ginger
grapefruit
grape
guava
goat cheese
hazelnut
honey
kiwi
lemongrass
lime
mango
mascarpone
mint
nectarine
orange
papaya
passion fruit
peach
pear
pecan
persimmon
pine nut
pistachio
plum
prickly pear
prune
quince
raspberry
rhubarb
rum
sour cream

walnut
yogurt

LEMONGRASS
black tea
cherry
cinnamon
clove
coconut
ginger
guava
honey
lime
mint
raspberry
strawberry
vanilla

LEMON VERBENA
apricot
blueberry
cherry
cinnamon
ginger
grape
green tea
honey
lavender
lemon
lemongrass
lime
melon
mint
nectarine
peach
plum
raspberry
strawberry
yogurt

LIME
apricot
blueberry
buttermilk
caramel
chocolate (white)
cream cheese
date
fig
ginger
grapefruit
green tea
guava
hazelnut
honey
kiwi
lemon
mango
mascarpone
melon
mint
orange

papaya
pecan
plum
raspberry
rum
strawberry
tequila
vanilla
yogurt

LOQUAT
ginger
grapefruit
lemon
lime
mango
orange
papaya
vanilla

LYCHEE (LITCHI)
blackberry
coconut
cream cheese
ginger
honey
kiwi
lemon
lemongrass
lime
mango
melon
orange
passion fruit
pear
pineapple
plum
raspberry
rum
strawberry
yogurt

MACADAMIA
NUT
apricot
banana
caramel
cashew
chocolate (dark,
  milk, or white)
coconut
coffee
date
fig
ginger
goat cheese
grapefruit
guava
honey
lemon
lime
mango

maple
mint
orange
papaya
passion fruit
peach
pineapple
prune
raspberry
rum

MANGO
almond
anise
apple
blackberry
blueberry
buttermilk
caramel
cashew
chocolate (white)
cinnamon
coconut
coffee
ginger
grapefruit
honey
kiwi
kumquat
lemon
lime
macadamia nut
mascarpone
melon
mint
orange
papaya
passion fruit
pineapple
raspberry
rum
star anise
strawberry
vanilla
yogurt

MAPLE
almond
apple
apricot
banana
blueberry
buttermilk
caramel
chestnut
chocolate (dark,
  milk, or white)
cinnamon
coffee
cream cheese
date
fig

ginger
hazelnut
lemon
lime
macadamia
nectarine
orange
peach
pear
pecan
persimmon
pineapple
plum
prune
pumpkin
quince
raspberry
rhubarb
rum
strawberry
walnut

MINT

apple
apricot
chocolate (dark
    or white)
cinnamon
coconut
ginger
grapefruit
honey
lavender
lemon
lemongrass
lime
mango
melon
nectarine
orange
peach
pear

pineapple
plum
raspberry
strawberry
vanilla

NECTARINE

almond
black pepper
blackberry
blueberry
caramel
Champagne
cherry
cinnamon
fig
ginger
orange
peach
raspberry
vanilla

ORANGE

allspice
basil
cardamom
cherry
chocolate (dark,
    milk, or white)
cinnamon
coconut
coffee
fig
ginger
mango
nutmeg
olive
pecan
star anise
strawberry
vanilla

PAPAYA

black pepper
caramel
cashew
chocolate (white)
cinnamon
coconut
ginger
grapefruit
honey
kiwi
kumquat
lemon
lime
macadamia nut
mango
melon
mint
nectarine
orange
passion fruit
peach
pineapple
raspberry
strawberry
vanilla
yogurt

PASSION FRUIT

almond
banana
caramel
cashew
chocolate (white)
coconut
cream cheese
ginger
kiwi
lemon
lime
macadamia nut
mango

orange
papaya
peach
pear
pineapple
rum
strawberry
tequila
vanilla
yogurt

PEACH

allspice
almond
apple
apricot
basil
black pepper
black tea
blackberry
blueberry
bourbon
brandy
buttermilk
caramel
cardamom
cherry
cinnamon
clove
coconut
crème fraîche
fig
ginger
green tea
hazelnut
honey
lavender
lemon
lime
maple
mascarpone
mint

molasses
nectarine
orange
papaya
passion fruit
pecan
pineapple
pistachio
plum
raspberry
red currant
red wine
rum
star anise
strawberry
tarragon
walnut
white wine
vanilla
yogurt

PEANUT

apple
banana
caramel
chocolate (dark,
    milk, or white)
coconut
coffee
ginger
honey
lemon
lime
pear
raisin
raspberry
strawberry
vanilla

PEAR
allspice
almond
anise
apple
blackberry
blueberry
bourbon
brandy
caramel
cardamom
crème de cassis
cherry
chestnut
chocolate (dark
 or white)
cinnamon
clove
cream cheese
date
fennel
fig
ginger
hazelnut
honey
lemon
macadamia
maple
mint
nutmeg
orange
passion fruit
pecan
pine nut
pistachio
Port
prune
quince
raisin
raspberry
red wine
rosemary
rum
star anise
strawberry
vanilla
walnut

PECAN
almond
apple
apricot
banana
blackberry
blueberry
bourbon
brandy
caramel
cherry
chocolate (dark,
 milk, or white)

cinnamon
date
ginger
goat cheese
grapefruit
hazelnut
honey
kumquat
lemon
maple
mascarpone
molasses
nectarine
nutmeg
orange
peach
pear
persimmon
plum
prune
pumpkin
quince
raisin
raspberry
red wine
rum
strawberry
vanilla

PERSIMMON
almond
apple
black pepper
bourbon
brandy
caramel
chocolate (white)
cinnamon
clove
coffee
ginger
honey
kiwi
kumquat
lemon
lime
maple
orange
pear
pecan
pomegranate
rum
vanilla
walnut
yogurt

PINEAPPLE
allspice
apricot
banana
basil
black pepper
brandy
caramel
cardamom
chocolate (dark)
cilantro
cinnamon
clove
coconut
fennel
ginger
grapefruit
honey
kiwi
kumquat
lemon
lime
macadamia nut
mango
maple
mint
orange
papaya
passion fruit
pistachio
pomegranate
raspberry
rosemary
rum
star anise
strawberry
tamarind
vanilla
yogurt

PINE NUT
apple
apricot
basil
caramel
fig
goat cheese
honey
lemon
nectarine
orange
peach
pear
plum
prune
raspberry
red wine
rum
vanilla
walnut

PISTACHIO
apple
apricot
banana
basil
cardamom
cherry
chocolate (dark
 or white)
coconut
cranberry
date
fig
ginger
goat cheese
honey
kumquat
lavender
lemon
lemongrass
mango
melon
nectarine
orange
peach
pear
plum
prune
quince
raspberry
vanilla

PLANTAIN
allspice
black pepper
caramel
chocolate (dark)
cinnamon
coconut
cranberry
dark rum
ginger
honey
lemon
lime
Madeira
orange
star anise

PLUM
allspice
almond
anise
apricot
black pepper
brandy
buttermilk
caramel
cardamom
cherry
cinnamon

clove
ginger
honey
lavender
lemon
maple
mint
nectarine
orange
peach
Port
raisin
raspberry
rum
strawberry
walnut
vanilla
yogurt

PRUNE
allspice
almond
anise
apple
apricot
Armagnac
black pepper
brandy
caramel
chestnut
chocolate (dark
 or white)
cinnamon
clove
coffee
Cognac
date
fig
ginger
honey
lemon
maple
orange
pear
pecan
pine nut
pistachio
quince
rum
star anise
vanilla
walnut

PUMPKIN
allspice
apple
black pepper
brandy
caramel
cardamom

chocolate (dark or white)
cinnamon
clove
coconut
cranberry
cream cheese
ginger
honey
kumquat
lemon
lime
maple
molasses
nutmeg
orange
pecan
pine nut
quince
raisin
sour cream
vanilla
walnut

QUINCE
almond
apple
black pepper
brandy
caramel
cardamom
cherry
cinnamon
clove
cranberry
date
fennel
fig
ginger
hazelnut
kumquat
lemon
maple
mascarpone
nutmeg
orange
pear
pecan
pistachio
raisin
raspberry
star anise
walnut

RASPBERRY
almond
apricot
blackberry
blueberry
caramel
chocolate (dark or white)
cinnamon
citrus
crème fraîche
fig
ginger
goat cheese
honey
lemon
lime
mango
mascarpone
melon
mint
nectarine
peach
pear
pineapple
plum
rhubarb
orange
red currant
rhubarb
sour cream
strawberry
thyme
vanilla

RHUBARB
almond
apple
apricot
black pepper
chocolate (white)
cinnamon
fennel
ginger
lemon
nectarine
orange
peach
plum
Port
raspberry
sour cream
star anise
strawberry
vanilla

ROSEMARY
apple
grapefruit
honey
lemon
lime
orange
pear

SAFFRON
ginger
lemon
orange
vanilla

SESAME SEED
apple
banana
ginger
honey
lemon
vanilla

STRAWBERRY
almond
apricot
banana
balsamic vinegar
black pepper
ginger
honey
lemon
lime
mango
melon
mint
papaya
passion fruit
peach
pineapple
pink peppercorn
pistachio
plum
pomegranate
Port
raspberry
rhubarb
rum
vanilla

TAMARIND
almond
banana
cinnamon
clove
coconut
date
fennel
ginger
honey
lime
mango
mint
orange
peach
pear
pineapple
star anise

TARRAGON
anise
apple
grapefruit
lemon
lime
melon
mint
nectarine
orange
peach

THYME
apple
chocolate (dark)
grapefruit
lemon
mint
orange
pear
raspberry

VANILLA
almond
apple
apricot
caramel
chocolate (dark)
cinnamon
coconut
coffee
cream cheese
fig
ginger
honey
lavender
lemon

lemongrass
melon
mint
orange
peach
pear
plum
rhubarb
rosemary
saffron
strawberry
tea

WALNUT
apple
apricot
banana
caramel
chocolate (dark)
cinnamon
nectarine
peach
pear
plum
pumpkin
rum

YOGURT
almond
apricot
banana
blackberry
blueberry
cinnamon
coconut
honey
lemon
lime
mango
maple
mint
nectarine
orange
peach
pineapple
pistachio
strawberry
vanilla

The Recipes

Christopher Boos

Phil Gormley

Glenn Bossie

BANANA AND MALTED MILK CHOCOLATE MOUSSE WITH CHERRY SAUCE

This classic plated dessert from Team Boos for the NPTC in 2000 featured the pairing of a Banana and Malted Milk Chocolate Mousse on an almond Jaconde cake. The dessert was frozen, unmolded, and then sprayed with a mixture of chocolate and cocoa butter before being sliced for serving. The rich mousse dessert was accented by a tart cherry sauce and served with sablé cookies and an elegant, flowing tuile.

MAKES 12 SERVINGS

Jaconde

90 g (3.2 oz/1 cup) almond flour

90 g (3.2 oz/scant ½ cup) granulated sugar

15 g (0.5 oz/2¼ tsp) invert sugar

150 g (5.3 oz/3 large) whole eggs

30 g (1.1 oz/¼ cup) all-purpose flour

90 g (3.2 oz/3 large) egg whites

45 g (1.6 oz/3 Tbsp plus ¾ tsp) unsalted butter, melted

1. Preheat the oven to 350°F (175°C).

2. Combine the almond flour, 30 g (1.1 oz/2 Tbsp plus 1½ tsp) of the granulated sugar, the invert sugar, eggs, and all-purpose flour in a food processor.

3. In the bowl of a stand mixer fitted with the whisk attachment, whip the egg whites with the remaining 60 g (2.1 oz/¼ cup plus 2¾ tsp) granulated sugar on high speed until they just hold a soft shape and fold into the almond flour mixture.

4. Fold in the melted butter. Spread out the batter in a parchment paper–lined sheet pan and bake for 8 minutes, or until set. Cool.

Banana Mousse

100 g (3.5 oz/2 large) whole eggs

85 g (3 oz/4½ large) egg yolks

85 g (3 oz/⅓ cup plus 1 Tbsp plus 2½ tsp) granulated sugar

16 g (0.56 oz/10 sheets) gelatin (platinum grade), bloomed and drained

57 g (2 oz/½ cup) freeze-dried banana powder

170 g (6 oz/¾ cup) banana purée

100 g (3.5 oz/⅓ cup plus 2 Tbsp plus 1 tsp) dark rum

454 g (16 oz/2 cups) heavy cream (40% butterfat)

1. In the bowl of a stand mixer fitted with the whisk attachment, begin beating the eggs and egg yolks on medium-low speed.

2. In a saucepan, combine the sugar with some water (about 2 Tbsp) and cook over high heat to the soft ball stage, 238°F (114°C). With the mixer running, pour the hot syrup onto the eggs, add the drained gelatin, and mix on high speed until cool.

3. In a bowl, combine the banana powder, banana purée, and rum and blend into the egg mixture.

4. Whip the cream on high speed to medium peaks and gently fold into the egg mixture. Pour into a 1-in (2.54-cm) diameter x 10-in- (25.4-cm-) long acetate plastic tube and freeze until set.

Malted Milk Chocolate Mousse

680 g (1.5 lb) bittersweet chocolate, chopped

200 g (7 oz) milk chocolate, chopped

142 g (5 oz/1¼ cups) malt powder

113 g (4 oz/⅓ cup plus 2 Tbsp plus 2 tsp) water

14 g (0.5 oz/9 sheets) gelatin (platinum grade), bloomed and drained

200 g (7 oz/6½ large) egg whites

200 g (7 oz/1 cup) granulated sugar

454 g (16 oz/2 cups) heavy cream (40% butterfat), whipped to medium peaks

1. Place the chopped dark and milk chocolate in a large bowl and set aside.

2. In a small saucepan, combine the malt powder and water and place over medium heat, whisking until the malt is dissolved. Add the drained gelatin and stir to dissolve. Pour the hot mixture over the chopped chocolate in the bowl and whisk to emulsify. Cool to room temperature.

3. In the bowl of a stand mixer fitted with the whisk attachment, begin beating the egg whites on medium-low speed. In a saucepan, combine the sugar with some water (about 2 Tbsp) and cook to the soft ball stage, 238°F (114°C). With the mixer running, pour the hot syrup onto the egg whites, and beat on high speed until cool to form a meringue.

4. Fold the meringue into the cooled chocolate mixture. Fold in the whipped cream.

5. Line a triangular mold that has 3-in (7.6-cm) sides and is 10 in (25.4 cm) long with acetate. Fill the mold halfway with the Malted Milk Chocolate Mousse. Unmold a tube of frozen Banana Mousse and place it on top, in the center. Fill the mold with the remaining Malted Milk Chocolate Mousse. Cut a rectangle of Jaconde cake to fit the base of the mold and place it on top. Freeze for several hours, or until firm.

Hippenmasse

57 g (2 oz/⅓ cup plus 2 Tbsp plus 2 tsp) all-purpose flour

57 g (2 oz/½ cup) confectioners' sugar

Pinch of salt

57 g (2 oz/2 large) egg whites

57 g (2 oz/½ stick) unsalted butter, melted

Pure vanilla extract

1. In a bowl, sift together the flour, sugar, and salt. Add the egg whites, melted butter, and vanilla to taste. Whisk just until combined. Set the batter aside to rest for 1½ hours before using.

2. Preheat the oven to 325°F (163°C).

3. Spread the batter over a 7-in- (17¾-cm-) long x 1¼-in- (3-cm-) wide stencil, placed on a silicone baking mat–lined sheet pan. Bake until golden brown around the edges, about 5 minutes. Shape while warm.

Cherry Sauce

57 g (2 oz/¼ cup) cherry juice

42 g (1.5 oz/3 Tbsp plus 1 tsp) granulated sugar

14 g (0.5 oz/1 Tbsp plus 2½ tsp) modified food starch

25 cherries in kirsch

1. In a saucepan, bring the cherry juice to a boil over high heat. Add the sugar and starch and cook, whisking, until thickened. Strain and stir in the cherries.

Caramelized Bananas

2 bananas, peeled and sliced

Granulated sugar, as needed

1. Place the banana slices on a sheet pan and sprinkle with sugar. Caramelize each banana slice with a torch.

Chocolate Spray

85 g (3 oz) bittersweet chocolate
85 g (3 oz/½ cup) cocoa butter

1. Melt the chocolate with the cocoa butter in a stainless steel bowl set over a pot of barely simmering water; the bottom of the bowl should not touch the water. Pour the melted chocolate in a spray gun canister. Unmold the mousse triangle and spray with the chocolate and cocoa butter mixture. Let set.

ASSEMBLY

Red-tinted cocoa butter
Sablé cookies (see page 309)

1. Place a cherry stencil on each white plate and spray it with the red-tinted cocoa butter. Carefully remove the stencil.

2. Cut the mousse triangle into 1¼-in (3-cm) slices. Arrange a slice, standing up, on each plate, near the cherries. Garnish each plate with a Hippenmasse cookie, sablé cookies, Cherry Sauce, and Caramelized Bananas.

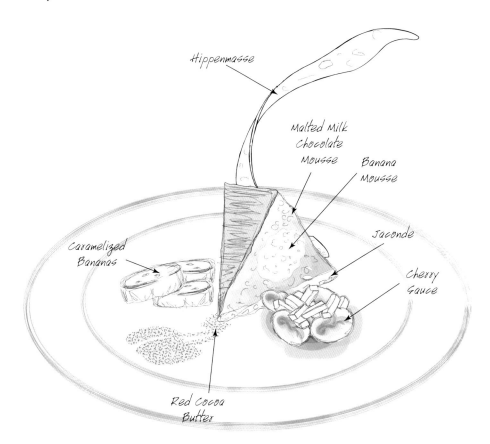

Hippenmasse

Malted Milk Chocolate Mousse

Banana Mousse

Jaconde

Cherry Sauce

Caramelized Bananas

Red Cocoa Butter

Stanton Ho

Donald Wressel

Michael Hu

CITRUS

As its name reflects, Team Ho's plated dessert from the 2000 National Pastry Team Championship celebrates the bold flavors of citrus fruits, including limequats, Buddha's Hand lemons, Meyer lemons, citron, Uniq fruit, and limes. At its center is a Meyer Lemon Curd Tart, topped with a crunchy meringue round, Uniq Citrus Granité, and a quenelle of Meyer Lemon Sorbet. Citron-flavored ravioli and a Citrus Herb Soup, flavored with lemongrass and peppermint, surrounds the flavorful tart.

MAKES 8 SERVINGS

Candied Fruit Confit

454 g (1 lb) limequats or kumquats, halved

1 Buddha's Hand lemon, thinly shaved on a mandoline

Granulated sugar, as needed

Glucose syrup, as needed

1. Three days in advance, place the fruit in a saucepan with cold water and bring to a boil over high heat. Strain and repeat four more times. Taste fruit for bitterness. If it is still bitter, repeat another time.

2. In a saucepan, combine equal parts of sugar and water and bring to a boil. Add the blanched fruit, reduce the heat to low, and simmer gently for 30 minutes. Cool and let stand in the refrigerator overnight.

3. Add another part of sugar to the syrup and bring to a boil. Simmer for 10 minutes, then remove from the heat and cool. Let stand overnight.

4. On the third day, add one part glucose to the syrup and bring to a boil. Remove from the heat and cool. Let stand overnight.

5. Bring the syrup to a boil. Remove from the heat and cool. The fruit confit is now ready to use.

Citron Gel for Ravioli

Zest of 4 lemons, removed in strips without the white pith

600 g (21.16 oz/2½ cups plus 2 tsp) Evian water

10 g (0.35 oz/½ bunch) fresh mint sprigs

250 g (8.8 oz/1¼ cups) granulated sugar

24 g (0.84 oz/12 sheets) gelatin (silver grade), bloomed and drained

400 g (14.1 oz/1½ cups plus 1 Tbsp plus 2 tsp) freshly squeezed lemon juice, passed through a coffee filter

1. The night before using, blanch the lemon zest in boiling water for 1 minute and strain.

2. In a saucepan over high heat, combine the Evian water, blanched zest, and fresh mint and bring to a boil. Remove from the heat, cover, and allow to infuse for 15 minutes. Strain, discard the zest and mint, and return the infused liquid to the saucepan.

3. Heat the infusion and whisk in the sugar and drained gelatin until dissolved. Strain through a chinois lined with a coffee filter. Cool. Stir in the lemon juice.

4. Line a perfectly flat sheet pan with plastic wrap, making the plastic wrap fit as smoothly as possible. Pour in enough of the gel liquid to cover the plastic wrap; you want a thin layer, about ¹⁄₁₆ in (1½ mm) thick. Allow to set on a level surface before transferring to the refrigerator. Let set in the refrigerator until firm, about 2 hours.

Meyer Lemon Curd

114 g (4 oz/⅓ cup plus 2 Tbsp plus 1 tsp) freshly squeezed Meyer lemon juice

92 g (3.24 oz/⅓ cup plus 2 Tbsp plus 1 tsp) granulated sugar

104 g (3.66 oz/2 large) whole eggs

38 g (1.34 oz/2 large) egg yolks

86 g (3 oz/¾ stick) unsalted butter

1. Place all of the ingredients in a stainless steel bowl, set over a pot of simmering water, and whisk until thickened. Transfer to a clean container and cool to room temperature. Cover and store in the refrigerator.

Minced fresh mint leaves

1. Place some of the Meyer Lemon Curd in a cornet. Pipe out small portions of the curd, about ½-in (1¼-cm) dollops, onto the Citron Gel on half of the sheet pan, leaving about 1½ in (3.75 cm) between portions.

2. Top each dollop with a small amount of the Candied Fruit Confit and some minced mint leaves. Fold over the other half of the gel. Using a 2-in (5-cm) round cutter, cut out each ravioli; you will need a total of 24. Set the ravioli aside.

Citrus Herb Soup

100 g (3.5 oz/½ cup) granulated sugar
6 g (0.21 oz/2 tsp) apple pectin
500 g (17.6 oz/2 cups plus 1 Tbsp plus 2¼ tsp) Evian water
10 g (0.35 oz/½ bunch) fresh peppermint
1 stem lemongrass, coarsely chopped
8 whole black peppercorns
1 vanilla bean, split lengthwise and seeds scraped
Zest and juice of 1 lemon

1. Combine 33 g (1.16 oz/2 Tbsp plus 2 tsp) of the sugar with the pectin and set aside.

2. In a saucepan, combine the remaining 67 g (2.34 oz/5 Tbsp plus 1 tsp) sugar with the water, peppermint, lemongrass, peppercorns, vanilla bean seeds and pod, lemon juice, and lemon zest. Cover the saucepan with plastic wrap and refrigerate overnight to let the flavors infuse.

3. Remove the plastic wrap and place the saucepan over medium-low heat. As the mixture becomes hot, add the sugar-pectin mixture. Reduce the heat to low and continue to cook, stirring occasionally, for another 5 minutes. Remove from the heat and cool.

4. Strain the soup through a chinois lined with a coffee filter and refrigerate until chilled.

Uniq Citrus Granité

500 g (17.6 oz/2 cups) Uniq fruit juice
14 g (0.5 oz/1 Tbsp plus ⅓ tsp) superfine granulated sugar

1. Combine both ingredients. Using a refractometer, gauge the mixture at 15° Brix.

2. Pour the mixture into a quarter-sheet pan and immediately freeze. Once frozen, use a fork to scrape it into a finely grated shaved ice. Freeze until ready to use.

Meyer Lemon Sorbet

460 g (16.22 oz/2¼ cups plus 2¼ tsp) granulated sugar

200 g (7 oz/1¼ cups) powdered glucose

3 g (0.1 oz/1¼ tsp) sorbet stabilizer

925 g (32.6 oz/scant 4 cups) water

500 g (17.6 oz/2 cups) freshly squeezed Meyer lemon juice

1. In a bowl, combine half of the sugar with the glucose powder. In another bowl, combine the remaining sugar with the sorbet stabilizer.

2. In a saucepan, bring the water to a boil over high heat. Whisk in the sugar-glucose mixture and continue to cook for 1 minute. Whisk in the sugar-stabilizer mixture. Cook for another minute to activate the stabilizer.

3. Stir in the lemon juice, transfer to a container, cover, and refrigerate for at least 4 hours.

4. Process the sorbet base in an ice cream machine according to the manufacturer's instructions.

Lime Tart Dough

344 g (12.13 oz/3 sticks plus 1 tsp) unsalted butter

172 g (6 oz/¾ cup plus 1 Tbsp plus 2¼ tsp) granulated sugar

Finely grated zest of 1 lime

1 vanilla bean, split lengthwise and seeds scraped

42 g (1.48 oz/2¼ large) egg yolks

52 g (1.8 oz/1 large) whole egg

510 g (18 oz/4½ cups) pastry flour, sifted

1. In the bowl of a stand mixer fitted with the paddle attachment, blend the butter with the sugar, lime zest, and vanilla bean seeds on medium speed. Gradually add the egg yolks and whole egg and mix on medium speed until blended. Add the flour and mix just until blended. Scrape the dough out onto a work surface and shape it into 2 disks. Wrap the disks in plastic wrap and refrigerate for at least an hour.

2. Preheat the oven to 375°F (190°C).

3. Roll the dough out on a lightly floured work surface to a thickness of ⅒ in (2.5 mm). Line four 3-in (7.6-cm) flan rings with the dough. Prick the bottom of the dough and bake for 10 minutes, until lightly golden. Cool.

Meringue Disks

114 g (4 oz/3¾ large) egg whites

114 g (4 oz/½ cup plus 1 Tbsp plus ½ tsp) granulated sugar

114 g (4 oz/1 cup) confectioners' sugar, sifted

1. Preheat the oven to 180°F (82°C).

2. In the bowl of a stand mixer fitted with the whisk attachment, beat the egg whites on high speed to soft peaks. Gradually add the granulated sugar and beat until stiff. Fold in the confectioners' sugar.

3. Scrape the meringue into a pastry bag fitted with a medium plain tip. Pipe out 3-in (7.6-cm) rounds onto a silicone baking mat–lined sheet pan. Bake until dry, at least 1 hour.

ASSEMBLY

Kite-shaped phyllo garnishes

1. Fill each lime tart shell with Meyer Lemon Curd. Arrange each tart in the center of a plate and top with a Meringue Disk. Top with a large scoop of the Uniq Citrus Granité, then a quenelle of Meyer Lemon Sorbet. Arrange 3 ravioli around each dessert and spoon some of the Citrus-Herb Soup around the plate. Top each dessert with a kite-shaped phyllo garnish.

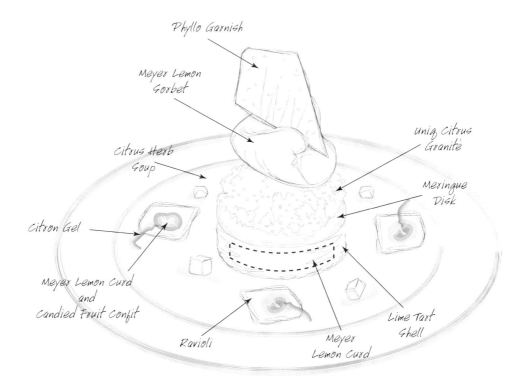

STRAWBERRY AND ALMOND MILK DELIGHT, RED CURRANT AND WINE JUS

Knowing that the dégustation *judges would be tasting a* lot *of desserts, Pastry Chef Sébastien Canonne decided to present a light dessert with clean and classic flavors for the 2000 National Pastry Team Competition. The gold medal–winning creation features a dome of Strawberry Sorbet and Almond Milk Ice Cream on top of an almond paste–topped sablé. A simple Red Currant and Wine Jus adds acidity and a touch of innovation to this beautiful dessert.*

MAKES 12 SERVINGS

Almond Paste

90 g (3.17 oz/⅓ cup) almond paste (70%)
35 g (1.23 oz/¼ cup plus 1½ tsp) roasted almonds (skin on), chopped
4.5 g (0.15 oz/1 tsp) almond liqueur

1. In the bowl of a stand mixer fitted with the paddle attachment, mix together the almond paste, roasted almonds, and almond liqueur on low speed until blended.

2. Roll the paste out thinly, to a thickness of about ⅛ in (3.17 mm), and cut out at least twelve 3-in (7.6-cm) rounds. Store in an airtight container at room temperature until ready to serve.

Sablé Cookies

140 g (5 oz/1 stick plus 2 Tbsp) unsalted butter (82% butterfat)

0.37 g (0.01 oz/pinch) sea salt

50 g (1.76 oz/½ cup plus 1 tsp) almond tant pour tant

47 g (1.65 oz/⅓ cup plus 1 Tbsp plus 1½ tsp) confectioners' sugar

½ Tahitian vanilla bean, split lengthwise and seeds scraped

30 g (1.05 oz/1½ large) hard-boiled egg yolks, passed through a fine-mesh sieve

30 g (1.05 oz/1½ large) egg yolks

175 g (6.17 oz/1½ cups plus 1½ tsp) pastry flour, sifted

1. In the bowl of a stand mixer fitted with the paddle attachment, cream the butter with the salt on high speed. Add the tant pour tant, sugar, and vanilla bean seeds and mix well. Add the hard-boiled egg yolks and raw egg yolks and mix until blended. Remove the bowl from the mixer stand and fold in the sifted flour. Shape the dough into a disk, wrap in plastic wrap, and refrigerate for at least 1 hour.

2. Preheat the oven to 300°F (150°C).

3. Roll the dough out to a thickness of 0.1 in (2.5 mm) and cut out at least twelve 3-in (7.6-cm) rounds from the dough. Place the rounds on a silicone baking mat–lined sheet pan and bake for 20 minutes, or until golden. Transfer the cookies to a wire rack to cool.

Red Clear Glaze

400 g (14.1 oz/3½ cups) fresh strawberries, washed and hulled

200 g (7 oz/1 cup) granulated sugar

50 g (1.76 oz/2 Tbsp plus 1½ tsp) glucose syrup

225 g (7.9 oz/¾ cup) neutral glaze

1. In a saucepan, combine the strawberries and 100 g (3.5 oz/½ cup) of the sugar and bring to a boil over medium-high heat, stirring frequently, until the strawberries release their juice. Strain and return the juice to the saucepan. Add the remaining 100 g (3.5 oz/½ cup) sugar and the glucose and bring to a boil. Add the neutral glaze, stirring to combine. Transfer the glaze to a covered container and let stand at room temperature until ready to use.

Almond Milk Ice Cream

6 g (0.21 oz/scant 1 Tbsp) ice cream stabilizer

124 g (4.37 oz/⅔ cup) granulated sugar

1080 g (38 oz/4½ cups) whole milk

45 g (1.58 oz/⅓ cup plus 2 Tbsp plus 1½ tsp) nonfat dry milk

68 g (2.4 oz/3 Tbsp plus 1½ tsp) Trimoline (invert sugar)

85 g (3 oz/⅓ cup plus 2½ tsp) heavy cream (35% butterfat)

250 g (8.8 oz/¾ cup plus 2 Tbsp) almond paste (70%)

A few drops of bitter almond essence

1. In a small bowl, combine the stabilizer with 62 g (2.18 oz/⅓ cup) of the sugar.

2. In a saucepan over low heat, bring the milk to a temperature of 40°F (4°C) and mix with the dry milk. Bring the milk to 78°F (25°C) and stir in the remaining 62 g (2.18 oz/⅓ cup) sugar, and the Trimoline. Bring the mixture to 97°F (35°C) and stir in the cream. At 99°F (37°C), whisk in the almond paste. At 114°F (45°C), add the stabilizer and sugar mixture. Heat to 185°F (85°C), stirring constantly, and cook for 2 minutes. Cool down rapidly in an ice water bath to 40°F (4°C). Stir in the bitter almond essence. Cover and refrigerate the base for 4 to 12 hours.

3. Using an immersion blender, homogenize the base. Process in an ice cream machine according to manufacturer's instructions. Transfer the ice cream to an airtight container and freeze until ready to use.

Strawberry Sorbet

247 g (8.7 oz/1 cup plus 3 Tbsp plus 2¼ tsp) granulated sugar

1 kg (35.27 oz/4⅓ cups) fresh strawberry purée

91 g (3.2 oz/⅓ cup plus 1 Tbsp plus ½ tsp) water

86 g (3 oz/½ cup plus 2 tsp) glucose powder

4.3 g (0.15 oz/1½ tsp) sorbet stabilizer

1. Add 100 g (3.5 oz/½ cup) of the sugar to the strawberry purée and whisk to combine. Refrigerate until ready to use.

2. In a saucepan over medium heat, bring the water to 105°F (40°C) and whisk in the remaining sugar, glucose powder and sorbet stabilizer. Heat to 185°F (85°C), then cool down rapidly to 68°F (20°C) in an ice water bath. Cover and refrigerate for at least 3 hours.

3. Fold in the strawberry purée and blend with an immersion blender. Process the base in an ice cream machine according to the manufacturer's instructions. Transfer the sorbet to an airtight container and freeze until ready to use.

Red Currant and Wine Jus

37 g (1.3 oz/⅓ cup) fresh raspberries

37 g (1.3 oz/¼ cup) fresh blueberries

45 g (1.5 oz/3 Tbsp plus 2 tsp) granulated sugar

190 g (6.7 oz/¾ cup plus 1 Tbsp plus 1½ tsp) red wine

60 g (2.1 oz/¼ cup) water

⅛ Tahitian vanilla bean, split lengthwise

⅓ bay leaf

3 whole black peppercorns

Grated zest of 1 orange

Grated zest of 1 lemon

Cornstarch, as needed

1. In a saucepan, combine the raspberries, blueberries, sugar, red wine, water, vanilla bean, bay leaf, peppercorns, and citrus zest. Bring to a boil over high heat and continue to boil until the berries start to break down a bit. Strain and return the juice to the saucepan.

2. If necessary, thicken the sauce by adding a small amount of cornstarch dissolved in a small amount of water. Bring to a boil to activate the cornstarch. Remove from the heat and cool.

ASSEMBLY

Colored white chocolate garnishes
Pulled sugar S-shaped garnishes (see page 308)
Red currants

1. Line twelve 3-in (7.6-cm) demisphere molds with Strawberry Sorbet, leaving a cavity in the center of each mold. Fill the cavities with Almond Milk Ice Cream. Top each with a round of the Almond Paste and then a Sablé Cookie. Freeze until firm.

2. Unmold the demisphere molds and glaze with the Red Clear Glaze. Arrange each dessert in the center of a plate. Garnish each dessert with the white chocolate and pulled sugar decorations. Spoon some of the Red Currant and Wine Jus onto each plate, and garnish with some fresh red currants.

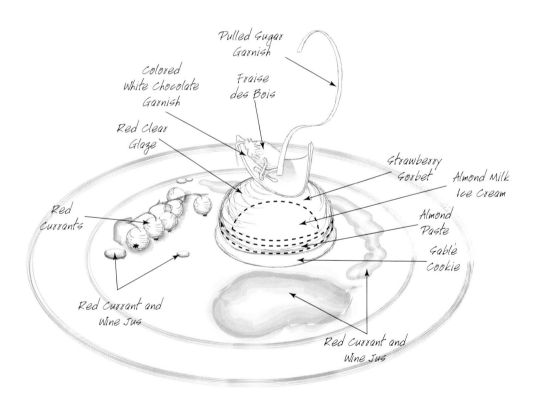

VANILLA AND PASSION FRUIT DOME WITH MIXED BERRY COULIS

At the 2000 NPTC, Team Settepani chose passion fruit as the featured flavor for their plated dessert because of its natural acidity, which cuts through the sweetness of many pastry elements. This dome-shaped dessert is made of layers of Passion Crémeux, Vanilla Mousse, and Mixed Berry Coulis, set on a crunchy Pistachio Dacquoise. A triangular tuile, Caramelized Pistachios, and a pulled sugar loop give the dessert a sophisticated finish. **MAKES 12 SERVINGS**

Passion Crémeux

375 g (13.22 oz/1½ cups plus 2 Tbsp) passion fruit purée

186 g (6.56 oz/3¾ large) whole eggs

75 g (2.64 oz/4 large) egg yolks

75 g (2.64 oz/⅓ cup plus 1 Tbsp) granulated sugar

93 g (3.28 oz/¾ stick plus 1½ tsp) unsalted butter

22.5 g (0.79 oz/11¼ sheets) gelatin (silver grade), bloomed and drained

1. In a saucepan, whisk together the passion fruit purée, whole eggs, egg yolks, and sugar. Cook over medium-high heat, whisking constantly, until the mixture comes to a boil. Remove from the heat and whisk in the butter and drained gelatin until both are melted. Strain the mixture through a fine-mesh sieve and pour into twelve 1-in (2.54-cm) demisphere molds. Freeze until firm.

Vanilla Mousse

375 g (13.2 oz) white chocolate, chopped

254 g (8.8 oz/1 cup plus 1 Tbsp plus 1½ tsp) heavy cream

3 vanilla beans, split lengthwise and seeds scraped

90 g (3.15 oz/about 4¾ large) egg yolks

12.75 g (0.45 oz/6⅓ sheets) gelatin (silver grade), bloomed and drained

561 g (19.78 oz/2⅓ cups plus 1 Tbsp plus 1½ tsp) heavy cream, whipped to medium peaks

282 g (9.9 oz/3 cups) pâte à bombe

1. Place the chopped white chocolate in a large bowl and set aside.

2. In a saucepan, combine the cream and vanilla bean seeds and pods and bring to a boil over high heat. Meanwhile, in a bowl, whisk the egg yolks. Gradually whisk about half of the hot cream into the egg yolks to temper, then return the entire mixture to the saucepan and cook, stirring constantly, until thickened. Strain through a fine-mesh sieve over the white chocolate in the bowl and allow to stand for 2 minutes.

3. Place the drained gelatin in a small cup and melt it in the microwave on low power, stirring every 10 seconds. Add the melted gelatin to the chocolate mixture and whisk until completely smooth. Cool until tepid.

4. Fold half of the whipped cream into the chocolate mixture. Fold the remaining half of the whipped cream into the pâte à bombe. Fold the two mixtures together. Refrigerate, covered, until ready to use.

Caramelized Pistachios

600 g (21.16 oz/4 cups) whole shelled pistachios

225 g (7.93 oz/1 cup plus 2 Tbsp) granulated sugar

38 g (1.34 oz/2 Tbsp plus 1½ tsp) water

23 g (0.81 oz/1 Tbsp plus 2 tsp) unsalted butter

1. Preheat the oven to 350°F (175°C).

2. Scatter the pistachios on a sheet pan and bake until warm, about 4 minutes.

3. Place the sugar and water in a copper sugar pot over high heat and cook to 240°F (115°C). Add the pistachios and stir until the mixture turns sandy. Continue cooking until the sugar melts and caramelizes evenly around the nuts. Add the butter and mix well until melted. Pour the mixture onto a silicone baking mat–lined sheet pan and separate the nuts. Cool completely, then store in an airtight container.

Pistachio Dacquoise

60 g (2.11 oz/½ cup plus 1¼ tsp) cake flour

170 g (6 oz/1½ cups plus 1 Tbsp plus 1 tsp) ground pistachios

300 g (10.5 oz/1½ cups) granulated sugar

10 g (0.35 oz/1 Tbsp plus 1 tsp) powdered egg whites

280 g (9.87 oz/9⅓ large) egg whites

1. Preheat the oven to 355°F (180°C).

2. Sift together the flour, ground pistachios, and 200 g (7 oz/1 cup) of the sugar.

3. In a small bowl, combine the remaining 100 g (3.5 oz/½ cup) sugar with the powdered egg whites.

4. In the bowl of a stand mixer fitted with the whisk attachment, beat the egg whites on high speed while adding the sugar and powdered egg white mixture; whip until stiff. Fold in the flour mixture.

5. Transfer the batter to a pastry bag fitted with a medium, plain tip. Pipe into twelve 3-in (7.6-cm) disks onto a silicone baking mat–lined sheet pan and bake until set. Cool completely.

Chocolate Spray

300 g (10.58 oz/1¾ cups) cocoa butter

300 g (10.58 oz) dark chocolate (64%), chopped

1. Melt the cocoa butter in a stainless steel bowl set over a saucepan of barely simmering water; the bottom of the bowl should not touch the water. Add the chocolate and stir until melted.

2. Pour the mixture into a spray gun canister.

Tuiles

50 g (1.76 oz/3 Tbsp plus 1½ tsp) unsalted butter

50 g (1.76 oz/⅓ cup plus 2 Tbsp) confectioners' sugar

50 g (1.76 oz/1⅔ large) egg whites

50 g (1.76 oz/⅓ cup plus 1 Tbsp plus 2 tsp) all-purpose flour

1. In the bowl of a stand mixer fitted with the whisk attachment, cream together the butter and sugar on high speed. Add the egg whites and mix until blended. Add the flour and mix just until blended. Let the batter rest 1 hour before using.

2. Preheat the oven to 350°F (175°C).

3. Spread the batter over a 6-in- (15.24-cm-) long triangular stencil with a 1½-in (3.81-cm) base, placed on a silicone baking mat–lined sheet pan. You will need to make at least 12 triangles. Bake until golden around the edges, about 5 minutes. Cool completely.

Mixed Berry Coulis

200 g (7 oz/scant 2 cups) fresh raspberries

200 g (7 oz/1½ cups) fresh blueberries

200 g (7 oz/scant 2 cups) fresh strawberries, washed and hulled

280 g (9.8 oz/1⅓ cups plus 1 Tbsp plus 1½ tsp) granulated sugar

30 g (1 oz/2 Tbsp) freshly squeezed lime juice

1. Place all of the ingredients in a saucepan and bring to a boil over high heat. Reduce the heat to medium and cook for a few minutes, until the berries release their juice.

2. Strain and cool completely. Store in a covered container in the refrigerator until ready to use.

ASSEMBLY

Pulled sugar loops for garnish (see page 308)
Fresh raspberries for garnish

1. Transfer the Vanilla Mousse to a pastry bag fitted with a medium, plain tip. Pipe a layer of Vanilla Mousse into twelve 3-in (7.6-cm) demisphere molds and spread it around the sides of the domes to the top. Freeze until set.

2. Spoon some of the Mixed Berry Coulis into the center of each mold and top with a demisphere of Passion Crémeux. Fill each mold with Vanilla Mousse and top with a Pistachio Dacquoise disk. Freeze until firm.

3. Unmold each dessert and coat evenly with the Chocolate Spray. Place on a dessert plate and garnish with some of the Mixed Berry Coulis, a tuile, some Caramelized Pistachios, a raspberry, and a pulled sugar loop.

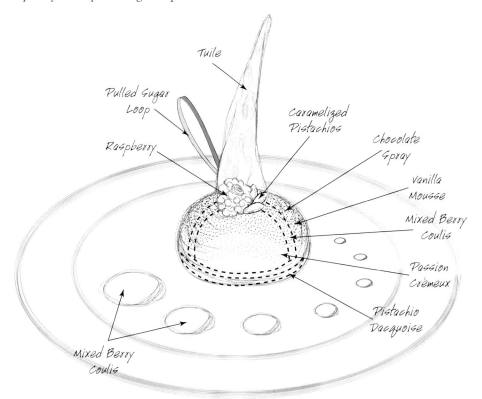

Andrew Shotts

Rémy Fünfrock

Patrice Caillot

CHOCOLATE DOME WITH SUMMER BERRY COMPOTE

Though the dominant flavor in this dome-shaped dessert is dark chocolate, accents of lime, mixed red berries, and vanilla give it a refreshing endnote. This dessert was created by Rémy Fünfrock, who had a variation of it on the menu at Café Boulud in New York, where he was the pastry chef in 2000. The dome is composed of layers of a glazed Chocolate Mousse, Vanilla Mousseline, Lime Dacquoise, and a mixed red berry compote. A chocolate tuile, caramel stick, and a pulled sugar loop give this dessert a refined finish. **MAKES 12 SERVINGS**

Lime Dacquoise

175 g (6.17 oz/1½ cups plus 1 tsp) confectioners' sugar

175 g (6.17 oz/2 cups) almond flour

Finely grated zest of 3 limes

225 g (7.9 oz/7½ large) egg whites

Juice of 1 lime

75 g (2.64 oz/⅓ cup plus 1 Tbsp) granulated sugar

150 g (5.3 oz/1¼ cups) toasted almonds, chopped

1. Preheat the oven to 380°F (193°C). Line a half-sheet pan with parchment paper.

2. In a bowl, combine the confectioners' sugar, almond flour, and lime zest and set aside.

3. In the bowl of a stand mixer fitted with the whisk attachment, whip the egg whites and lime juice on high speed to soft peaks. Gradually add the granulated sugar and whip until stiff and glossy. Remove the bowl from the mixer stand and fold in the almond flour mixture. Spread the batter onto the prepared pan and sprinkle the chopped almonds over the top. Bake for 12 minutes, or until golden. Cool.

4. Cut out twelve 1¾-in (4.4-cm) disks from the dacquoise and twelve ¾-in (2-cm) disks.

Summer Berry Compote

90 g (3.17 oz/scant ½ cup) granulated sugar

6 g (0.21 oz/2¼ tsp) Vitpris powdered apple pectin (see Sources page 310)

480 g (17 oz/4 cups) fresh mixed red berries

Juice of 1½ limes

1 vanilla bean, split lengthwise and seeds scraped

1. In a small bowl, combine the sugar and Vitpris and set aside.

2. Place the berries in a saucepan and sprinkle with the lime juice and sugar mixture. Add the vanilla bean seeds and pod and cook, stirring occasionally, over medium-high heat for about 4 minutes, until the berries release their juice and the mixture thickens. Cool, remove the vanilla bean pod, then store covered in the refrigerator.

Chocolate Mousse

100 g (3.5 oz/½ cup) granulated sugar

160 g (5.64 oz/8½ large) egg yolks

160 g (5.64 oz/¾ cup) heavy cream

330 g (11.64 oz) chocolate (64%), melted and cooled to tepid

680 g (24 oz/3 cups) heavy cream, whipped to medium peaks

1. In a stainless steel medium bowl, whisk together the sugar, egg yolks, and heavy cream. Place the bowl over a pot of simmering water and heat, whisking constantly, until thickened. Remove from the heat and stir until cool.

2. Fold the whipped cream into the melted chocolate, then fold in the egg yolk mixture.

3. Transfer the mousse to a pastry bag fitted with a medium, plain tip. Pipe a layer of Chocolate Mousse into twelve 2-in (5-cm) dome molds. Spread the mousse around the sides of the domes to the top. Freeze until set.

Vanilla Mousseline

400 g (14.1 oz/1⅔ cups plus 1½ tsp) whole milk

4 vanilla beans, split lengthwise and seeds scraped

60 g (2.1 oz/3¼ large) egg yolks

110 g (3.8 oz/½ cup plus 2¼ tsp) granulated sugar

30 g (1.05 oz/⅓ cup) pastry cream powder

4 g (0.14 oz/2 sheets) gelatin (silver grade), bloomed and drained

90 g (3.17 oz/¾ stick plus 1 tsp) unsalted butter

250 g (8.8 oz/1 cup plus 1 Tbsp plus ¾ tsp) heavy cream, whipped

1. In a saucepan, combine the milk and vanilla bean seeds and pods and bring to a boil over high heat.

2. In a bowl, whisk together the egg yolks, sugar, and pastry cream powder until light. Gradually whisk about half of the milk mixture into the egg yolk–sugar mixture, then return the entire mixture to the saucepan. Continue to cook over medium-high heat, whisking constantly, until thickened, about 3 minutes. Remove from the heat and whisk in the drained gelatin. Whisk in the butter until melted. Cool to room temperature. Remove the vanilla beans.

3. Fold the whipped cream into the cooled mixture.

4. Transfer the mousseline to a pastry bag fitted with a medium, plain tip. Pipe a layer of Vanilla Mousseline into the Chocolate Mousse–filled molds and spread it around the sides of the domes to the top. Place a ¾-in (2-cm) disk of dacquoise on the mousseline in each dome. Top with 20 g (0.7 oz/1 Tbsp plus 1½ tsp) of the Summer Berry Compote. Top with the 1¾-in (4.4-cm) dacquoise disks and freeze until set.

Chocolate Tuile

120 g (4.23 oz/1 stick plus 1½ tsp) unsalted butter, at room temperature
100 g (3.5 oz/¾ cup plus 2 Tbsp) confectioners' sugar
120 g (4.23 oz/4 large) egg whites
70 g (2.46 oz/½ cup plus 1 Tbsp plus 1 tsp) all-purpose flour, sifted
10 g (0.35 oz/1 Tbsp plus 2⅛ tsp) cocoa powder, sifted

1. Preheat the oven to 375°F (190°C).

2. In the bowl of a stand mixer fitted with the paddle attachment, cream together the butter and sugar on high speed until light. Gradually add the egg whites, mixing until blended. Add the flour and cocoa powder and mix until smooth. Spread the batter into a 10 x 3-in (25 x 7.6-cm) rectangle on a silicone baking mat–lined sheet pan. Bake for 7 minutes.

3. Immediately cut into 4 triangles, each with a ½-in (1¼-cm) base. Wrap around a dome mold while warm to curve. Cool completely. Repeat to make 12 tuiles. Store in an airtight container until ready to serve.

Caramel Sticks

300 g (10.58 oz/¾ cup plus 2 Tbsp) fondant
150 g (5.3 oz/⅓ cup plus ½ tsp) glucose syrup

1. In a saucepan, combine the fondant and the glucose and cook over medium-high heat until a golden brown caramel. Spoon the caramel onto a silicone baking mat, forming twelve 6-in- (15¼-cm-) long sticks. Cool and store in an airtight container.

Chocolate Glaze

375 g (13.22 oz/1¾ cups plus 2 Tbsp) granulated sugar

500 g (17.63 oz/1⅔ cups) apricot glaze

250 g (8.8 oz/1 cup plus 1 Tbsp) water

75 g (2.64 oz/¾ cup plus 1 Tbsp) cocoa powder

75 g (2.64 oz) pâte à glacer (brun)

75 g (2.64 oz) cocoa paste

20 g (0.7 oz/10 sheets) gelatin (silver grade), bloomed and drained

1. In a saucepan, combine the sugar, apricot glaze, and water and bring to a boil over high heat. Add the cocoa powder, pâte à glacer, and cocoa paste and stir until melted. Continue to cook over medium-high heat for about 4 minutes. Add the drained gelatin and stir until melted. Strain and store covered.

ASSEMBLY

Pulled sugar loops for garnish (see page 308)

1. Unmold the domes and coat with the Chocolate Glaze. Place each dome in the center of a plate and garnish with a tuile, Caramel Stick, and a pulled sugar loop.

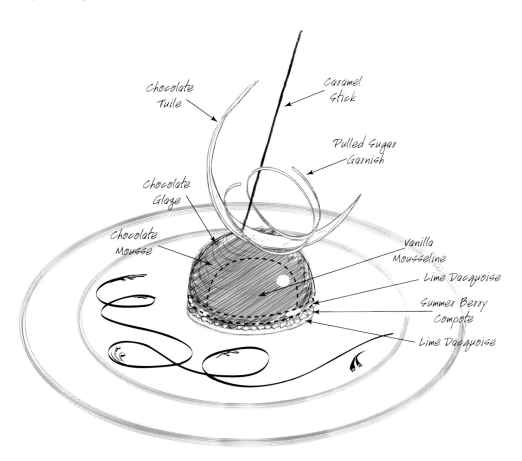

TEAM KLOCKO 2003

Jody Klocko

Chris Hamner

Patrick Coston

WARM ALMOND SAVARIN

WITH RASPBERRY GELÉE CENTER, AND RASPBERRY SORBET SERVED WITH MASCARPONE MOUSSE, VANILLA FOAM, AND CANDIED ALMOND DUST

A clever white chocolate garnish representing a Broadway show ticket may be the star of this plated dessert, but Team Klocko's primary focus was on its vibrant combination of flavors. The team wanted to keep it light, and chose to feature almond and raspberry in a multilayer dessert with both hot and cold elements. The star design was made by spraying colored cocoa butter directly onto the plate.

MAKES 12 SERVINGS

Raspberry Gelée

90 g (3.17 oz/⅓ cup plus 2 Tbsp plus ¾ tsp) granulated sugar

8 g (0.28 oz/2½ tsp) powdered pectin

250 g (8.8 oz/1 cup plus 1 Tbsp plus 1 tsp) raspberry purée

4 g (0.14 oz/2 sheets) gelatin (silver grade), bloomed and drained

1. Combine the sugar with the pectin. Heat the raspberry purée in a saucepan over medium-high heat and add the sugar and pectin. Bring to a boil, then add the drained gelatin, and mix until melted. Pour the gelée into 12 Flexipan mini tartlet molds and freeze until set.

Almond Savarin

100 g (3.5 oz/¾ stick plus 1 Tbsp) unsalted butter

70 g (2.5 oz/generous ⅓ cup) granulated sugar

60 g (2.1 oz/3 Tbsp plus 1½ tsp) almond paste

100 g (3.5 oz/2 large) eggs

72 g (2.5 oz/½ cup plus 2 Tbsp) cake flour, sifted

1. Preheat the oven to 400°F (205°C).

2. In the bowl of a stand mixer fitted with the paddle attachment, cream the butter, sugar, and almond paste on medium-high speed until light. Add the eggs, one at a time, mixing well after each addition and scraping down the sides of the bowl as necessary. Add the cake flour on low speed, mixing just until blended.

3. Transfer the batter to a pastry bag fitted with a medium, plain tip. Pipe a layer of the batter into twelve 3-in (7.62-cm) Flexipan savarin molds. Arrange a disk of frozen Raspberry Gelée in the center of each mold and pipe more almond batter on top to cover.

4. Bake the savarins until golden, about 20 minutes. Cool completely.

Mascarpone Mousse

455 g (1 lb/1¾ cups plus 1 Tbsp plus 1½ tsp) mascarpone cheese

115 g (4 oz/½ cup) heavy cream (35% butterfat)

20 g (0.7 oz/1 Tbsp plus 1½ tsp) granulated sugar

1 vanilla bean, split lengthwise and seeds scraped

1. In the bowl of a stand mixer fitted with the whisk attachment, whip the cheese, cream, sugar, and vanilla bean seeds on medium-high speed to soft peaks. Cover and chill until ready to use.

Raspberry Sorbet

20 g (0.7 oz/1 Tbsp plus 1 tsp) spring water

90 g (3.17 oz/⅓ cup plus 2 Tbsp plus ¾ tsp) granulated sugar

40 g (1.4 oz/⅓ cup plus 1 Tbsp plus 2 tsp) glucose powder

10 g (0.35 oz/1 Tbsp plus 2 tsp) dextrose powder

3 g (0.1 oz/1¼ tsp) sorbet stabilizer

500 g (17.6 oz/2 cups plus 2 Tbsp plus 2¼ tsp) raspberry purée

1. Place the water in a saucepan and heat to 105°F (40°C). Whisk in the sugar, glucose powder, dextrose powder, and sorbet stabilizer. Heat the mixture to 185°F (85°C) and stir in the raspberry purée. Cool and chill.

2. Process the sorbet base in an ice cream machine according to the manufacturer's instructions.

Raspberry Coulis

300 g (10.58 oz/1⅓ cups) raspberry purée
10 g (0.35 oz/1½ tsp) freshly squeezed lemon juice
50 g (1.76 oz/¼ cup) granulated sugar

1. Whisk together the raspberry purée, lemon juice, and sugar. Store, covered, in the refrigerator until ready to serve.

Candied Almond Dust

150 g (5.3 oz/¾ cup) granulated sugar
75 g (2.6 oz/⅓ cup) spring water
200 g (7 oz/1⅔ cups) blanched almonds

1. Preheat the oven to 400°F (205°C).

2. Combine the sugar and water and toss the nuts in the mixture. Spread out the nuts on a silicone baking mat–lined sheet pan and bake, stirring frequently, until golden, about 10 minutes. Cool completely.

3. In a food processor fitted with the steel blade, grind the nuts to a fine powder.

Vanilla Foam

20 g (0.7 oz/1 Tbsp plus 1 tsp) spring water
20 g (0.7 oz/1 Tbsp plus 2 tsp) granulated sugar
2 vanilla beans, split lengthwise
2 g (0.07 oz/1 sheet) gelatin (silver grade), bloomed and drained
300 g (10.58 oz/1¼ cups) skim milk
120 g (4.2 oz/½ cup) heavy cream (35% butterfat)

1. In a saucepan, combine the water, sugar, and vanilla beans and bring to a boil over high heat, stirring to dissolve the sugar. Remove from the heat, add the drained gelatin, and stir to dissolve. Add the milk and cream and transfer to a siphon. Charge the siphon.

2. Refrigerate the syrup for 1 hour.

ASSEMBLY

Red cocoa butter spray

White chocolate Broadway show–ticket plaque garnishes

Pulled sugar garnishes (see page 308)

1. Create a stencil for the star pattern shown on the plate in the photo. Spray the red cocoa butter over the stencil directly onto each dessert plate and allow to set.

2. Using a round stencil that is the same size as the base of the savarins, sprinkle a circle of Candied Almond Dust in the center of each plate. Unmold a savarin onto the circle, letting one portion of the dust show at the edge. Top with a scoop of Raspberry Sorbet. Top the sorbet with a quenelle of the Mascarpone Mousse and garnish with a Broadway show–ticket plaque and the pulled sugar.

3. Garnish each plate with the Raspberry Coulis and Vanilla Foam.

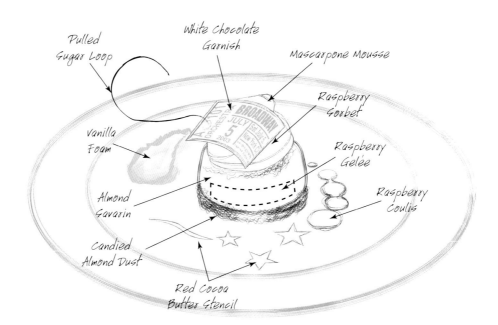

TEAM LHUILLIER 2003

Laurent Lhuillier

Regis Courivaud

Javier Mercado

JAPANESE-STYLE CHEESECAKE WITH CARAMELIZED APPLES AND APPLE SORBET

Team Lhuillier's plated dessert for the 2003 NPTC features a Japanese-Style Cheesecake, a dessert that is less sweet and considerably lighter than its fat-laden American cousin. The cake sits on a sablé round that is topped with caramelized apples, and has a Chocolate Tuile wrapped around it. A scoop of light Apple Sorbet and a crispy Apple Chip top off this elegant dessert.

MAKES 14 SERVINGS

Chocolate Tuiles

100 g (3.5 oz/¾ stick plus 1 Tbsp) unsalted butter, softened

100 g (3.5 oz/¾ cup plus 2 Tbsp) confectioners' sugar

100 g (3.5 oz/3⅓ large) egg whites

100 g (3.5 oz/¾ cup plus 2 Tbsp) pastry flour

40 g (1.4 oz/⅓ cup plus 2 Tbsp) cocoa powder

1. Preheat the oven to 350°F (175°C).

2. In the bowl of a stand mixer fitted with the paddle attachment, cream together the butter and sugar on high speed. Add the egg whites and mix until blended.

3. In a separate bowl, whisk together the flour and cocoa powder. Fold into the butter mixture until blended.

4. Spread the batter over an 11 x 1½-in (28 x 3¾-cm) rectangular stencil, placed on a silicone baking mat–lined sheet pan, to form 6 rectangles. Bake until set, about 5 minutes. While still warm, wrap each tuile around a 3-in (7.6-cm) ring mold. Repeat to make 8 more tuiles.

Honey Jelly

120 g (4.2 oz/⅓ cup plus 2 tsp) honey
120 g (4.2 oz/½ cup plus 1½ tsp) water
3 g (0.1 oz/1½ sheets) gelatin (silver grade), bloomed and drained

1. In a saucepan, combine the honey, water, and the drained gelatin and heat over medium-low heat until the gelatin is dissolved.

2. Pour the mixture into a shallow pan and refrigerate until set.

Yogurt Sauce

118 g (4.16 oz/½ cup) water
100 g (3.5 oz/½ cup) granulated sugar
150 g (5.3 oz/½ cup plus 2 Tbsp) nonfat yogurt

1. In a saucepan, combine the water and sugar and cook over high heat, stirring just to dissolve the sugar, until the syrup comes to a boil. Remove the pan from the heat and cool the syrup completely.

2. Whisk enough of the simple syrup into the yogurt just to bring it to sauce consistency.

Japanese-Style Cheesecake

150 g (5.3 oz/¾ cup) cream cheese
50 g (1.76 oz/3 Tbsp plus 1 tsp) whole milk
80 g (2.82 oz/4⅓ large) egg yolks
120 g (4.2 oz/½ cup plus 1 Tbsp plus 1 tsp) granulated sugar
32 g (1.13 oz/¼ cup plus 1½ tsp) pastry flour
10 g (0.35 oz/1 Tbsp plus 1 tsp) cornstarch
120 g (4.2 oz/4 large) egg whites

1. Preheat the oven to 300°F (150°C).

2. Place the cream cheese and milk in a stainless steel bowl set over a saucepan of simmering water and whisk until smooth.

3. In the bowl of a stand mixer fitted with the paddle attachment, beat the egg yolks with half (60 g/2.1 oz/¼ cup plus 2 tsp) of the sugar on high speed until well blended and light. Add the flour and cornstarch and mix until blended. Add the cream cheese mixture and mix until combined.

4. In the bowl of a stand mixer fitted with the whisk attachment, whip the egg whites on high speed to soft peaks. Gradually add the remaining sugar and whip until stiff and glossy. Fold the whipped whites into the cream cheese batter and scrape the mixture into fourteen 3-in (7.6-cm) Flexipan round molds. Bake for about 20 minutes, or just until set. Cool completely and store in an airtight container at room temperature until ready to serve.

Apple Sorbet

850 g (30 oz/3½ cups plus 1 Tbsp plus 1½ tsp) water
300 g (10.6 oz/1½ cups) granulated sugar
150 g (5.3 oz/1½ cups) glucose powder
8 g (0.28 oz/2¾ tsp) sorbet stabilizer
1 kg (2 lb, 3.27 oz/4⅓ cups) apple purée

1. In a saucepan, combine the water, sugar, glucose powder, and sorbet stabilizer. Allow to macerate in the refrigerator overnight.

2. Whisk in the apple purée and process the sorbet base in an ice cream machine according to the manufacturer's instructions.

Sablé Fondant

140 g (4.9 oz/1 stick plus 2 Tbsp) unsalted butter
30 g (1.05 oz/¼ cup plus 1½ tsp) confectioners' sugar
30 g (1.05 oz/1½ large) hard-boiled egg yolks
150 g (5.3 oz/1⅓ cups) cake flour
25 g (0.88 oz/¼ cup plus 1½ tsp) almond flour
1 g (0.03 oz/scant ¼ tsp) baking powder
5 g (0.17 oz/¾ tsp) salt

1. In the bowl of a stand mixer fitted with the paddle attachment, beat the butter and sugar on high speed until light. Add the egg yolks and beat until blended.

2. In a separate bowl, whisk together the cake flour, almond flour, baking powder, and salt. Add the flour mixture to the butter mixture and beat just until incorporated. Transfer the dough to a lightly floured work surface, knead the dough a few times to bring it together, and then divide the dough in half. Wrap each half in plastic wrap and refrigerate until firm (at least an hour).

3. Preheat the oven to 350°F (175°C).

4. Remove one portion of the dough from the refrigerator and place on a lightly floured work surface. Roll out the dough to a thickness of ¼ in (6.35 mm). Using a lightly floured 3-in (7.6-cm) round cookie cutter, cut out at least 14 cookies, and place them on a silicone baking mat–lined sheet pan. Bake for 12 to 14 minutes until golden brown around the edges. Cool completely.

Apple Jelly

400 g (14.1 oz/1⅔ cups) green apple juice

60 g (2.1 oz/¼ cup plus 2½ tsp) granulated sugar syrup

8 g (0.28 oz/4 sheets) gelatin (silver grade), bloomed and drained

1. In a saucepan, combine the apple juice, sugar, and drained gelatin and heat over medium-low heat until the gelatin is dissolved.

2. Pour the mixture into a shallow pan and refrigerate until set.

Apple Chips

300 g (10.58 oz/1½ cups) granulated sugar

300 g (10.58 oz/1¼ cups) water

100 g (3.5 oz/¼ cup plus 2 tsp) glucose

150 g (5.3 oz/½ cup) fondant

1 green apple

1. In a saucepan, combine the sugar, water, glucose, and fondant and bring just to a boil over high heat, stirring to dissolve the sugar.

2. Peel and core the apple and slice very thinly on a mandoline. Add the apple slices to the syrup and allow them to soak for at least 2 hours.

3. Preheat the oven to 200°F (94°C).

4. Strain the apple slices and arrange them on a silicone baking mat–lined sheet pan. Dry in the oven for 2 hours. Store in an airtight container with desiccant at room temperature until ready to use.

Caramelized Apples

500 g (17.6 oz/2½ cups) granulated sugar

200 g (7 oz/1¾ sticks) unsalted butter, cut into tablespoons

14 Golden Delicious, Washington State apples, cored, peeled, and cut into ½-in (1.27-cm) wedges

1. Heat half the sugar in a skillet over medium-high heat until it turns to a light caramel. Add half the butter and half the apples and cook over high heat until the apple wedges are tender. Repeat with the remaining ingredients and set aside to cool.

ASSEMBLY

Pulled sugar spirals (see page 308)

1. Place a sablé in the bottom of each of fourteen 3-in (7.6-cm) ring molds and top with a layer of Caramelized Apples. Top with a Japanese-Style Cheesecake and place a Chocolate Tuile ring around it. Spoon a quenelle of Apple Sorbet on and top and garnish with an Apple Chip. Spoon some Apple Jelly, Honey Jelly, and Yogurt Sauce on each plate. Garnish with a pulled sugar spiral.

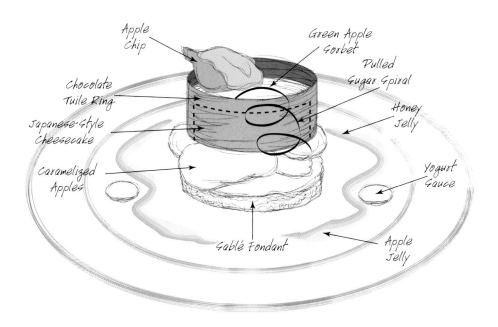

Brian Schoenbeck

Cyril Chaminade

Bill Foltz

FRAÎCHEUR DE CAVAILLON

For the 2003 NPTC, Cyril Chaminade, who was in charge of the dégustation *for Team Schoenbeck, decided to do something that was "way outside of the box." Since the judges had to taste sixteen different plates, he anticipated they would have "tired taste buds" by the time they got to Team Schoenbeck's dessert. So he chose to offer something "bold, clean, crisp, refreshing," something that didn't include whipped cream or chocolate. This innovative dessert showcases the flavors of the French Riviera, with a tomato—the fruit that is often mistaken for a vegetable—as its star element. The poached tomato is filled with a Cantaloupe Sorbet, and is served on a lavender-infused sablé Brêton with fresh cantaloupe and an Ice Wine Granité.* **MAKES 12 SERVINGS**

Poached Tomatoes

12 medium tomatoes

2 kg (70.5 oz/2 qt plus 4 oz/8½ cups) water

500 g (17.6 oz/3 cups plus 2 Tbsp) glucose powder

10 g (0.35 oz/1 Tbsp plus 2 tsp) citric acid

100 g (3.5 oz/2 cups packed) fresh mint leaves, chopped

Grated zest of 1 lemon

1. Core, blanch, and peel the tomatoes. Remove the seeds and pulp, keeping the tomatoes intact.

2. Combine the remaining ingredients in a saucepan and place over medium-low heat until warm. Pour the warm syrup over the tomatoes and vacuum-pack them for 3 hours.

Cantaloupe Sorbet

152 g (5.3 oz/¾ cup) granulated sugar

114 g (4 oz/½ cup) water

46 g (1.6 oz/¼ cup plus 2 tsp) glucose powder

7.5 g (0.26 oz/2¼ tsp) dextrose powder

0.7 g (0.02 oz/¼ tsp) sorbet stabilizer

500 g (17.6 oz/2 cups plus 2 Tbsp plus 2¼ tsp) cantaloupe purée

1. Combine the sugar and water in a saucepan and bring to a boil over high heat. Add the glucose powder, dextrose powder, and sorbet stabilizer and continuing boiling for 2 minutes. Remove from the heat, add the cantaloupe purée, and cool down as quickly as possible to 38°F (3°C).

2. Process the sorbet base in an ice cream machine according to the manufacturer's instructions.

Lavender Tuile Lace

75 g (2.6 oz/⅓ cup plus 1 Tbsp) granulated sugar

1.5 g (0.05 oz/⅛ tsp) pectin

25 g (0.88 oz/1 Tbsp plus 2 tsp) water

50 g (1.7 oz/1¼ sticks plus 1¼ tsp) unsalted butter

25 g (0.88 oz/1 Tbsp plus ¾ tsp) glucose syrup

2.5 g (0.88 oz/1 Tbsp) lavender, chopped

1. Preheat the oven to 390°F (200°C).

2. Mix together the sugar and pectin. Place the water in a saucepan over low heat until warm, then add the pectin mixture. Add the butter, glucose, and lavender, increase the heat to high, and bring to a boil.

3. Spread into twelve 2-in (5-cm) rounds onto a silicone baking mat–lined sheet pan and bake until just set, about 5 minutes. Press each tuile over a small cup while still warm to form a slight cup shape. Cool completely. Store in an airtight container until ready to serve.

Lavender Sablé Brêton

120 g (4.2 oz/1 cup plus 2¾ tsp) cake flour

120 g (4.2 oz/1 cup) all-purpose flour

12 g (0.42 oz/2½ tsp) baking powder

180 g (6.34 oz/1½ sticks plus 1¼ tsp) unsalted butter, cut into cubes and chilled

160 g (5.6 oz/¾ cup plus 2½ tsp) granulated sugar

4 g (0.14 oz/1 tsp) fleur de sel

1 Tahitian vanilla bean, split lengthwise and seeds scraped

80 g (2.82 oz/4⅓ large) egg yolks

6 g (0.21 oz/1 Tbsp) dried lavender

1. In the bowl of a stand mixer, sift together the cake flour, all-purpose flour, and baking powder. Add the cold cubed butter and mix with the paddle attachment on low speed until it forms a fine, crumbly mixture. Add the sugar, fleur de sel, vanilla bean seeds, and egg yolks and mix on medium speed until combined. Add the lavender and mix until blended. Scrape the dough into a disk, wrap in plastic wrap, and refrigerate for at least 4 hours.

2. Preheat the oven to 320°F (160°C).

3. Roll out the dough and cut into twelve 3-in (7.6-cm) rounds. Bake for 15 minutes, or until golden. Cool completely.

Marinated Cantaloupe Balls

Cantaloupe Sorbet
Dash of Pernod

1. With a small melon baller, scoop out 84 balls of sorbet and place them in a container that will allow them to fit tightly. Sprinkle with the Pernod, cover, and freeze for several hours.

Ice Wine Granité

One 750-ml (25 fl oz/3 cups plus 2 Tbsp) bottle ice wine

1. Pour the wine into a shallow pan and freeze until set.

ASSEMBLY

Fresh thyme sprigs for garnish

1. Fill each Poached Tomato with Cantaloupe Sorbet and arrange it on top of a Lavender Sablé Brêton round in the center of a shallow bowl. Top it with a Lavender Tuile Lace and a sprig of thyme.

2. Arrange 7 Marinated Cantaloupe Balls around the base of each tomato. Using a fork, scrape the Ice Wine Granité, and place a spoonful of it between the cantaloupe balls. Serve immediately.

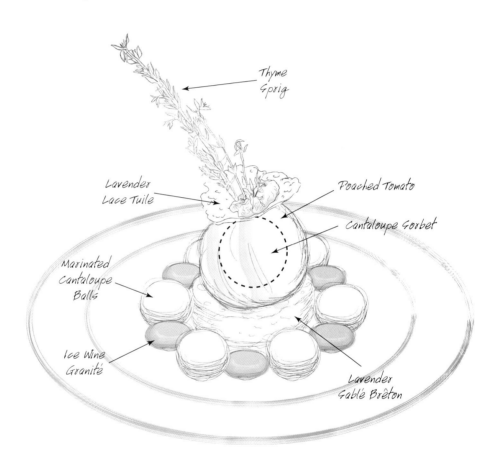

Thyme Sprig

Lavender Lace Tuile

Poached Tomato

Cantaloupe Sorbet

Marinated Cantaloupe Balls

Ice Wine Granité

Lavender Sablé Brêton

TEAM WEIDER 2003

Rudi Weider

Don Holtzer

Siribane Noudaranouvong

CHOCOLATE BANANA CARAMEL CRUNCH

The theme of the 2003 National Team Pastry Championship was Broadway, and Team Weider used the show 42nd Street *as the inspiration for their plated dessert. A dancing couple is depicted in a tuile that is perched on top of a cylinder of chocolate caramel mousse with a chocolate banana center. A sugar-dusted, red sugar heart and a baked* feuille de bric *ring surround the mousse, along with a creamy banana sauce and caramelized banana slices.*

MAKES 12 SERVINGS

Chocolate Banana Centers

396 g (13.96 oz/1½ cups plus 2 Tbsp plus 2½ tsp) water

228 g (8 oz/1 cup plus 2 Tbsp plus ¾ tsp) granulated sugar

77 g (2.71 oz) bittersweet chocolate couverture, chopped

45 g (1.58 oz/⅓ cup plus 2 Tbsp plus 2¼ tsp) cocoa powder

11 g (0.38 oz/1½ tsp) Clearjel

30 g (1.05 oz/2 Tbsp) banana compound

1. In a saucepan, combine 226 g (7.97 oz/¾ cup plus 3 Tbsp plus 1 tsp) of the water, the sugar, and the couverture and bring to a boil over medium-high heat, stirring to melt the chocolate. Remove from the heat.

2. In a bowl, combine the cocoa powder, Clearjel, banana compound, and remaining 170 g (6 oz/⅔ cup plus 1 Tbsp plus 1½ tsp) water. Whisk in half of the hot chocolate mixture, then return the entire mixture to the saucepan, and return it to the heat, stirring constantly, until the mixture comes to a boil. Remove from the heat and strain through a fine-mesh sieve. Cool.

3. Pour the mixture into a bowl, cover, and freeze until firm.

4. Shape the chocolate mixture into ¾-in (2-cm) balls and freeze until ready to use.

Chocolate Mousse Caramel

225 g (8 oz/1 cup plus 2 Tbsp) granulated sugar

75 g (2.64 oz/½ stick plus 1⅓ Tbsp plus 1 tsp) unsalted butter, cut into tablespoons

712 g (25.11 oz/ 3 cups plus 1 Tbsp) heavy cream

187 g (6.6 oz) bittersweet chocolate, chopped

1. In a heavy-bottomed saucepan over medium-high heat, cook the sugar dry to a deep caramel. Add the butter and stir until melted.

2. Place 150 g (5.3 oz/⅓ cup plus 1 tsp) of the cream in the bowl of a stand mixer fitted with the whisk attachment and whip slightly on high speed, just until thickened. Stir the cream into the caramel. Pour the hot caramel over the chopped chocolate and whisk until smooth. Cool to 97°F (35°C).

3. Meanwhile, whip the remaining 562 g (19.82 oz/2⅔ cups plus 2 tsp) cream on high speed to medium peaks. When the caramel mixture reaches 97°F, gently fold the cream into it. Pour the mousse into 12 parchment paper–lined 2-in (5-cm) ring molds, filling them to ½ in (1.25 cm) from the top. Press a Chocolate Banana Center into the center of each mousse-filled mold. Freeze until firm.

Florentine Almond Crunch

130 g (4.58 oz/1 stick plus 1 Tbsp plus ¾ tsp) unsalted butter, cut into tablespoons

215 g (7.58 oz/1 cup plus 1 Tbsp plus ¾ tsp) granulated sugar

185 g (6.52 oz/2 cups plus 3 Tbsp) chopped almonds

45 g (1.58 oz/⅓ cup plus 1 Tbsp) all-purpose flour

70 g (2.46 oz/3 Tbsp plus 1¾ tsp) light corn syrup

1. In a saucepan, melt the butter over medium heat, then add the sugar and cook until the sugar is dissolved. Remove from the heat.

2. In a bowl, combine the almonds and flour and add to the butter mixture. Stir in the corn syrup and refrigerate for at least 1 hour.

3. Preheat the oven to 375°F (190°C).

4. Drop the dough by level teaspoons, about 3 in (7.6 cm) apart, onto silicone baking mat–lined sheet pans. Spread thinly with a rubber spatula. Bake for 6 to 8 minutes, or until golden brown. Cut each cookie with a 2-in (5-cm) round cutter. Cool completely.

Banana Sauce

150 g (5.3 oz/¾ cup) granulated sugar

150 g (5.3 oz/⅔ cup plus ½ tsp) water

300 g (10.58 oz/1¼ cups plus 2 tsp) heavy cream

200 g (7 oz/¾ cup plus 2 Tbsp) banana purée

1. In a saucepan, bring the sugar and water to a boil over high heat and cook to a deep caramel. Remove from the heat and add the cream and banana purée. Return to the heat and bring to a boil. Strain the mixture through a fine-mesh sieve into a bowl and chill in an ice bath.

Tuile Garnish

225 g (7.9 oz/2 sticks) unsalted butter, softened

225 g (7.9 oz/2 cups) confectioners' sugar

125 g (4.4 oz/about 4 large) egg whites

225 g (7.9 oz/1⅔ cups plus 1 Tbsp plus 1½ tsp) bread flour, sifted

1. Preheat the oven to 350°F (175°C).

2. In a bowl, mix together the butter and sugar by hand with a wooden spoon. Very gradually mix in the egg whites. Gradually mix in the sifted flour just until combined.

3. Spread the batter over a stencil of a dancing couple, placed on a silicone baking mat–lined sheet pan. Bake until golden brown around the edges. Repeat to make 12 dancing couple tuiles.

Sugar Heart Garnish

Granulated sugar, as needed

Isomalt, as needed

Red food coloring

1. Fill a half-sheet pan with granulated sugar and level it with a ruler so that it is even. Using a 5-in- (12.7-cm-) wide heart-shaped cutter, place the thick-edged side down and make an indentation in the sugar.

2. Ready a double-lined parchment paper cornet.

3. In a saucepan, cook the Isomalt over high heat until melted, then stir in the food coloring. Using gloves, pour the hot Isomalt into the cornet and pipe it directly into the heart-shaped indentation in the sugar. Let cool for several minutes until hardened. Turn it over so that the sugar crystals are on top. Repeat to make 12 hearts.

ASSEMBLY

Chocolate spray mixture (50% dark chocolate melted with 50% cocoa butter)
Apricot nappage, as needed
Twelve 4½-in (11½-cm) diameter x 1-in- (2½-cm-) thick baked *feuille de bric* rings
Chocolate ganache, as needed
Caramelized banana slices for garnish (see page 103)

1. Unmold each Chocolate Mousse Caramel dessert and spray with the chocolate-cocoa butter mixture. Allow to set.

2. Place a Florentine Almond Crunch round at each open end of the dessert.

3. Spread a small amount of nappage in the center of each plate and attach the *feuille de bric* ring as shown in the photo. Arrange a mousse dessert on its side inside the ring. Lay a sugar heart against the ring. Attach a Tuile Garnish onto the mousse dessert with some ganache.

4. Using a spoon, spread some Banana Sauce around each dessert. Top with some caramelized banana slices.

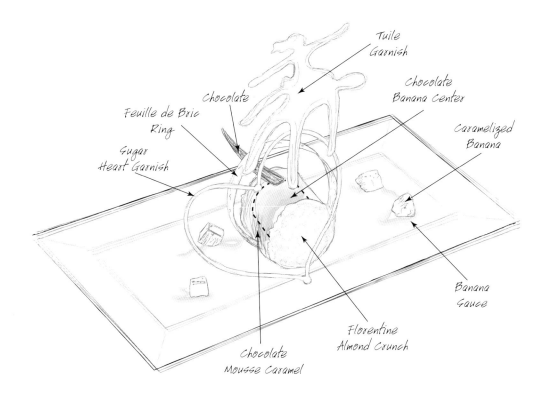

Tuile Garnish

Chocolate

Chocolate Banana Center

Feuille de Bric Ring

Caramelized Banana

Sugar Heart Garnish

Banana Sauce

Chocolate Mousse Caramel

Florentine Almond Crunch

Matt McBain

Diane Loewenguth

Kirsten Tibballs

VOLCANIC ERUPTION

The theme for the 2004 World Pastry Team Competition centered on the four elements of nature: earth, wind, fire, and water. Team Australia chose a dramatic rendering of an erupting volcano for their plated dessert, presenting an iced chocolate parfait overflowing with lavalike chocolate sauce.

MAKES 14 SERVINGS

Raspberry Confiture

300 g (10.6 oz/2⅔ cups) fresh raspberries

200 g (7 oz/1 cup) granulated sugar

1 vanilla bean, split lengthwise and seeds scraped

1. Combine all of the ingredients in a saucepan and cook over medium heat, stirring frequently, until the berries have released their juices and the mixture is thickened. Remove from the heat and cool completely. Remove the vanilla bean pod.

Crumble

150 g (5.3 oz/1 stick plus 2⅔ Tbsp plus 2 tsp) unsalted butter

75 g (2.6 oz/⅓ cup packed) brown sugar

190 g (6.7 oz/1½ cups plus 1 Tbsp plus 1 tsp) all-purpose flour

20 g (0.7 oz) bittersweet chocolate, melted

1. Preheat the oven to 350°F (175°C).

2. Mix the butter and sugar lightly together. Add the flour and mix until crumbly. Spread the crumble out onto a silicone baking mat–lined sheet pan and bake until golden brown. Cool.

3. Toss with the melted chocolate. Set aside in a covered container at room temperature until ready to use.

Iced Chocolate Parfait

350 g (12.3 oz) bittersweet chocolate couverture, chopped

260 g (9.17 oz/1 cup plus 1 Tbsp plus 1½ tsp) whole milk

180 g (6.3 oz/¾ cup plus 2 Tbsp plus 1½ tsp) granulated sugar

100 g (3.5 oz/5½ large) egg yolks

650 g (23 oz/2¾ cups) heavy cream, whipped to medium peaks

1. Place the chopped couverture in a large bowl and set aside.

2. In a saucepan, combine the milk with 110 g (3.8 oz/½ cup plus 1 Tbsp) of the sugar and bring to a boil over high heat, stirring occasionally.

3. In a bowl, whisk together the egg yolks with the remaining 70 g (2.5 oz/scant ⅓ cup) sugar. Whisk about 250 g (8 oz/1 cup) of the hot milk mixture into the egg yolk–sugar mixture to temper the eggs, then return the entire mixture to the saucepan. Cook the mixture over medium-high heat, stirring constantly with a wooden spoon, until the mixture thickens enough to coat the back of the spoon and reaches 180°F (82°C).

4. Strain the mixture over the chocolate couverture in the bowl and let stand for 1 minute. Whisk until smooth and emulsified. Cool completely.

5. Fold the whipped cream into the chocolate mixture, then scrape into fourteen 2¾-in (7-cm) diameter x 2⅜-in- (6-cm-) deep, Flexipan cone molds, filling them almost to the top. Top off each mold with the Crumble, then place in the freezer for 2 hours.

Chocolate Velvet Spray

454 g (1 lb) bittersweet chocolate, melted

227 g (8 oz/1⅓ cups) cocoa butter, melted

1. Combine the chocolate and cocoa butter and warm to 120°F (49°C) over a hot water bath. Allow the mixture to cool to 90°F (32°C), stirring frequently.

2. Strain the mixture through a cheesecloth-lined sieve and then pour into a spray gun canister.

3. Unmold the Iced Chocolate Parfaits and spray them with the chocolate coating. Return the desserts to the freezer until ready to serve.

Chocolate Sauce

250 g (8.8 oz/1 cup plus 1½ tsp) whole milk

40 g (1.4 oz/2 Tbsp plus 2¼ tsp) heavy cream

30 g (1.05 oz/2 Tbsp plus 1½ tsp) granulated sugar

250 g (8.8 oz) dark chocolate couverture (70%), chopped

1. In a saucepan, combine the milk, cream, and sugar and bring to a gentle boil over medium heat, stirring occasionally. Put the couverture in a bowl. Pour the milk mixture over the chocolate couverture and let stand for 1 minute.

2. Whisk the chocolate mixture until smooth. Strain through a fine-mesh sieve. Store in a covered container in the refrigerator until ready to serve. Reheat in the microwave before serving.

Sautéed Pears

3 pears

75 g (2.6 oz/1 stick plus 1⅓ Tbsp plus 1 tsp) unsalted butter

75 g (2.6 oz/⅓ cup plus 1 Tbsp) granulated sugar

1 vanilla bean, split lengthwise and seeds scraped

98 g (3.45 oz/¼ cup plus 3 Tbsp) Poire William

1. Peel, core, and dice the pears.

2. Melt the butter in a sauté pan over medium-high heat and add the sugar and vanilla bean seeds and pod. Cook until the sugar is melted. Add the pears to the mixture and cook until tender. Deglaze the pan with the liqueur. Strain out the pears, set aside, and continue to cook the syrup until it has reduced slightly. Remove the vanilla pod. Store the pears and sauce separately in covered containers in the refrigerator until ready to serve. Reheat each before serving.

Crisp Sesame Biscuits

130 g (4.6 oz/1 cup plus 2 Tbsp) confectioners' sugar

35 g (1.2 oz/¼ cup plus 1½ tsp) all-purpose flour

50 g (1.76 oz/3 Tbsp plus 1 tsp) whole milk

50 g (1.7 oz/3 Tbsp plus 1½ tsp) unsalted butter, at room temperature

50 g (1.7 oz/⅓ cup) sesame seeds

1. Preheat the oven to 340°F (170°C).

2. Combine the sugar, flour, milk, and butter.

3. Spread the mixture over a stencil with a wavy design placed on a silicone baking mat–lined sheet pan to form 4 biscuits, then sprinkle with the sesame seeds. Bake for 8 to 10 minutes. Repeat to make 14 biscuits. Cool and store in an airtight container until ready to serve.

ASSEMBLY

1. Fill each parfait center one-third of the way with Raspberry Confiture and arrange on a plate. Spoon some of the Sautéed Pears and syrup on the plate a few inches from the parfait. Fill each parfait with Chocolate Sauce, letting it flow down the sides of the parfait. Garnish each parfait with a Crisp Sesame Biscuit.

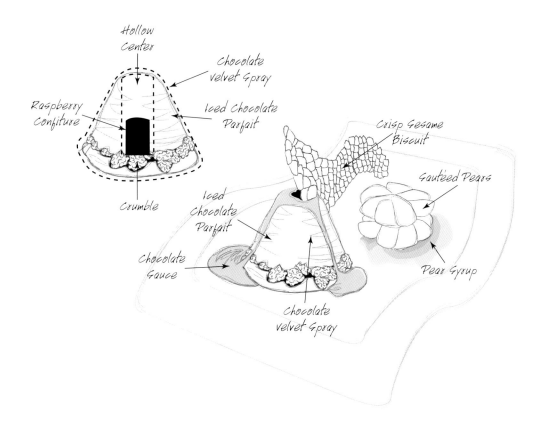

TEAM BELGIUM 2004

Serge Alexandre

Philippe Rheau

Stéphane Leroux

HOT CHOCOLATE SOUFFLÉ, GINGER MOUSSE, AND TROPICAL PARFAIT

For the 2004 World Pastry Team Championship, Team Belgium presented a plated dessert that combined both hot and cold elements, a feat that would require precise timing to execute perfectly—which they did. The dessert consists of three components: a Hot Chocolate Soufflé; a delicate parfait with layers of Campari Jelly, Orange Granité, and Ginger Mousse; and a tart Lime Cream topped with cubes of fresh mango and a Lychee Sorbet. **MAKES 14 SERVINGS**

Confectioners' Custard

140 g (4.9 oz/½ cup plus 1 Tbsp plus 1½ tsp) whole milk

1 vanilla bean, split lengthwise and seeds scraped

28 g (1 oz/1½ large) egg yolks

21 g (0.74 oz/1 Tbsp plus 1¾ tsp) granulated sugar

6 g (0.21 oz/2⅛ tsp) all-purpose flour

4 g (0.14 oz/1½ tsp) cornstarch

1. In a saucepan, combine the milk and vanilla bean seeds and pod and bring to a gentle boil over medium-high heat.

2. Meanwhile, in a bowl, whisk together the egg yolks, sugar, flour, and cornstarch. Whisk a small amount of the hot milk mixture into the yolk mixture and then return the entire mixture to the saucepan and cook, whisking constantly, until the mixture boils for 1 minute. Remove from the heat and cool. Remove the vanilla bean. Set the custard aside.

Hot Chocolate Soufflé

Softened butter and granulated sugar, as needed, for dusting ramekins

Reserved Confectioners' Custard (page 89)

130 g (4.58 oz) bittersweet chocolate (70%), chopped

10 g (0.35 oz/2 Tbsp) cocoa powder

50 g (1.7 oz/2½ large) egg yolks

160 g (5.6 oz/1⅓ cups plus 1 Tbsp plus 1 tsp) confectioners' sugar

120 g (4.2 oz/4 large) egg whites

50 g (1.7 oz/¼ cup) granulated sugar

5 g (0.17 oz/1 tsp) Cointreau

1. Preheat the oven to 350°F (175°C). Coat the inside of 14 ramekins with softened butter and dust them with granulated sugar.

2. Add the chocolate and cocoa powder to the hot Confectioners' Custard, stirring until the chocolate is melted. Whisk in the egg yolks and the confectioners' sugar.

3. In the bowl of a stand mixer fitted with the whisk attachment, beat the egg whites on high speed to soft peaks. Gradually add the remaining 50 g (1.7 oz/¼ cup) granulated sugar and continue to whip until the meringue forms medium peaks.

4. Gently blend one-third of the meringue along with the Cointreau into the chocolate base. Fold in the remaining meringue. Divide the mixture among the prepared ramekins and bake the soufflés until fully risen, about 20 minutes. Serve immediately; the soufflés should be prepared right before serving.

Campari Jelly

175 g (6.17 oz/¾ cup) water

50 g (1.76 oz/¼ cup) granulated sugar

Finely grated zest of 1 orange

Finely grated zest of 1 lemon

4 g (0.14 oz/⅓ tsp) powdered gelatin, softened in water

25 g (0.88 oz/1 Tbsp plus 1½ tsp) Campari

1. In a saucepan, combine the water, sugar, and citrus zests and heat to 122°F (50°C). Add the softened gelatin and stir until dissolved. Remove from the heat and cool slightly, then stir in the Campari. Pour the jelly into a small hotel pan and refrigerate until set, about 2 hours.

Orange Granité

200 g (7 oz/1 cup) granulated sugar

700 g (24.7 oz/2¾ cups plus 2 Tbsp plus 1 tsp) freshly squeezed orange juice

Finely grated zest of 1 orange

Finely grated zest of 1 lemon

30 g (1.05 oz/2 Tbsp) Cointreau

30 g (1.05 oz/2 Tbsp) Campari

1. In a saucepan, combine the sugar with the orange juice and place over medium heat, stirring just to dissolve the sugar. Cool. Add the remaining ingredients and chill in the refrigerator for several hours.

2. Pour into a prechilled hotel pan and freeze, stirring the mixture every 15 to 20 minutes with a whisk until it resembles crushed ice. Cover tightly and freeze until needed.

Ginger Mousse

345 g (12.17 oz/1⅓ cups plus 2 Tbsp) whole milk

75 g (2.6 oz/⅓ cup plus 1 Tbsp) granulated sugar

10 g (0.35 oz/2 Tbsp plus 1½ tsp) ground ginger

7 g (0.24 oz/2⅓ tsp) powdered gelatin, softened in water

150 g (5.3 oz/⅔ cup) heavy cream, whipped to medium peaks

1. In a saucepan, combine the milk, sugar, and ground ginger and bring to a gentle boil over medium-high heat. Remove from the heat and add the gelatin, stirring to dissolve the gelatin. Cool completely.

2. Gently fold the whipped cream into the mousse mixture and refrigerate until needed.

Chocolate Powder

180 g (6.3 oz/¾ cup) heavy cream

90 g (3.17 oz/⅓ cup plus 1 Tbsp) whole milk

27 g (0.95 oz/⅓ cup) cocoa powder, sifted

27 g (0.95 oz/2 Tbsp plus ½ tsp) granulated sugar

36 g (1.27 oz) bittersweet chocolate (70%), chopped

180 g (6.3 oz) milk chocolate, chopped

1. In a saucepan, combine the cream, milk, cocoa powder, and sugar and bring to a boil over high heat. Put the milk and bittersweet chocolate in a bowl. Pour the hot mixture over the chocolate and let stand for 1 minute to melt the chocolate. Whisk until smooth. Pour onto a sheet pan and chill for at least 4 hours.

2. Using a microplane grater, grate the chilled chocolate mixture to a fine powder.

Lime Cream

75 g (2.6 oz/1½ large) whole eggs

50 g (1.76 oz/¼ cup) granulated sugar

45 g (1.58 oz/1½ large) egg whites

250 g (8.8 oz/1 cup) mascarpone cheese

Finely grated zest of 1 lime

1. Combine the whole eggs and half of the sugar (25 g/0.88 oz/2 Tbsp) in the bowl of a stand mixer. Set the bowl over a saucepan of simmering water and whisk the mixture until warm. Place the bowl on the mixer stand and, using the whisk attachment, beat on high speed until light.

2. In a separate mixer bowl, using the whisk attachment, beat the egg whites at high speed until they form soft peaks. Gradually add the remaining sugar and beat until stiff.

3. Fold the mascarpone cheese into the egg mixture, then fold in the meringue and lime zest. Refrigerate, covered, until ready to use.

Lychee Sorbet

364 g (12.8 oz/1½ cups) water

251 g (8.8 oz/1¼ cups) granulated sugar

126 g (4.4 oz/¾ cup) atomized glucose

3 g (0.1 oz/1 tsp) sorbet stabilizer

1 vanilla bean, split lengthwise

1.256 kg (44.3 oz/5½ cups) lychee pulp

1. In a saucepan, combine the water, sugar, glucose, sorbet stabilizer, and vanilla bean and bring to a boil over high heat, stirring frequently. Add the lychee pulp and chill for at least 4 hours.

2. Remove the vanilla bean and process the sorbet base in an ice cream machine according to the manufacturer's instructions.

Tuile

125 g (4.4 oz/1 stick plus 2¼ tsp) unsalted butter, melted

40 g (1.4 oz/2 Tbsp plus 1½ tsp) freshly squeezed orange juice

Finely grated zest of 1 lime

150 g (5.3 oz/1¼ cups plus 1 Tbsp) confectioners' sugar

75 g (2.6 oz/½ cup plus 2 Tbsp) all-purpose flour

Pinch of salt

25 g (0.88 oz/⅓ cup) sliced blanched almonds

1. Preheat the oven to 350°F (175°C).

2. In a bowl, whisk together the melted butter, orange juice, and lime zest. Stir in the sugar, flour, salt, and sliced almonds and mix until blended.

3. Spread the batter thinly into 2-in (5-cm) circles on a silicone baking mat–lined sheet pan. Bake until set, about 5 minutes. Cool completely. Store in an airtight container at room temperature.

ASSEMBLY

Confectioners' sugar
14 fresh raspberries
Cubed flesh of 2 mangoes
Candied orange zest colored with grenadine

1. Arrange a layer of the Lime Cream in a small glass and top with a layer of the mango cubes and then a scoop of the Lychee Sorbet. Top with a Tuile and a piece of candied orange zest.

2. Dust each baked soufflé lightly with sugar and place in the center of a rectangular plate. Top with a fresh raspberry.

3. Cut the Campari Jelly into small cubes and arrange a layer in the bottom of a martini glass. Top with a layer of the Orange Granité, and then with a layer of the Ginger Mousse. Top with a layer of the Chocolate Powder.

TEAM SWITZERLAND 2004

| Franz Ziegler |
| Rolf Mürner |
| Adrian Bader |

APPLE SAVARIN WITH MASCARPONE CREAM AND CRANBERRY GELÉE

Team Switzerland's plated dessert from the 2004 WPTC showcases the flavors of autumn—apple and cranberry, with accents of cassis, mascarpone cheese, and yogurt. The main element in the dessert is an apple liqueur–soaked savarin, which is topped with Mascarpone Cream and a round of Cranberry Gelée and then wrapped in white chocolate. A tart Cranberry Yogurt Ice Cream, Cassis Sauce, and Apple Chip are flavorful accompaniments. **MAKES 12 SERVINGS**

Savarin Dough

20 g (0.7 oz/1 Tbsp plus 1½ tsp) granulated sugar

8 g (0.28 oz/2⅔ tsp) active dry yeast

200 g (7 oz/1⅔ cups) all-purpose flour

150 g (5.3 oz/½ cup plus 2 Tbsp) whole milk

120 g (4.2 oz/2½ large) eggs

4 g (0.14 oz/½ tsp) salt

100 g (3.5 oz/¾ stick plus 1 Tbsp) unsalted butter, softened

50 g (1.76 oz/½ cup) toasted walnuts, chopped

1. In a small bowl, combine the sugar and yeast and let stand for 15 minutes.

2. In the bowl of a stand mixer fitted with the paddle attachment, mix the flour, milk, eggs, and salt on low speed until blended. Add the butter and the sugar-yeast mixture and mix until combined. Add the walnuts and mix just until combined. Let stand in a warm place for 30 minutes.

3. Preheat the oven to 390°F (200°C).

4. Pipe the dough into 12 Flexipan mini savarin molds and bake until golden brown and baked through, about 12 minutes. Unmold and cool completely.

Savarin Syrup

300 g (10.5 oz/1⅓ cups) apple wine
170 g (5.9 oz/¾ cup plus 1 Tbsp plus 1½ tsp) granulated sugar
130 g (4.6 oz/½ cup) apple liqueur

1. In a saucepan, combine the apple wine and sugar and bring to a boil over medium-high heat. Remove from the heat and cool completely.

2. Stir in the apple liqueur. Soak each savarin in the warm syrup long enough to absorb as much liquid as possible. Place upside-down on a cooling rack, set over a sheet pan. Reheat the syrup as necessary to soak the remaining savarin.

Mascarpone Cream

75 g (2.6 oz/2½ large) egg whites
75 g (2.6 oz/¼ cup plus 2 Tbsp) granulated sugar
250 g (8.8 oz/1 cup) mascarpone cheese
20 g (0.7 oz/1 Tbsp plus 1 tsp) freshly squeezed lemon juice
60 g (2.1 oz/3 extra-large) egg yolks, whisked until foamy
150 g (5.3 oz/½ cup plus 2 Tbsp) heavy cream, whipped to medium peaks
25 g (0.88 oz/1 Tbsp plus 1½ tsp) apple liqueur

1. In the bowl of a stand mixer, combine the egg whites and sugar, set over a saucepan of simmering water, and whisk together until warm. Transfer the bowl to the mixer stand and, using the whisk attachment, beat on high speed until a stiff and glossy meringue forms.

2. In a separate bowl, combine the mascarpone cheese and lemon juice. Fold the egg yolk into the mixture, then fold in the meringue. Fold in the whipped cream, then the apple liqueur. Cover and refrigerate until ready to use.

Cranberry Gelée

227 g (8 oz/2 cups) fresh cranberries
100 g (3.5 oz/½ cup) granulated sugar
60 g (2.1 oz/¼ cup) freshly squeezed orange juice
3 g (0.1 oz/1½ sheets) gelatin (gold grade), bloomed and drained

1. In a saucepan, combine the cranberries with 113 g (4 oz/½ cup) of water and cook over moderate heat until they begin to pop, about 5 minutes. Remove from the heat and let cool. Transfer to a blender and purée until smooth. Strain the purée through a fine-mesh sieve. Rinse out the saucepan.

2. Add the sugar and 57 g (2 oz/¼ cup) of water to the saucepan and bring to a boil, stirring, until dissolved. Let cool. Stir in the orange juice and cranberry purée, then the drained gelatin. Keep warm in a bowl set over a saucepan of hot water until ready to use.

Cranberry Yogurt Ice Cream

100 g (3.5 oz/⅓ cup plus 1 Tbsp plus 1½ tsp) whole milk

300 g (10.5 oz/1½ cups) granulated sugar

50 g (1.76 oz/3 Tbsp plus 1½ tsp) unsalted butter, cut into tablespoons

6 g (0.21 oz/3 sheets) gelatin (silver grade), bloomed and drained

150 g (5.3 oz/⅔ cup) apple juice

450 g (15.8 oz/4 cups) fresh cranberries

375 g (13.2 oz/1½ cups) plain full-fat yogurt

1. Place the milk, sugar, and butter in a saucepan and bring to a boil over medium-high heat, stirring until the sugar is dissolved. Remove from the heat, add the drained gelatin, and stir until dissolved.

2. In a separate saucepan, combine the apple juice and cranberries and bring to a boil over high heat. Combine with the milk mixture and chill the base in an ice bath. Fold in the yogurt and process in an ice cream machine according to the manufacturer's instructions.

Cassis Sauce

10 g (0.35 oz/1 Tbsp plus 1 tsp) cornstarch

100 g (3.5 oz/scant ½ cup) apple juice

200 g (7 oz/1 cup) granulated sugar

300 g (10.5 oz/1¼ cups) cassis purée

1. In a saucepan, whisk the cornstarch into the apple juice and bring to a boil over medium-high heat. Boil for 1 minute, then remove from the heat and add the sugar, stirring to dissolve it. Cool.

2. Stir the cassis purée into the cooled mixture. Cover the bowl and refrigerate until ready to use.

Raw Apple Purée

2 g (0.07 oz/1 sheet) gelatin (silver grade), bloomed and drained

150 g (5.3 oz/1 medium) apple, peeled, cored, and cut into chunks

20 g (0.7 oz/1 Tbsp plus 1 tsp) freshly squeezed lemon juice

40 g (1.4 oz/3 Tbsp plus 1 tsp) granulated sugar

1. Fill a small saucepan halfway with water and bring to a boil over medium-high heat. Place the drained gelatin in a bowl set over a saucepan of hot water and heat until melted.

2. Meanwhile, process the apple chunks and lemon juice in a blender. Add the sugar and dissolved gelatin and mix until blended. Cover and hold at room temperature until ready to use.

Apple Chips

220 g (7.76 oz/scant 1 cup) apple purée

110 g (3.8 oz/½ cup plus 2 tsp) granulated sugar

10 g (0.35 oz/1¾ tsp) freshly squeezed lemon juice

10 g (0.35 oz/2¼ tsp) unsalted butter

1. Preheat the oven to 300°F (150°C).

2. Combine all of the ingredients in a nonstick pan and cook over medium-high heat until slightly reduced. Cool.

3. Spread the mixture paper-thin over a wavy stencil, placed on a silicone baking mat–lined sheet pan, and bake until set, about 5 minutes. Repeat to make 12 Apple Chips.

Apple Compote

500 g (17.6 oz/2 cups plus 1 Tbsp plus 2 tsp) water

100 g (3.5 oz/⅓ cup plus 2 Tbsp) apple juice

500 g (17.6 oz/3⅓ medium) apples, cored, peeled, and scooped into Parisienne balls with a melon baller

30 g (1.05 oz/2 Tbsp) freshly squeezed lemon juice

200 g (7 oz/1 cup) granulated sugar

30 g (1.05 oz/1 Tbsp plus 2 tsp) apple liqueur

1. In a saucepan, combine the water, apple juice, and apple balls and cook over medium heat until the apples are tender. Add the lemon juice and sugar and cook, stirring, until the sugar is dissolved. Cool.

2. Stir in the apple liqueur. Cover and refrigerate until ready to use. Reheat in the microwave until warm before serving.

ASSEMBLY

Red-colored cocoa butter

Tempered white chocolate for wrapping desserts

Pulled sugar sticks (see page 308)

1. Place each savarin in the bottom of a 2-in (5-cm) diameter x 3-in- (7.6-cm-) high ring mold and top with a layer of Raw Apple Purée. Fill the ring mold almost to the top with the Mascarpone Cream and top off with some Cranberry Gelée. Freeze until firm.

2. Unmold each dessert. Decorate an acetate strip, 3 in (7.6 cm) high and wide enough to wrap around the ring mold, with red-tinted cocoa butter and let set (or use a transfer sheet). Spread some tempered white chocolate over the strip. Let set slightly, then wrap around the ring mold. Refrigerate until set.

3. Peel off the acetate strip and arrange each dessert on a plate. Place a quenelle of Cranberry Yogurt Ice Cream next to the dessert. Arrange three balls from the Apple Compote next to the ice cream and garnish with an Apple Chip and a pulled sugar stick.

4. Decorate the plate with dots of Cassis Sauce.

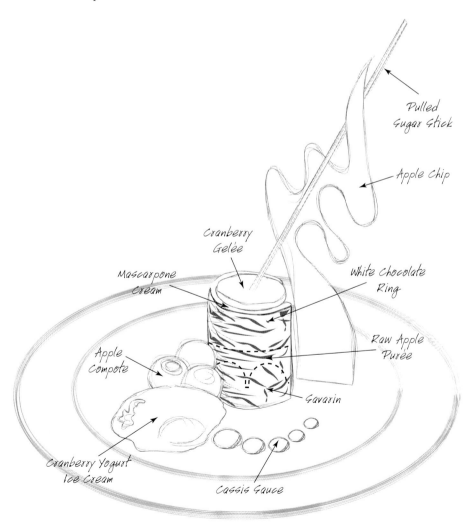

Pulled Sugar Stick

Apple Chip

Cranberry Gelée

Mascarpone Cream

White Chocolate Ring

Raw Apple Purée

Apple Compote

Savarin

Cranberry Yogurt Ice Cream

Cassis Sauce

Patrice Caillot

Claude Escamilla

Chris Hanmer

TASTE OF PARADISE

Prompted by a belief that other teams would choose more traditional flavors, Team USA chose to use tropical ones in their plated dessert for the 2004 WPTC competition. Each member of the team contributed at least one recipe for this dessert, which features a warm Almond Cake surrounded by Mango Sauce and topped with a Banana Tuile and a quenelle of Coconut Sorbet.

MAKES 12 SERVINGS

Almond Cake

120 g (4.2 oz/1⅓ cups plus 1 Tbsp) almond flour

100 g (3.5 oz/¾ cup plus 2 Tbsp) cake flour

2 g (0.07 oz/¼ tsp) salt

1 g (0.03 oz/¼ tsp) baking powder

160 g (5.6 oz/1 stick plus 3⅓ Tbsp plus 1 tsp) unsalted butter

100 g (3.5 oz/½ cup) granulated sugar

200 g (7 oz/4 large) eggs

1 vanilla bean, split lengthwise and seeds scraped

1. Preheat the oven to 350°F (175°C).

2. In a medium bowl, combine the flours, salt, and baking powder and set aside. In the bowl of a stand mixer fitted with the paddle attachment, cream together the butter and sugar on high speed. Add the eggs, one at a time, and mix until blended. Add the dry ingredients and vanilla bean seeds and mix on low speed until blended. Scrape the batter into twelve 3-in (7.6-cm) savarin molds and bake until golden, about 15 minutes. Cool completely.

Caramel Base

350 g (12.3 oz/1¾ cups) granulated sugar

150 g (5.3 oz/⅓ cup plus 2 Tbsp) glucose syrup

150 g (5.3 oz/½ cup plus 2 Tbsp) water

1. In a saucepan over high heat, stir together all of the ingredients and heat to the caramel stage (see page 10). Measure out 140 g (5 oz/¼ cup plus 3 Tbsp) of the base and place it in a saucepan for the Caramelized Bananas (see page 103).

Exotic Coulis

125 g (4.4 oz/½ cup) mango purée

125 g (4.4 oz/½ cup) passion fruit purée

40 g (1.4 oz/3 Tbsp) granulated sugar

8 g (0.3 oz/2½ tsp) pectin powder

2 g (0.08 oz/1 sheet) gelatin (gold grade), bloomed and drained

1. In a saucepan, heat the mango and passion fruit purées with the sugar over medium-high heat, stirring to dissolve the sugar. Add the pectin and drained gelatin and stir until the gelatin is dissolved. Cool completely. Cover and refrigerate until ready to use.

Mango Sauce

450 g (15.8 oz/2 cups) mango purée

450 g (15.8 oz/2 cups) passion fruit purée

150 g (5.3 oz/¾ cup) granulated sugar

150 g (5.3 oz/scant ½ cup) glucose syrup

1 vanilla bean, split lengthwise and seeds scraped

1 fresh mango, peeled, pitted, and cubed

1. Process all of the ingredients, except the fresh mango, in a food processor fitted with the steel blade until smooth.

2. Stir in the mango cubes. Cover and refrigerate until ready to use.

Pastry Cream

1 kg (2.2 lb/1 qt plus 2 Tbsp) whole milk

180 g (6.3 oz/¾ cup plus 2 Tbsp) granulated sugar

3 vanilla beans, split lengthwise and seeds scraped

180 g (6.3 oz/9½ large) egg yolks

70 g (2.5 oz/½ cup) pastry cream powder

8 g (0.28 oz/4 sheets) gelatin (gold grade), bloomed and drained

250 g (8.8 oz/1 cup plus 1 Tbsp) heavy cream, whipped

1. In a saucepan, heat the milk with half the sugar and the vanilla bean seeds and pods over medium-high heat until scalding.

2. Meanwhile, in a bowl, whisk together the egg yolks, the remaining sugar, and the pastry cream powder. Add some of the hot milk to the bowl to temper the eggs, then return the mixture to the saucepan. Heat until the mixture is boiling and thickened. Remove from the heat, add the drained gelatin, and stir until dissolved. Strain the pastry cream into a bowl and cool in an ice bath.

3. Fold the whipped cream into the cooled pastry cream. Cover and refrigerate until ready to use.

Caramelized Bananas

200 g (7 oz/1 cup) granulated sugar

140 g (5 oz/⅓ cup plus 1 Tbsp plus 1½ tsp) reserved Caramel Base

130 g (4.5 oz/⅓ cup plus 1 Tbsp) glucose syrup

110 g (3.8 oz/¾ cup) cocoa butter

300 g (10.6 oz/1¼ cups) heavy cream

45 g (1.6 oz/3 Tbsp) unsalted butter

6 g (0.2 oz/scant 1 tsp) salt

2 vanilla beans, split lengthwise and seeds scraped

4 bananas, peeled and sliced

25 g (0.8 oz/2 Tbsp) dark rum

1. In a sauté pan, combine all of the ingredients, except for the bananas and rum, and cook over medium-high heat until the butter is melted and the mixture is smooth.

2. Stir in the banana slices and rum. Transfer to an airtight container and refrigerate until ready to use. Reheat before serving.

Gaufrette

110 g (3.8 oz/scant 1 cup) cake flour

38 g (1.3 oz/⅓ cup plus 2 Tbsp) almond flour

90 g (3.1 oz/¾ stick plus 1 tsp) unsalted butter

130 g (4.6 oz/1 cup plus 2 Tbsp) confectioners' sugar

2 g (0.07 oz/¼ tsp) salt

110 g (3.8 oz/3½ large) egg whites

1. Preheat the oven to 350°F (175°C).

2. In a bowl, sift together the cake flour and almond flour and whisk gently to combine.

3. In the bowl of a stand mixer fitted with the paddle attachment, cream the butter with the sugar and salt on high speed. Slowly add the egg whites and mix on low speed until combined. Add the flour mixture on low speed and mix until blended.

4. Spread the mixture onto a silicone baking mat in rectangular shapes, about 2 x 5 in (5 x 12.7 cm). Bake until golden around the edges, about 5 minutes. While still warm, roll each rectangle into a cigarette shape. Cool completely. Repeat to make a total of 12 gaufrettes.

Banana Tuile

390 g (13.8 oz/3⅓ cups plus 1 Tbsp) confectioners' sugar

100 g (3.5 oz/¾ cup plus 2 Tbsp) cake flour

140 g (5 oz/½ cup plus 1 Tbsp plus 2¼ tsp) banana purée

140 g (5 oz/1 stick plus 2 Tbsp) unsalted butter, melted

1 vanilla bean, split lengthwise and seeds scraped

1 g (0.03 oz/⅛ tsp) pectin powder

1. Preheat the oven to 350°F (175°C).

2. Combine all of the ingredients in a bowl and whisk by hand until smooth.

3. Spread the batter thinly onto a silicone baking mat in a triangular shape, with a 3-in (7.6-cm) base with 6-in (15.24-cm) sides.

4. Bake until golden around the edges, about 5 minutes. Repeat to make 12 tuiles and cool completely.

Coconut Sorbet

1 kg (2.2 lb/4⅓ cups) coconut purée

410 g (14.4 oz/2 cups plus 1 Tbsp) granulated sugar

885 g (31 oz/3¾ cups) water

150 g (5.3 oz/¾ cup plus 3 Tbsp) glucose powder

50 g (1.8 oz/⅓ cup) dextrose powder

5 g (0.2 oz/1½ tsp) sorbet stabilizer

1. In a saucepan, combine the coconut purée and sugar and cook over medium-high heat, stirring until the sugar is dissolved. Add the remaining ingredients and refrigerate, covered, until chilled.

2. Process the sorbet base in an ice cream machine according to the manufacturer's instructions.

ASSEMBLY

Pulled sugar spikes (see page 308)

1. Spoon some Mango Sauce around the perimeter of each plate, about 2 in (5 cm) from the edge. Spoon some Exotic Coulis around the perimeter of the sauce. Unmold the warm Almond Cakes and place one in the center of each plate. Spoon some Caramelized Bananas in the center of each cake, and then pipe some Pastry Cream on top. Top with a Banana Tuile. Top with a quenelle of Coconut Sorbet. Top with a Gaufrette, and garnish with pulled sugar spikes.

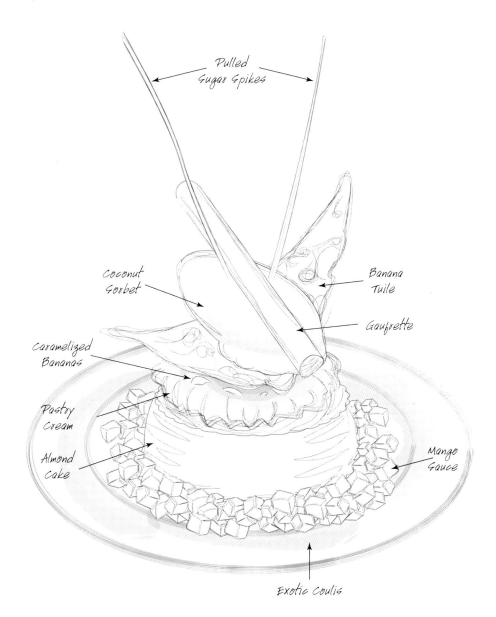

TEAM ANGNARDO 2005

Michael Angnardo

Don Holtzer

Manfred Schmidtke

PEACH MINT FINANCIER WITH ROASTED PEACHES AND APRICOT SORBET

Featuring a warm, buttery, peach- and mint-studded financier as its base, Team Angnardo's dessert from the 2005 NPTC alternates layers of Lemon Crème Fraîche–Mascarpone Cream with crisp Almond Cookies. Roasted peach slices and an Apricot Sorbet highlight the stone fruit–flavor profile of this dessert, while a Mint Syrup and Crème Fraîche Sauce offer complementary flavor accents.

MAKES 12 SERVINGS

Apricot Sorbet

227 g (8 oz/1 cup plus 2 Tbsp plus ½ tsp) granulated sugar

16 g (0.56 oz/1 Tbsp plus 1½ tsp) sorbet stabilizer

454 g (1 lb/2 cups) apricot purée

454 g (1 lb/1¾ cups plus 2 Tbsp plus 2 tsp) water

1. In a saucepan, combine all of the ingredients over medium-high heat and cook until the sugar is dissolved. Refrigerate for at least 3 hours until well chilled.

2. Process the sorbet base in an ice cream machine according to the manufacturer's instructions.

Peach Mint Financier

114 g (4 oz/1 stick) unsalted butter
142 g (5 oz/1¼ cups) confectioners' sugar
57 g (2 oz/⅔ cup) almond flour
57 g (2 oz/½ cup) pastry flour
114 g (4 oz/4 large) egg whites
2 peaches, peeled and cut into small dice
6 fresh mint leaves, cut into chiffonade

1. Preheat the oven to 350°F (175°C).

2. In a saucepan over medium heat, heat the butter until it is melted. Continue to cook the butter until the solids at the bottom of the pan begin to turn brown and the butter is fragrant, about 5 minutes.

3. Sift together the sugar and flours. Stir in the beurre noisette until it is partially blended. Add the egg whites, peaches, and mint leaves and mix thoroughly.

4. Spray twelve 3-oz (90-ml) financier molds with nonstick cooking spray. Divide the batter among the prepared molds and bake until set, about 15 minutes. Cool completely.

Almond Cookie

100 g (3.5 oz/¾ stick plus 1 Tbsp) unsalted butter
200 g (7 oz/1 cup) granulated sugar
30 g (1 oz/1 large) egg white
90 g (3.17 oz/¾ cup) all-purpose flour
12 g (0.4 oz/2 Tbsp plus ½ tsp) almond flour
63 g (2.2 oz/¼ cup plus 1 tsp) water
165 g (5.8 oz/1½ cups) ground almonds

1. Preheat the oven to 350°F (175°C).

2. In a stand mixer fitted with the paddle attachment, cream the butter and sugar together on high speed until smooth. Gradually add the egg whites, scraping down the sides of the bowl as necessary.

3. Sift together the flours and add to the butter mixture on low speed. Add the water and ground almonds and mix until combined.

4. Spread the batter over a 2¼-in (5.7-cm) round stencil, placed on a silicone baking mat–lined sheet pan, to form 12 cookies. Bake until light golden brown, about 7 minutes. Cool completely.

Lemon Crème Fraîche–Mascarpone Cream

454 g (1 lb/1¾ cups plus 2 Tbsp) mascarpone cheese

227 g (8 oz/¾ cup plus 2 Tbsp plus 1½ tsp) crème fraîche

Finely grated zest of 2 lemons

1. In the bowl of a stand mixer fitted with the paddle attachment, beat the mascarpone and crème fraîche on medium speed until smooth. Mix in the lemon zest. Scrape the cream into a disposable pastry bag fitted with a #5 star tip and refrigerate until ready to serve.

Honey Tuiles

85 g (3 oz/¾ stick) unsalted butter

227 g (8 oz/scant 2 cups) confectioners' sugar

85 g (3 oz/3 regular) egg whites

227 g (8 oz/1¾ cups plus 2 Tbsp plus ¾ tsp) all-purpose flour, sifted

85 g (3 oz/¼ cup) honey

1. Preheat the oven to 350°F (175°C).

2. In the bowl of a stand mixer fitted with the paddle attachment, cream the butter and sugar on high speed until smooth. Gradually add the egg whites, scraping down the sides of the bowl as necessary. Reduce the speed to low and mix in the flour and honey until just blended.

3. Spread the batter over an 8 x ½-in (20.32 x 1¼-cm) stencil, placed on a silicone baking mat–lined sheet pan, to form 8 tuiles. Bake until light golden brown. After cooling slightly, shape each tuile around a cylinder to create a circle.

Roasted Peaches

2 vanilla beans, split lengthwise and seeds scraped

227 g (8 oz/1 cup plus 2 Tbsp plus ½ tsp) granulated sugar

8 ripe peaches

½ bunch fresh mint

1. Preheat the oven to 350°F (175°C).

2. Toss the vanilla bean seeds and pods with the sugar.

3. Blanch the peaches in boiling water for 20 to 30 seconds, depending on ripeness (riper peaches will take less time). Cool in an ice bath, then remove the skins. Cut each peach in half and remove the pit.

4. Spread the sugar over the bottom of a half-sheet pan and arrange the peaches on top. Scatter the vanilla beans and mint around the peaches and roast until soft, about 30 minutes. Cool, then slice 6 of the peaches (reserve the remaining 2 for the Peach Sauce). Refrigerate, covered, until ready to use.

Peach Sauce

2 roasted peaches (see page 109)
114 g (4 oz/scant ½ cup) water
85 g (3 oz/⅓ cup plus 2 Tbsp) granulated sugar

1. Combine the roasted peaches with the water and sugar and purée in a food processor until smooth. Transfer the sauce to a squeeze bottle and reserve in the refrigerator.

Mint Syrup

20 fresh spearmint leaves
227 g (8 oz/⅔ cup) light corn syrup
10 g (0.35 oz/2 tsp) water

1. Combine all of the ingredients and blend with an immersion blender. Transfer the syrup to a squeeze bottle and reserve.

Crème Fraîche Sauce

114 g (4 oz/scant ½ cup) crème fraîche
59 g (2 oz/¼ cup plus 2 tsp) granulated sugar
59 g (2 oz/¼ cup) whole milk

1. Whisk together all of the ingredients. Transfer the sauce to a squeeze bottle and reserve in the refrigerator until ready to use.

ASSEMBLY

Melted bittersweet chocolate, as needed

1. Pour the melted chocolate into a small parchment paper cone (cornet) and pipe a long stem and a leaf outline on each plate. Fill in the leaf portion with Mint Syrup.

2. Warm the Peach Mint Financiers in a 350°F (175°C) oven for about 4 minutes.

3. Pipe the Lemon Crème Fraîche–Mascarpone Cream onto an Almond Cookie and top with another cookie.

4. Arrange a warm financier at the end of the stem on each plate. Place an Almond Cookie on top of the financier. Arrange a Honey Tuile on top of the Almond Cookie and place a scoop of Apricot Sorbet on the tuile to hold it in place. Place a few slices of Roasted Peach next to each dessert.

5. Pipe the Peach Sauce in a series of graduated dots, increasing in size, along the stem, starting from the bottom and working up.

6. Pipe the Crème Fraîche Sauce in a series of graduated dots, decreasing in size, starting from the top and working down.

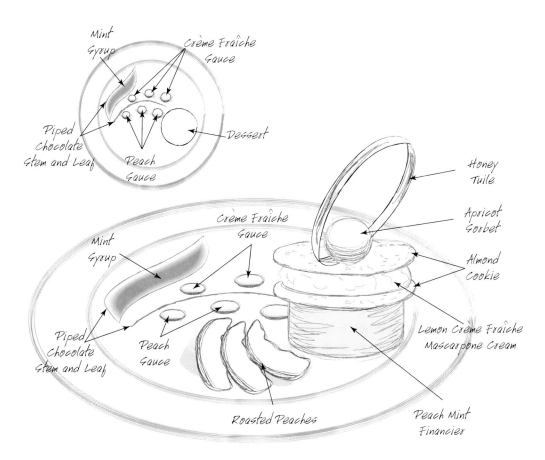

Lou Canillo

Klaus Hasmuller

Kimberley Schwethelm

ESPRIT

Team Canillo's simple tear-shaped dessert for the 2005 NPTC was made of alternating layers of Almond Sponge, raspberry-infused Sabayon, and a Wine Gelée. Fresh berries, mango cubes, mint, and colorful pulled sugar decorations serve as garnish. **MAKES 16 SERVINGS**

Almond Sponge

340 g (12 oz/1 cup plus 3 Tbsp) almond paste

397 g (14 oz/8 large) whole eggs

23 g (0.8 oz/1 Tbsp plus 1½ tsp) egg yolks

106 g (3.75 oz/½ cup plus 1½ tsp) granulated sugar

Pinch of salt

99 g (3.5 oz/¾ cup plus 1 Tbsp) all-purpose flour

1.2 g (0.04 oz/¼ tsp) baking powder

142 g (5 oz/1 stick plus 2 Tbsp) unsalted butter, melted

Finely grated zest of ½ lemon

1 vanilla bean, split lengthwise and seeds scraped

1. Preheat the oven to 325°F (163°C).

2. In the bowl of a stand mixer fitted with the whisk attachment, mix together the almond paste, whole eggs, and egg yolks on medium speed until smooth. Add the sugar and salt and beat on high speed until doubled in volume.

3. Sift the flour and baking powder together. Fold into the egg mixture. Fold in the butter, lemon zest, and vanilla bean seeds. Scrape the batter into three 8-in (20.3-cm) round pans and bake for 15 to 18 minutes until a toothpick inserted into the center of the cakes comes out clean. Cool completely.

Wine Gelée

170 g (6 oz/¾ cup) water

44 g (1.55 oz/22 sheets) gelatin (silver grade)

340 g (12 oz/1⅔ cups plus 1½ tsp) granulated sugar

1 lt (33.8 fl oz/4¼ cups) Gewürztraminer or dry Riesling wine

1. Place the water in a medium saucepan and add the gelatin leaves. Set aside to bloom.

2. Add the sugar to the saucepan and place over low heat, stirring occasionally, until the sugar is dissolved. Remove from the heat.

3. Whisk in the wine and pour the mixture into a sheet pan. Refrigerate until set.

Sabayon

595 g (20.12 liq oz/2½ cups) heavy cream

210 g (7.4 oz/¾ cup plus 2 Tbsp) Gewürztraminer or dry Riesling wine

198 g (7 oz/1 cup) granulated sugar

113 g (4 oz/6 large) egg yolks

24 g (0.84 oz/12 sheets) gelatin (silver grade), bloomed and drained

17 g (0.6 oz/1 Tbsp) raspberry liqueur

1. In the bowl of a stand mixer fitted with the whisk attachment, whip the cream on high speed to medium peaks. Refrigerate until needed.

2. In a medium bowl, combine the wine, sugar, egg yolks, drained gelatin, and liqueur. Place the bowl over a saucepan of simmering water; the bottom of the bowl should not touch the water. Whisk the mixture until thickened and airy. Cool to room temperature.

3. Fold the egg yolk mixture into the reserved whipped cream. Cover and refrigerate until ready to use.

ASSEMBLY

Fresh berries

Mango cubes

Fresh mint

Pulled sugar garnishes (see page 308)

1. Cut each Almond Sponge cake round into three layers. Line sixteen 3-in- (7.6-cm-) long teardrop molds with acetate strips; this will make unmolding the finished dessert easier.

2. Using the same size teardrop mold, cut out 32 pieces of the sponge and 16 pieces of the Wine Gelée.

3. Arrange a sponge piece in the bottom of each lined teardrop mold. Pipe a thick layer of Sabayon over the sponge, then top with another piece of sponge. Top with fresh berries and mango cubes, then top with the gelée piece. Freeze slightly before unmolding. Garnish with fresh berries, mango cubes, mint, and a pulled sugar garnish.

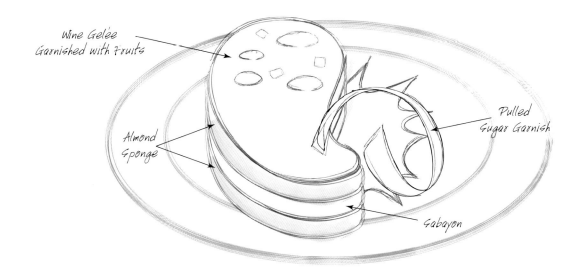

Wine Gelée Garnished with Fruits

Almond Sponge

Pulled Sugar Garnish

Sabayon

Jared Danks

Paul Bodrogi

Natasha Capper

DYAUS

The name of Team Danks's plated dessert for the 2005 National Pastry Team Championship refers to Dyaus Pita, *or "Sky Father," one of the early Hindu deities. The belief was that he took the form of a red bull during the day (symbolized by the red cherries in the Cherry Port Compote) and a black horse at night (represented by the Chocolate Mousse). The sweet cherry compote sits atop an Almond Financier and is crowned with a tangy Sour Cream Ice Cream. Alongside is a dessert made of alternating layers of Chocolate Mousse and Caramel Jelly. The compote perfectly complements and balances the flavors of both components.* **MAKES 12 SERVINGS**

Almond Financier

80 g (2.82 oz/½ stick plus 1⅔ Tbsp plus 2 tsp) unsalted butter, cut into cubes

37 g (1.38 oz/⅓ cup plus 1 Tbsp plus 2¼ tsp) blanched almond flour

80 g (2.82 oz/⅔ cup plus 1 Tbsp plus ½ tsp) confectioners' sugar (10-X)

25 g (0.88 oz/3 Tbsp plus 1½ tsp) cake flour

0.5 g (0.017 oz/⅛ tsp) baking powder

80 g (2.82 oz/2⅔ large) egg whites

1. Preheat the oven to 350°F (175°C).

2. To make beurre noisette, place the butter in a saucepan and cook over medium heat until it stops foaming and the solids fall to the bottom of the pan and begin to brown. Strain and let cool.

3. In a bowl, combine the almond flour, sugar, cake flour, and baking powder.

4. In a bowl, whisk the egg whites until frothy. Stir the egg whites into the dry ingredients. Slowly stir in the beurre noisette. Pour the mixture into twelve 3-in (7.6-cm) round silicone molds or buttered flan rings set on a silicone baking mat and bake until golden and baked through, about 20 minutes. Cool.

Cherry Port Compote

360 g (12.7 oz/1¾ cups plus 2 tsp) granulated sugar

12 g (0.42 oz/2 tsp) pectin

390 g (13.75 oz/2½ cups) pitted cherries

360 g (12.6 oz/1½ cups) Port wine

1½ cinnamon sticks

18 g (0.63 oz/1 Tbsp plus ½ tsp) freshly squeezed lemon juice

1. In a saucepan, combine the sugar and pectin. Add the cherries, Port, and cinnamon sticks. Bring to a boil over high heat, then add the lemon juice. Remove the cinnamon sticks and set aside at room temperature.

Chocolate Mousse

180 g (6.3 oz/¾ cup plus 3 Tbsp) granulated sugar

90 g (3.18 oz/⅓ cup plus 1 Tbsp) water

126 g (4.44 oz/scant ½ cup) pasteurized egg yolks

450 g (15.87 oz) bittersweet chocolate couverture (64%), chopped

810 g (28.56 oz/3½ cups) heavy cream (40% butterfat)

13.5 g (0.42 oz/6¾ sheets) gelatin (silver grade), bloomed and drained

54 g (1.9 oz/3 Tbsp plus 2 tsp) vanilla Cognac

1. In a medium saucepan, cook the sugar and water over high heat to 240°F (115°C). While the sugar is cooking, begin whipping the egg yolks in a stand mixer fitted with a whisk attachment on medium-low speed. When the sugar is to temperature, add it to the egg yolks and whip on high speed until cool to make a pâte à bombe.

2. Melt the chocolate couverture. Whip the heavy cream on high speed to soft peaks. In a small saucepan, melt the gelatin with the vanilla Cognac over low heat. Fold one-fourth of the whipped cream into the pâte à bombe mixture. Fold in the melted chocolate. Fold in the melted gelatin mixture. Fold in the remaining cream. Set aside while you prepare the Caramel Jelly.

Caramel Jelly

444 g (15.66 oz/2 cups plus 3 Tbsp plus 1½ tsp) granulated sugar

72 g (2.5 oz/3 Tbsp plus 1½ tsp) glucose syrup

3 vanilla beans, split lengthwise and seeds scraped

798 g (28.15 oz/3⅓ cups plus 2 Tbsp) heavy cream (40% butterfat)

192 g (6.7 oz/¾ cup) pasteurized egg yolks

15 g (0.53 oz/7½ sheets) gelatin (silver grade), bloomed and drained

1. In a medium saucepan, combine the sugar and glucose and cook over high heat until caramelized. Remove from the heat and add the vanilla bean seeds and heavy cream. Return to the heat, if necessary, to smooth the mixture out. Whisk a small amount of the

hot cream mixture into the egg yolk mixture to temper the eggs, then return the entire mixture to the saucepan and cook, stirring constantly, to 179°F (81°C). Add the drained gelatin and stir until dissolved. Strain the mixture and pour a layer into twelve 3 x 1¼-in (7.6 x 3-cm) rectangular Flexipan molds.

2. Pipe a layer of Chocolate Mousse on top, then top with another layer of Chocolate Mousse, leaving a hole in the center. Spoon a few cherries from the compote into the center. Top with another layer of Caramel Jelly and refrigerate until set.

Sour Cream Ice Cream

342 g (12 oz/1½ cups) heavy cream (40% butterfat)

342 g (12 oz/1⅓ cups plus 1 Tbsp plus 1½ tsp) whole milk

36 g (1.3 oz/1 Tbsp plus 2¼ tsp) Trimoline (invert sugar)

1½ vanilla beans, split lengthwise and seeds scraped

102 g (3.6 oz/⅓ cup plus 1 Tbsp plus 1 tsp) pasteurized egg yolks

318 g (11.22 oz/1½ cups plus 1 Tbsp plus 1½ tsp) granulated sugar

510 g (18 oz/2 cups plus 1 Tbsp plus 2 tsp) sour cream

1. In a saucepan, bring the heavy cream, milk, Trimoline, and vanilla bean seeds and pods just to a boil over medium-high heat. In a bowl, whisk together the egg yolks and sugar. Whisk a small amount of the hot cream mixture into the egg yolk mixture to temper the eggs, then return the entire mixture to the saucepan and cook, stirring constantly, to 170°F (77°C). Cool in an ice bath, then refrigerate for at least 4 hours.

2. Strain the mixture and whisk in the sour cream. Process in an ice cream machine according to the manufacturer's instructions.

3. Spread the ice cream into twelve flexible silicone demisphere molds and freeze until ready to plate.

Honey Tuile Cookie

85 g (3 oz/¾ cup) confectioners' sugar

53 g (1.87 oz/3 Tbsp plus 2¼ tsp) unsalted butter

11 g (0.38 oz/1½ tsp) honey

75 g (2.6 oz/⅓ cup) all-purpose flour

0.5 g (0.017 oz/½ tsp) ground cinnamon

0.5 g (0.017 oz/pinch) salt

53 g (1.87 oz/1¾ large) egg whites

1. In a stand mixer fitted with the paddle attachment, cream together the sugar, butter, and honey on high speed.

2. Sift together the flour, cinnamon, and salt. Slowly add the egg whites to the butter mixture. Add the dry ingredients and mix on low speed until blended. Chill the mixture until firm.

3. Preheat the oven to 350°F (175°C).

4. Spread the batter over a long triangular stencil, placed on a silicone baking mat–lined sheet pan. Bake until golden brown, about 5 minutes. Shape into a curve while still warm. Repeat to make a total of 12 cookies.

ASSEMBLY

Chocolate plaquette rectangles
Pulled sugar spirals (see page 308)

1. Spoon the Cherry Port Compote on top of each Almond Financier cake and arrange it on a plate. Top with a Honey Tuile Cookie, and unmold a Sour Cream Ice Cream demisphere on top. Top the ice cream with a pulled sugar spiral. Unmold the Chocolate Mousse dessert next to the financier and top with a cherry on one end and then a chocolate plaquette. Spoon a small amount of the sauce, without the cherries, in the front of each plate.

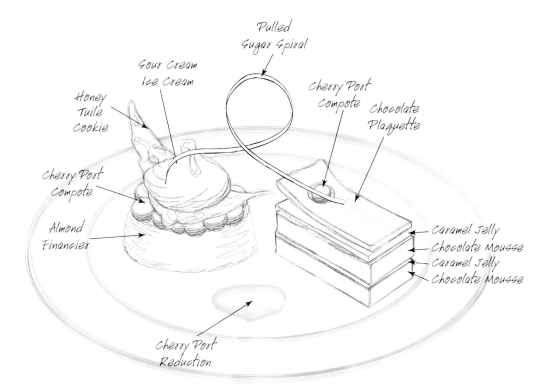

Mohan De Silva

Julie Jangali

Fabrice Bendano

STRAWBERRY TIAN

Team De Silva's dessert for the 2005 NPTC was their take on a classic French orange tian. Instead of oranges, they decided to feature fraises des bois—*small, intensely flavorful wild strawberries—in the dessert. But the day before the competition, their precious produce order did not show up, so they resorted to using ordinary strawberries—a huge disappointment for team member Fabrice Bendano. But Bendano carried on, topping a round of buttery Brêton shortcrust with a Strawberry-Mint Whipped Cream and a circle of ripe strawberry slices. A Mascarpone Ice Cream served in an Orange Tuile cup and a Strawberry-Mint Sauce accompany what turned out to be a simple, elegant dessert.*   **MAKES 12 SERVINGS**

Shortcrust Brêton

> 500 g (17.6 oz/4 sticks plus 3 Tbsp plus 1½ tsp) unsalted butter
>
> 400 g (14.1 oz/2 cups) granulated sugar
>
> 9 g (0.3 oz/½ large) egg yolk
>
> 600 g (21.16 oz/5 cups) all-purpose flour
>
> 40 g (1.4 oz/2 Tbsp plus 2⅛ tsp) baking powder
>
> 10 g (0.35 oz/1½ tsp) salt
>
> 2 vanilla beans, split lengthwise and seeds scraped

1. Preheat the oven to 350°F (175°C).

2. In a stand mixer fitted with the paddle attachment, cream the butter and sugar together on high speed. Add the egg yolk and mix until blended.

3. Combine the flour, baking powder, and salt and add to the butter mixture, along with the vanilla bean seeds, mixing on low speed. Shape the dough into a disk and roll it out to a thickness of ⅛ in (3.17 mm). Cut out twelve 3-in (7.6-cm) rounds from the dough and arrange them on a silicone baking mat–lined sheet pan. Bake for 8 to 10 minutes. Cool completely.

Strawberry-Mint Whipped Cream

1 kg (35.27 oz/1 qt plus ⅓ cup) heavy cream

150 g (5.3 oz/1 cup plus 3 Tbsp plus ¾ tsp) confectioners' sugar

100 g (3.5 oz/⅓ cup plus 2 Tbsp) strawberry-mint purée

1. In the bowl of a stand mixer fitted with the whisk attachment, whip the cream with the sugar on high speed to firm peaks. Fold the whipped cream into the strawberry-mint purée. Cover and refrigerate until ready to use.

Orange Tuile

125 g (4.4 oz/1 stick plus 2¼ tsp) unsalted butter

250 g (8.8 oz/1¼ cups) granulated sugar

100 g (3.5 oz/⅓ cup plus 1 Tbsp plus 1½ tsp) freshly squeezed orange juice

63 g (2.2 oz/½ cup plus 1¼ tsp) all-purpose flour

125 g (4.4 oz/1½ cups) sliced almonds

1. Preheat the oven to 375°F (190°C).

2. In the bowl of a stand mixer fitted with the paddle attachment, cream together the butter and sugar on high speed. Add the orange juice and mix until combined. Reduce the speed to low, add the flour, and mix just until blended.

3. Spread the batter over a 5-in (12.7-cm) round stencil, placed on a silicone baking mat–lined sheet pan, to form 12 tuiles. Sprinkle with some sliced almonds and bake for 8 to 10 minutes. While still warm, ease each tuile into a muffin cup to form a cup shape.

Strawberry-Mint Sauce

500 g (17.6 oz/2 cups plus 2 Tbsp plus 2¼ tsp) strawberry-mint purée

100 g (3.5 oz/½ cup) granulated sugar

15 g (0.5 oz/1 Tbsp) raspberry liqueur

15 g (0.5 oz/1 Tbsp) orange liqueur

15 g (0.5 oz/1 Tbsp) orange blossom water

1. In a double boiler, heat the strawberry-mint purée and sugar, stirring frequently until the sugar dissolves. Cool in an ice bath.

2. Stir in the raspberry and orange liqueurs and orange blossom water. Cover and refrigerate until ready to serve.

Mascarpone Ice Cream

2 vanilla beans, split lengthwise and seeds scraped

500 g (17.6 oz/2 cups plus 1 Tbsp) whole milk

500 g (17.6 oz/2 cups plus 2 Tbsp plus 1½ tsp) heavy cream

270 g (9.5 oz/1⅓ cups) granulated sugar

200 g (7 oz/10¾ large) egg yolks

475 g (16.7 oz/scant 2 cups) mascarpone cheese

50 g (1.7 oz/2 Tbsp plus 1 tsp) glucose syrup

20 g (0.7 oz/3 Tbsp plus 1 tsp) finely grated lime zest

1. In a medium saucepan, combine the vanilla seeds and pods, milk, cream, and half of the sugar and cook over low heat for about 12 minutes. Turn off the heat, but leave the saucepan on the stovetop.

2. In a medium bowl, combine the egg yolks with the remaining sugar, mascarpone cheese, glucose, and lime zest. Add some of the hot milk mixture to the egg yolk mixture to temper the eggs, then return the entire mixture to the saucepan. Cook over low heat, stirring with a wooden spoon until the sauce thickens enough to coat the back of the spoon and reaches 175°F (80°C). Strain the custard into a shallow pan and cover its surface with plastic wrap; keep the edges of the wrap raised so steam can escape. Chill for 4 hours.

3. Process the base in an ice cream machine according to the manufacturer's instructions.

ASSEMBLY

Fresh strawberries

Red sugar decorations

1. Place each shortcrust disk in a metal ring lined with acetate. Pipe a layer of Strawberry-Mint Whipped Cream on top. Slice some fresh strawberries and arrange them on top of the cream. Refrigerate for 10 minutes.

2. Decorate each plate with Strawberry-Mint Sauce. Remove the ring and acetate from each shortcrust and place one dessert on each plate. Place a scoop of Mascarpone Ice Cream in an Orange Tuile cup and place it on the plate. Garnish with a sugar decoration.

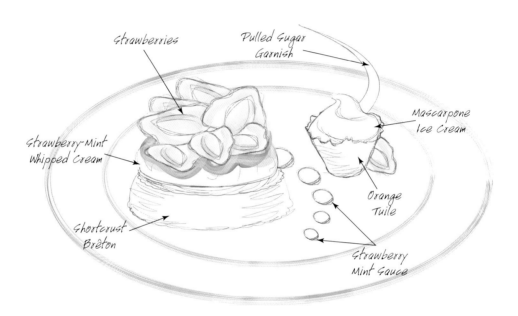

TEAM EDWARDS 2005

Jemal Edwards

Curt Wagner

Kimberly Bugler

FRUIT FOR THOUGHT

Team Edwards's plated dessert for the 2005 NPTC celebrates the fruits of summer—peaches, blueberries, and strawberries—in a light and refreshing combination of elements. At one end of the plate is a creamy Vanilla Panna Cotta topped with a Red Peach Gelée with Fresh Strawberries and accompanied by a light Basil-Mascarpone Crème Chantilly. Next to this is a colorful Peach and Blueberry Compote and, at the other end, a quenelle of Vanilla Cognac Ice Cream atop a square-shaped tuile. A ribbon of pink pulled sugar serves as a delicate garnish for this brightly flavored dessert.

MAKES 12 SERVINGS

Brown Sugar Shortcake

264 g (9.3 oz/2⅓ cups) cake flour

20 g (0.7 oz/4 tsp) baking powder

4 g (0.14 oz/¾ tsp) salt

4 g (0.14 oz/1⅛ tsp) cream of tartar

100 g (3.5 oz/¾ stick plus 1 Tbsp) unsalted butter

120 g (4.2 oz/½ cup plus 1 Tbsp packed) brown sugar

50 g (1.7 oz/2 large) eggs

90 g (3.17 oz/⅓ cup plus 1 Tbsp plus ½ tsp) heavy cream

Demerara sugar for sprinkling

1. Preheat the oven to 350°F (175°C).

2. In a bowl, sift together the flour, baking powder, salt, and cream of tartar.

3. In the bowl of a stand mixer fitted with the paddle attachment, cream the butter and brown sugar together on high speed until well blended. Beat in the eggs and cream, scraping down the sides of the bowl as necessary. Add the dry ingredients and mix on low speed until blended.

4. Press the dough into twelve 3-in (7.6-cm) square silicone molds, sprinkle with demerara sugar, and bake until golden, 12 to 15 minutes. Cool completely.

Red Peach Gelée with Fresh Strawberries

8 g (0.28 oz/4 sheets) gelatin (silver grade), bloomed and drained

400 g (14.1 oz/1¾ cups) red peach purée

60 g (2.1 oz/¼ cup plus 2½ tsp) granulated sugar

120 g (4.2 oz/1 cup) diced fresh strawberries

1. In a microwave-safe bowl, combine the drained gelatin, red peach purée, and sugar and heat in the microwave, stirring frequently, until well dissolved.

2. Pour 20 g (0.7 oz/1 Tbsp) of the gelée into each of 12 Flexipan dome molds. Add 10 g (0.35 oz/ 1 Tbsp) of the diced strawberries to each mold and allow to set in the freezer.

Vanilla Panna Cotta

750 g (26.45 oz/3 cup plus 3 Tbsp plus 2¼ tsp) heavy cream

250 g (8.8 oz/1 cup plus 1½ tsp) whole milk

120 g (4.2 oz/½ cup plus 1 Tbsp plus 1½ tsp) granulated sugar

1 Tahitian vanilla bean, split lengthwise and seeds scraped

1 Bourbon Madagascar vanilla bean, split lengthwise and seeds scraped

1 Indonesian vanilla bean, split lengthwise and seeds scraped

8 g (0.28 oz/4 sheets) gelatin (silver grade), bloomed and drained

1. In a medium saucepan, combine the cream, milk, sugar, and Tahitian, Bourbon, and Indonesian vanilla bean seeds and bring to a simmer over medium heat. Add the drained gelatin. Allow the mixture to cool enough so that the vanilla bean seeds stay suspended in the base.

2. Pour the mixture into twelve 3½-in (9-cm) round Flexipan molds or ramekins and freeze until set.

Vanilla Cognac Ice Cream

430 g (15.16 oz/1¾ cups plus 1 Tbsp plus 1½ tsp) heavy cream

500 g (17.6 oz/2 cups plus 1 Tbsp) whole milk

50 g (1.76 oz/3 Tbsp plus 1½ tsp) vanilla Cognac

252 g (8.8 oz/1¼ cups) granulated sugar

1 Tahitian vanilla bean, split lengthwise and seeds scraped

26 g (0.9 oz/1 Tbsp plus ¼ tsp) glucose syrup

1. In a saucepan, combine the cream, milk, vanilla Cognac, sugar, and vanilla bean seeds and pod and place over medium-high heat until the sugar is dissolved, stirring frequently. Stir in the glucose. Strain through a fine-mesh sieve and cool the mixture in an ice bath.

2. Process the base in an ice cream machine according to the manufacturer's instructions.

Peach and Blueberry Compote

150 g (5.3 oz/¾ cup) granulated sugar

75 g (2.6 oz/⅓ cup) water

Finely grated zest of 1 lemon

4 g (0.14 oz/1½ tsp) powdered pectin

6 ripe white peaches, sliced

292 g (10.3 oz/2 cups) fresh blueberries

1. In a saucepan, combine 50 g (1.76 oz/¼ cup) of the sugar with the water and lemon zest and cook over medium-high heat, stirring frequently, until the sugar is dissolved.

2. Combine the remaining 100 g (3.5 oz/½ cup) sugar with the pectin. Bring the sugar syrup to a simmer, add the pectin mixture, and let simmer for 2 minutes. Remove from the heat and add the sliced peaches and blueberries. Set aside.

Basil-Mascarpone Crème Chantilly

250 g (8.8 oz/1 cup plus 1 Tbsp plus ¾ tsp) heavy cream

30 g (1.05 oz/½ cup) chopped fresh basil leaves

25 g (0.88 oz/2 Tbsp) granulated sugar

1 g (0.03 oz/½ sheet) gelatin (silver grade), bloomed and drained

100 g (3.5 oz/⅓ cup plus 1 Tbsp plus 1½ tsp) mascarpone cheese

1. In a saucepan, combine the cream and basil and bring to a gentle boil over medium-high heat. Remove from the heat and let the mixture infuse for 20 minutes.

2. Strain the cream and discard the basil. Add the sugar and drained gelatin and heat until the sugar and gelatin are dissolved. Cool and then chill well.

3. In the bowl of a stand mixer fitted with the whisk attachment, whip the chilled basil cream on high speed to soft peaks. Stir the mascarpone in a bowl until smooth and fold into the whipped cream. Cover and refrigerate until ready to serve.

Croustillant Tuile

75 g (2.6 oz/½ stick plus 1⅓ Tbsp plus 1 tsp) unsalted butter

75 g (2.6 oz/⅓ cup packed) dark brown sugar

75 g (2.6 oz/⅓ cup plus 1 Tbsp) granulated sugar

75 g (2.6 oz/⅓ cup) freshly squeezed orange juice

75 g (2.6 oz/⅔ cup) all-purpose flour

1. Preheat the oven to 350°F (175°C).

2. In the bowl of a stand mixer fitted with the paddle attachment, cream the butter with the dark brown and granulated sugars on high speed. Add the orange juice and mix until blended. Reduce the speed to low, add the flour, and mix until blended. Refrigerate until chilled.

3. Spread the batter over a 2-in (5-cm) square stencil, placed on a silicone baking mat–lined sheet pan, to form 12 tuiles. Bake until set, about 5 minutes. Cool completely.

ASSEMBLY

Pulled sugar garnishes (see page 308)

1. Arrange each Croustillant Tuile at the end of a long plate and top with a quenelle of the Vanilla Cognac Ice Cream. Place a Brown Sugar Shortcake at the other end of each plate, and unmold a Vanilla Panna Cotta onto it. Top with the Red Peach Gelée with Fresh Strawberries, and pipe some Basil-Mascarpone Crème Chantilly at the base of the panna cotta. Spoon some Peach and Blueberry Compote in the center of each plate and decorate with a pulled sugar garnish.

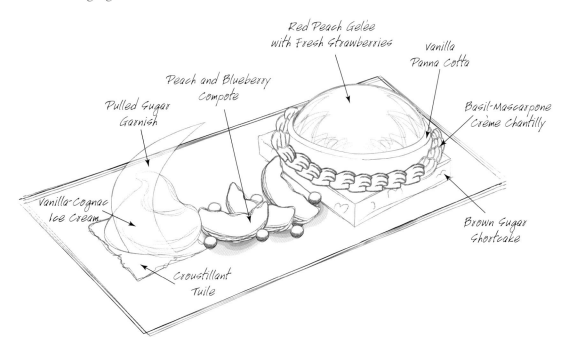

TEAM LHUILLIER 2005

Laurent Lhuillier

David Ramirez

James Mullaney

COCONUT CREAM WITH STRAWBERRY CONFIT AND FROMAGE BLANC ICE CREAM

This intricate plated dessert was created by Team Lhuillier for the 2005 NPTC in Phoenix. Pastry chef David Ramirez was responsible for making the dessert, and recalled the challenges it presented. "This dessert was very difficult to put together, especially making and filling the delicate honey tuile tubes. They had to be extremely thin in order to be easy for the judges to eat. On a scale of one to ten, this dessert is a 14 in difficulty." **MAKES 14 SERVINGS**

Fine Sugar Dough Base

165 g (5.8 oz/1 stick plus 3 Tbsp plus 2¼ tsp) unsalted butter, cut into ½-in (1.27-cm) chunks

60 g (2.1 oz/⅓ cup) confectioners' sugar

150 g (5.3 oz/1⅓ cups) cake flour

2 g (0.1 oz/scant ¼ tsp) salt

1. Preheat the oven to 340°F (170°C).

2. In the bowl of a stand mixer fitted with the paddle attachment, cream the butter and sugar together on high speed until well blended. Reduce the speed to low, add the cake flour and salt, and mix until combined.

3. Scrape the dough into a pastry bag fitted with a medium, plain tip and pipe it into twenty 2 x 4-in (5 x 10-cm) Flexipan molds and bake for about 12 minutes, or until golden. Cool completely. Set aside 14 of the pastry bases to use as a base for the Coconut Cream dessert. Place the remaining 6 bases in a bowl and crumble them with your hands and reserve for garnish.

Coconut Cream

110 g (3.9 oz/½ cup) coconut purée

1½ vanilla beans, split lengthwise and seeds scraped

36 g (1.3 oz/3 Tbsp) granulated sugar

50 g (1.8 oz/2½) egg yolks

4.5 g (.2 oz/2¼ sheets) gelatin (silver grade), bloomed and drained

154 g (5.4 oz/⅔ cup) heavy cream, whipped to soft peaks

1. In a saucepan, cook the coconut purée and vanilla bean seeds over medium heat until just beginning to boil. In a bowl, whisk together the sugar and egg yolks. Whisk about a third of the coconut purée into the egg yolks, then combine with the remaining purée in the saucepan. Cook, stirring constantly with a wooden spoon, until the mixture thickens slightly, coats the back of the spoon and reaches 175°F (80°C). Remove from the heat.

2. Add the drained gelatin to the hot coconut mixture and stir until dissolved. Transfer the mixture to a bowl and cool in an ice bath, stirring occasionally.

3. Fold the whipped cream into the cooled coconut mixture. Spoon the Coconut Cream into fourteen 2 x 4-in (5 x 10-cm) Flexipan molds. Top each with a Fine Sugar Dough Base and freeze.

Lemon Cream

70 g (2.5 oz/⅓ cup) granulated sugar

70 g (2.5 oz/3¾) egg yolks

70 g (2.5 oz/1½) whole eggs

70 g (2.5 oz/⅓ cup) freshly squeezed lemon juice

70 g (2.5 oz/½ stick plus 1 Tbsp) unsalted butter, cut into ½-in (1.27-cm) pieces

1. In a saucepan, combine all of the ingredients except for the butter and cook over medium heat, stirring constantly with a rubber spatula to prevent the eggs from cooking, until the mixture thickens.

2. Transfer to a deep container and blend with an immersion blender, gradually incorporating the butter. Cover and refrigerate until ready to use.

Fromage Blanc Ice Cream

156 g (5.5 oz/⅔ cup) water

170 g (6 oz/¾ cup plus 1 Tbsp plus 1½ tsp) granulated sugar

750 g (26.5 oz/3 cups) fromage blanc

280 g (9.9 oz/¾ cup plus 2 Tbsp) sweetened condensed milk

1. In a saucepan, combine the water and sugar and cook over medium-high heat until the sugar is dissolved. Measure out 225 g (7.9 oz/¾ cup) of the syrup and cool completely. Discard the remaining syrup.

2. Add the fromage blanc and the condensed milk to the syrup and blend with an immersion blender. Refrigerate until well chilled.

3. Process the base in an ice cream machine according to the manufacturer's instructions.

Strawberry Confit

150 g (5.3 oz/1⅓ cups) fresh strawberries, washed, hulled, and chopped

65 g (2.3 oz/scant ⅓ cup) granulated sugar

2 g (0.07 oz/¾ tsp) powdered pectin

30 g (1 oz/¼ cup) small, fresh strawberries

1. Combine the chopped strawberries and 35 g (1.2 oz/2 Tbsp plus 2¾ tsp) of the sugar in a saucepan and cook over medium-high heat until the berries give off their juice and the mixture comes to a boil. Boil for about 2 minutes. Add the pectin and the remaining 30 g (1 oz/2 Tbsp plus 1½ tsp) sugar and return the mixture to a boil for 2 minutes. Transfer to a bowl.

2. Hull the small strawberries. Add the strawberries to the confit mixture, cover with plastic wrap, and refrigerate until ready for plating.

Strawberry Sauce

130 g (4.6 oz/½ cup plus 1 Tbsp) strawberry purée

2 g (0.07 oz/¼ tsp) liquid pectin

18 g (0.6 oz/1 Tbsp plus 1½ tsp) granulated sugar

15 g (0.5 oz/2 tsp) glucose syrup

8 g (0.3 oz/1½ tsp) Trimoline (invert sugar)

1 g (0.04 oz/½ sheet) gelatin (silver grade), bloomed and drained

15 g (0.5 oz/1 Tbsp) water

1. In a saucepan, combine all of the ingredients and bring to a boil over high heat to activate the pectin. Remove from the heat and purée with an immersion blender. Cool completely.

2. Just before plating, mix again with an immersion blender and transfer the sauce to a squeeze bottle.

Strawberry Salpicon

50 g (1.8 oz/3 Tbsp plus 1½ tsp) strawberry purée

15 g (0.5 oz/2¼ tsp) Trimoline (invert sugar)

2 g (0.07 oz/1 sheet) gelatin (silver grade), bloomed and drained

200 g (7 oz/1¾ cups) fresh strawberries, washed, hulled, and cubed

1. Combine the strawberry purée and invert sugar in a saucepan and bring to a boil over medium heat. Remove from the heat and add the drained gelatin, stirring to dissolve. Transfer to a bowl.

2. Stir in the cubed strawberries and let cool. Refrigerate, covered, until ready to serve.

Honey Tuile

125 g (4.4 oz/2 Tbsp plus 1 tsp) unsalted butter

75 g (2.6 oz/3 Tbsp plus 1½ tsp) glucose syrup

50 g (1.8 oz/2 Tbsp plus 1 tsp) honey

125 g (4.4 oz/⅔ cup plus) granulated sugar

1. Preheat the oven to 340°F (170°C).

2. Combine all of the ingredients in a saucepan and cook over medium heat to 245°F (118°C).

3. Spread the mixture onto a silicone baking mat–lined half-sheet pan and bake until light brown in color, about 11 minutes. While still warm and pliable, cut it into 2 pieces and roll each around a wooden dowel to form 4-in- (10.16-cm-) long tubes, about 0.4 in (1 cm) in diameter. Cool completely and repeat to form 14 tuiles.

ASSEMBLY

Chocolate loop garnish

1. Draw a line of Strawberry Sauce down the length of each rectangular plate. Spoon some Strawberry Confit at each end of the line.

2. Invert the Coconut Cream onto the center of the plate, crust layer on the bottom.

3. Fill two pastry bags fitted with small, round tips with the Lemon Cream and the Strawberry Salpicon and pipe each into a Honey Tuile tube. Lay the tubes on top of the Coconut Cream. Garnish with the reserved crumbled Fine Sugar Dough.

4. Scoop a quenelle of Fromage Blanc Ice Cream on top. Garnish with a chocolate loop.

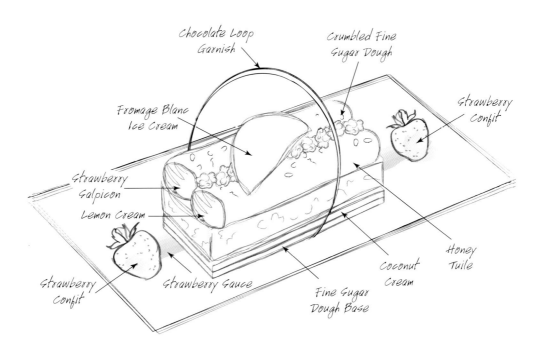

James McNamara

Thomas Bell

Kenneth Magana

VANILLA HONEY HAZELNUT MOUSSE WITH PEACH SORBET

For their plated dessert in the 2005 NPTC in Phoenix, Team McNamara chose to put their own spin on the classic pairing peaches and cream. Because peaches were so prominently featured, the team tracked down a great source in the area and made sure they had the peaches two days before the event, so that they would be perfectly ripe on the day of judging. The main element of this dessert is a layered rectangle made of tender buttermilk pound cake, Lacy Tuiles, Vanilla Honey Hazelnut Mousse, and a flavorful Peach Sorbet. A light Peach Consommé and dots of Mint Oil surround this pretty dessert.

MAKES 12 SERVINGS

Peach Sorbet

280 g (9.87 oz/1⅓ cups plus 1 Tbsp plus 1¼ tsp) granulated sugar

250 g (8.8 oz/1½ cups plus 1 Tbsp plus 1½ tsp) water

60 g (2.1 oz/2 Tbsp plus 2¾ tsp) glucose

8 g (0.28 oz/2½ tsp) sorbet stabilizer

1 kg (35.27 oz/4⅓ cups) peach purée

1. In a saucepan, combine 200 g (7 oz/1 cup) of the sugar with the water and glucose and bring to a boil over medium-high heat.

2. In a bowl, combine the remaining 80 g (2.8 oz/⅓ cup plus 1 Tbsp plus 1¼ tsp) sugar with the sorbet stabilizer and add to the boiling syrup. Remove from the heat and cool to room temperature.

3. Add the peach purée to the syrup and chill for 24 hours.

4. Process the sorbet base in an ice cream machine according to the manufacturer's instructions.

Mint Oil

454 g (1 lb/4 bunches) fresh mint leaves, washed and dried

537 g (18.9 oz/2½ cups) canola oil

1. In a saucepan, combine the mint with the oil. Place over high heat and cook until the temperature registers 302°F (151°C). Remove from the heat and cool.

2. Strain the oil through a cheesecloth-lined sieve. Set aside, covered, at room temperature until ready to use.

Peach Consommé

480 g (16.93 oz/2 cups) white wine

200 g (7 oz/1 cup) granulated sugar

5 unpeeled peaches, pitted and cut into eighths

1. In a saucepan, combine the wine with the sugar and bring to a boil over high heat. Add the peaches and reduce to a simmer. Cook until the peaches are tender. Remove from the heat and let cool.

2. Strain through a double cheesecloth; do not push it through the cloth; let gravity do the work. The resulting liquid should be flavorful and crystal clear with a tint of peach color.

Hazelnut Nougatine

600 g (21.16 oz/3 cups) granulated sugar

113 g (3.98 oz/⅓ cup plus 2 Tbsp plus 2 tsp) water

213 g (7.51 oz/1½ cups) toasted hazelnuts, chopped

Salt

1. In a saucepan, combine the sugar and water and cook over high heat to caramel stage (see page 10). Stir in the hazelnuts and salt to taste and pour onto a silicone baking mat. Cool completely.

Lacy Tuile

454 g (1 lb/4 cups) confectioners' sugar

360 g (12.69 oz/3 sticks plus 1 Tbsp plus 1½ tsp) unsalted butter

150 g (5.3 oz/⅓ cup plus 2 Tbsp plus 1 tsp) light corn syrup

150 g (5.3 oz/⅔ cup) water

150 g (5.3 oz/1¼ cups) all-purpose flour

1. In a food processor, blend together the sugar and butter. Add the corn syrup and water and mix until smooth. Add the flour and pulse to combine. Refrigerate the batter until ready to use.

2. Preheat the oven to 350°F (175°C).

3. Spread the batter over a 2 x 3-in (5 x 7.6-cm) rectangular stencil, placed on a silicone baking mat–lined sheet pan, to form 14 tuiles. Bake until lightly browned. Cool completely.

Pound Cake

1.02 kg (2 lb, 4 oz/8½ cups) all-purpose flour
44 g (1.5 oz/3 Tbsp) baking powder
3.75 g (0.13 oz/¾ tsp) baking soda
20 g (0.7 oz/3 tsp) salt
510 g (1 lb, 2 oz/4½ sticks) unsalted butter
1.02 kg (2 lb, 4 oz/5 cups plus 1 Tbsp plus 2 tsp) granulated sugar
750 g (26.45 oz/15 large) eggs
542 g (19.1 oz/2 cups plus 3 Tbsp plus 2¾ tsp) buttermilk

1. Preheat the oven to 350°F (175°C).

2. Sift together the flour, baking powder, baking soda, and salt.

3. In the bowl of a stand mixer fitted with the paddle attachment, cream the butter and sugar on high speed until light and creamy. Gradually add the eggs and mix until blended, scraping down the sides of the bowl as necessary. Reduce the speed to low, add the dry ingredients, and mix just until blended. Scrape the batter into a parchment paper–lined half-sheet pan and bake for 25 minutes, until a cake tester comes out clean. Cool.

Vanilla Honey Hazelnut Mousse

1 lt (33.8 oz/4 cups) heavy cream
1 vanilla bean, split lengthwise and seeds scraped
200 g (7 oz/½ cup plus 1 Tbsp plus 1½ tsp) honey
55 g (1.9 oz/2 Tbsp plus 2 tsp) glucose syrup
100 g (3.5 oz/½ cup) granulated sugar
500 g (17.6 oz/1⅔ cups) Hazelnut Nougatine
340 g (12 oz/11⅓ large) egg whites

1. In the bowl of a stand mixer fitted with the whisk attachment, whip the cream with the vanilla bean seeds on high speed to soft peaks. Reserve in the refrigerator.

2. In a saucepan, bring the honey, glucose, and sugar to a boil over medium-high heat. Remove from the heat.

3. In a food processor fitted with the steel blade, grind the nougatine finely.

4. In the bowl of a stand mixer fitted with the whisk attachment, beat the egg whites on high speed while gradually adding the honey syrup. Whip to soft peaks. Fold in the nougatine and the reserved whipped cream. Scrape the mousse into fourteen 2 x 3-in (5 x 7.6-cm) flexible silicone molds and freeze until firm.

ASSEMBLY

Pulled sugar garnishes (see page 308)

1. Cut the Pound Cake into 2 x 3-in (5 x 7.6-cm) pieces and place each piece in the center of a shallow soup bowl. Arrange a Lacy Tuile on top of the cake. Unmold the Vanilla Honey Hazelnut Mousses and place one on top of each tuile. Top each tuile with a spoonful of diced peaches. Place a quenelle of Peach Sorbet on top. Pour 57 g (2 oz/¼ cup) of the Peach Consommé around each dessert. Drizzle Mint Oil on the consommé. Place a sugar garnish on the sorbet.

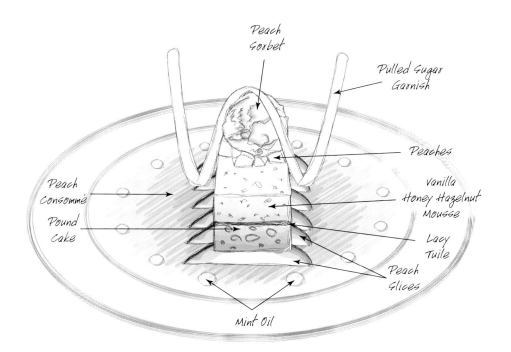

TEAM RUSKELL 2005

Richard Ruskell

Stephen Durfee

Louise Chien

STRAWBERRY FLOATING ISLAND

WITH FENNEL POLLEN, SPRING FRUIT SALAD AND MASCARPONE SHERBET

Pastry Chef Stephen Durfee, who prepared this dessert at the 2005 National Pastry Team Competition, said his team created it because it was a variation on a classic with light, bright flavors. He knew the judges would be tasting a lot of chocolate desserts, so in his mind this dessert would be a refreshing change. Durfee loves the combination of sweet strawberry and aromatic fennel, and the simple Mascarpone Sherbet gives the dessert a tangy richness. **MAKES 14 SERVINGS**

Meringue

225 g (7.9 oz/4½ large) egg whites

275 g (9.7 oz/1⅓ cups plus 1 Tbsp) granulated sugar

1. Preheat the oven to 250°F (122°C).

2. Combine the egg whites and sugar in the bowl of a stand mixer and place the bowl in a skillet of simmering water, whisking frequently, until the whites are hot and no longer viscous.

3. Remove from the heat and, using the whisk attachment, whip the whites on medium speed until they are full and fluffy. Transfer the meringue to a pastry bag fitted with a medium, plain tip.

4. Spray 14 baking cups with nonstick cooking spray. Pipe the meringue mixture into the cups and transfer them to a hotel pan. Surround the cups with water and cover the pan with foil. Bake until firm, about 12 minutes. Remove them from the water and chill in the refrigerator.

Strawberry Cream

140 g (4.9 oz/½ cup plus 1 Tbsp plus 1½ tsp) heavy cream

60 g (2.1 oz/¼ cup) strawberry-rhubarb purée

40 g (1.4 oz/⅓ cup) finely chopped, fresh strawberries

1. In the bowl of a stand mixer fitted with the whisk attachment, whip the cream on high speed to medium peaks and then fold in the strawberry-rhubarb purée and chopped strawberries. Transfer the strawberry cream to a pastry bag fitted with a medium, plain tip.

2. Using a #40 ice cream scoop, hollow out the bases of the Meringues and pipe in the Strawberry Cream. Refrigerate the Meringues.

Fruit Salad

380 g (13.4 oz/1¼ cups) grenadine syrup

75 g (2.6 oz/2 stalks) rhubarb, diced

1½ navel oranges, cut into suprêmes, then diced

146 g (5.14 oz/1 cup) fresh strawberries, washed, hulled, and cut into pea-size Parisienne balls

1. Place the grenadine syrup in a saucepan and bring to a gentle boil over medium-high heat. Add the diced rhubarb and simmer over medium-low heat until tender, 3 or 4 minutes; do not overcook, or it will be mushy. Cool and refrigerate in the syrup.

2. Store the diced orange and strawberry balls in the refrigerator.

Fennel-Scented Custard Sauce

305 g (10.6 oz/1¼ cups) whole milk

250 g (8.5 oz/1 cup plus 1 Tbsp plus 1 tsp) heavy cream

100 g (3.5 oz/5⅓ large) egg yolks

50 g (1.8 oz/¼ cup) granulated sugar

Pinch of salt

3 g (0.1 oz/1 Tbsp) fennel pollen

1. In a saucepan, combine 241 g (8.5 oz/1 cup) of the milk with the cream and bring to a gentle boil over medium-high heat. In a bowl, whisk together the egg yolks, sugar, and salt. Whisk some of the hot milk mixture into the egg yolk mixture to temper the eggs, then return the entire mixture to the saucepan. Cook over medium heat, stirring constantly with a wooden spoon until the custard coats the back of the spoon and reaches 175°F (80°C). Strain and measure out 100 g (3.5 oz/⅓ cup plus 2 Tbsp) of the finished sauce and chill.

2. In a saucepan, combine the remaining 64 g (2 oz/¼ cup) milk with the fennel pollen and bring to a simmer to infuse. Strain, chill, and combine with the reserved custard. Cover and refrigerate until ready to use.

Fennel Crisps

30 g (1 oz/just over ½ large) egg whites
150 g (5.3 oz/1¼ plus 1 Tbsp) confectioners' sugar
2 g (0.07 oz/2 tsp) fennel pollen

1. Preheat the oven to 250°F (122°C).

2. In the bowl of a stand mixer, stir together the egg whites and sugar. Place the bowl on the mixer stand and, using the whisk attachment, beat on high speed for 6 minutes until firm and thick. Transfer the mixture to a small dish and cover with plastic wrap.

3. Spray a silicone baking mat with nonstick cooking spray and wipe it clean. Place it on a sheet pan. Make a 3-in (7.6-cm) round stencil out of plastic. Spread the egg white mixture over the stencil, placed on the lined sheet pan, forming at least 14 circles. Sprinkle each disk with some fennel pollen. Bake for 6 minutes. Immediately remove the disks from the mat, cool, and store in an airtight container.

Candied Fennel Bulb

250 g (8.8 oz/¾ cup plus 1 Tbsp) simple syrup (made with equal parts sugar and water)
10 g (0.4 oz/2 tsp) anisette liqueur
75 g (2.6 oz/⅔ cup) finely chopped fennel bulb

1. In a saucepan, combine the syrup, anisette, and chopped fennel. Bring to a gentle simmer over medium-low heat and poach the fennel until tender, about 10 minutes. Cool and refrigerate the fennel in the syrup.

Candied Fennel Financier

62 g (2.2 oz/½ cup plus 1½ tsp) confectioners' sugar
20 g (0.7 oz/2 Tbsp plus 1½ tsp) all-purpose flour
18 g (0.6 oz/3 Tbsp plus 1 tsp) almond flour
50 g (1.8 oz/slightly more than 1½ large) egg whites
30 g (1.1 oz/2 Tbsp plus 1½ tsp) beurre noisette (see page 117)
2 g (0.07 oz/1 tsp) finely grated lemon zest

1. Preheat the oven to 325°F (163°C).

2. In a medium bowl, combine the sugar and the all-purpose and almond flours. Stir in the egg whites and butter, then stir in the lemon zest.

3. Transfer the batter to a pastry bag fitted with a medium, plain tip. Pipe the batter into fourteen greased 2 x 4-in (5 x 10-cm) financier molds. Arrange a few strips of Candied Fennel Bulb on top of each cake. Bake for 8 minutes, or until golden. Cool completely.

Fennel Oil

6 g (0.2 oz/1 Tbsp plus 1½ tsp) fennel seeds

20 g (0.7 oz/½ cup packed) fresh, flat-leaf parsley leaves

200 g (7 oz/¾ cup plus 3 Tbsp) canola oil

65 g (2.3 oz/2 cups) fennel fronds, chopped

1. Fill a saucepan one-third of the way with water and bring to a boil over high heat. Add the fennel seeds and parsley leaves and blanch in the boiling water for a few seconds. Drain, dry, and purée them with the oil in a blender. Add the chopped fennel fronds and chill.

Mascarpone Sherbet

250 g (8.8 oz/1 cup) mascarpone cheese

325 g (11.5 oz/1 cup plus 1 Tbsp) simple syrup (made with equal parts sugar and water)

35 g (1.2 oz/2 Tbsp plus ¾ tsp) freshly squeezed lemon juice

1. Purée the mascarpone cheese with the simple syrup in a blender or food processor. Process in an ice cream machine according to the manufacturer's instructions, adding the lemon juice when it is nearly frozen.

Fennel Chips

1 fennel bulb

Confectioners' sugar for dusting

1. Preheat the oven to 200°F. Cut the fennel bulb in half lengthwise. Set the mandoline on the thinnest setting and shave 14 pieces from one of the halves (save the remaining fennel for another use).

2. Line a half-sheet pan with a silicone baking mat and dust it liberally with confectioner's sugar. Lay the fennel slices on the mat and dust them with more sugar. Bake for 2 to 3 hours, or until the chips are dried and crisp. Cool and store in an airtight container.

ASSEMBLY

100 g (3.5 oz/⅓ cup plus 2 Tbsp) strawberry-rhubarb purée

1. Drain the fennel and rhubarb from the syrups. Strain the Fennel Oil.

2. Ladle a pool of Fennel-Scented Custard Sauce onto each plate. Unmold a Meringue into the puddle of sauce. Top with a Fennel Crisp.

3. Drizzle each plate with strawberry-rhubarb purée and Fennel Oil. Arrange some of the Fruit Salad on top.

4. Place a Candied Fennel Financier on each plate and top with a quenelle of Mascarpone Sherbet. Garnish with a fennel chip.

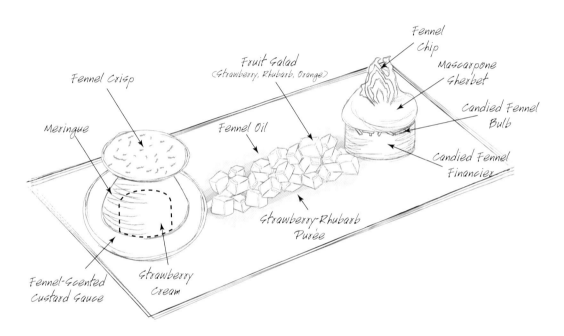

| Bruno Montcoudiol |
| Franck Michel |
| Franck Kestener |

LES POMMES

Team France's stunning plated dessert for the 2006 WPTC is an homage to the apple, presented in several forms. The centerpiece of the dessert is a poached apple stuffed with bits of caramel-coated fried apple. This anchors a light, orange-kissed cream, sandwiched between two orange tuiles, while a bright Green Apple Sorbet, molded to look like the stem-end of an apple, tops the layered dessert.

MAKES 14 SERVINGS

Poached Apples

14 apples

50 g (1.76 oz/3 Tbsp plus ½ tsp) freshly squeezed lemon juice

900 g (31.74 oz/4½ cups) superfine granulated sugar

1.5 kg (52.91 oz/6⅓ cups) water

1. Peel and core the apples and then cut each one into a square shape and spray with the lemon juice.

2. Place the sugar in a skillet and cook over medium heat, stirring occasionally, until the sugar liquefies and turns to a dark amber caramel. Add the water to stop the cooking process. Add the apple squares to the syrup and cook over medium heat for about 15 minutes, or until poached through. Cool the apples in the syrup.

Fried Apple

300 g (10.58 oz/2 medium) apples

Freshly squeezed lemon juice, as needed

80 g (2.82 oz/⅓ cup plus 1 Tbsp plus 1½ tsp) superfine granulated sugar

40 g (1.41 oz/2 Tbsp plus 2¼ tsp) unsalted butter

1. Peel, core, and dice the apples. Toss with the lemon juice.

2. Place the sugar in a saucepan and cook over medium heat, stirring occasionally, until the sugar liquefies and turns to a dark amber caramel. Remove from the heat and add half of the butter, stirring until melted.

3. Melt the remaining butter in a sauté pan over medium-high heat and add the diced apple. Sauté for a few minutes, then add the caramel syrup and bring to a simmer. Simmer for 15 minutes, then cool completely.

Crumble

100 g (3.5 oz/1 stick plus 1 Tbsp) unsalted butter

100 g (3.5 oz/⅓ cup plus 2 Tbsp plus 1½ tsp packed) brown sugar

1 g (0.03 oz/pinch) salt

130 g (4.58 oz/1½ cups) almond flour

100 g (3.5 oz/¾ cup plus 1 Tbsp plus 1 tsp) all-purpose flour

1. Preheat the oven to 300°F (150°C).

2. In the bowl of a stand mixer fitted with the paddle attachment, mix together the butter, sugar, and salt on medium speed until blended. Add the almond and all-purpose flours and mix on low speed until blended.

3. Pass the dough through a crosshatch-style wire rack or thick sieve and sprinkle onto a silicone baking mat–lined sheet pan. Bake until golden, about 15 minutes. Cool completely.

Light Cream

300 g (10.58 oz/1¼ cups plus 2 tsp) heavy cream

25 g (0.88 oz/2 Tbsp) superfine granulated sugar

3 g (0.1 oz/1½ sheets) gelatin (silver grade), bloomed and drained

10 g (0.35 oz/2 tsp) orange liqueur

1. In the bowl of a stand mixer fitted with the whisk attachment, whip 250 g (8.8 oz/1 cup plus 1 Tbsp plus ¾ tsp) of the cream on high speed to medium peaks and refrigerate until needed.

2. In a small saucepan, combine the remaining 50 g (1.76 oz/3 Tbsp plus 1¼ tsp) cream with the sugar and bring to a gentle boil over medium-high heat, stirring to dissolve the sugar. Add the drained gelatin and stir until melted. Cool the mixture down to 77°F (25°C) and stir in the orange liqueur. Fold in the reserved whipped cream. Spread the cream in a lined pan to a thickness of ¾ in (2 cm) and freeze until firm.

3. Cut into 2¾-in (7-cm) squares and refrigerate until ready to assemble the dessert.

Green Apple Sorbet

145 g (5.11 oz/⅔ cup plus 1 Tbsp plus 1½ tsp) superfine granulated sugar

60 g (2.1 oz/⅓ cup plus 1 Tbsp) glucose powder

5 g (0.17 oz/scant 1 Tbsp) nonfat dry milk

3 g (0.1 oz/1 tsp) sorbet stabilizer

155 g (5.46 oz/⅔ cup) water

25 g (0.88 oz/1 Tbsp plus 1 tsp) Trimoline (invert sugar)

600 g (21.16 oz/2⅔ cups) green apple purée

60 g (2.1 oz/3 Tbsp plus 2½ tsp) freshly squeezed lemon juice

1. In a bowl, mix together half of the superfine granulated sugar with the glucose and dry milk and set aside.

2. In a separate bowl, mix the remaining superfine granulated sugar with the sorbet stabilizer; set aside.

3. In a saucepan, combine the water and invert sugar. Bring the mixture to 68°F (20°C) and add the glucose mixture. Heat to 97°F (36°C) and add the sugar and stabilizer mixture. Heat to 185°F (85°C), stirring constantly, then cool completely.

4. Stir in the green apple purée and lemon juice and process the base in an ice cream machine according to the manufacturer's instructions. Scrape the sorbet into fourteen 2¾-in (7-cm) square silicone molds (Team France used a custom-made mold shaped like the top of an apple) and freeze until ready to serve.

Orange Tuile

100 g (3.5 oz/¾ cup plus 2 Tbsp) confectioners' sugar

35 g (1.2 oz/2 Tbsp plus 1 tsp) freshly squeezed orange juice

35 g (1.2 oz/2 Tbsp plus 1½ tsp) unsalted butter, softened

55 g (1.9 oz/⅓ cup plus 2 Tbsp plus 1 tsp) all-purpose flour

1. Preheat the oven to 355°F (180°C).

2. In a bowl, mix together the sugar and orange juice until blended. Add the softened butter and mix until blended. Stir in the flour until blended.

3. Spread the tuile batter over a 3-in (7.6-cm) square stencil, placed on a silicone baking mat–lined sheet pan, to form 14 tuiles. Bake until golden around the edges, about 5 minutes. Cool completely.

Caramel Coulis

250 g (8.8 oz/1 cup plus 1 Tbsp plus ¾ tsp) heavy cream

200 g (7 oz/1 cup) granulated sugar

50 g (1.76 oz/3 Tbsp plus 1½ tsp) unsalted butter

1 g (0.03 oz/pinch) salt

1 vanilla bean, split lengthwise and seeds scraped

1. In a small saucepan, heat the cream over low heat.

2. Meanwhile, pour the sugar into another saucepan and cook over medium heat, stirring occasionally, until the sugar liquefies and turns to a dark amber caramel. Add the butter to stop the cooking process and mix until blended. Stir in the warm cream, salt, and vanilla bean seeds.

Crispy Apple Balls

25 g (0.88 oz/1 Tbsp plus 2¼ tsp) unsalted butter

14 Parisienne apple balls (cut from peeled apples with a melon baller)

20 g (0.7 oz/½ medium) egg, lightly beaten

50 g (1.76 oz/½ cup) Crumble

1. Melt the butter in a sauté pan over medium-high heat and sauté the apple balls until slightly softened. Cool.

2. Dip the apple balls in the egg and then roll them in the Crumble. Set aside in the refrigerator for at least an hour before baking.

3. Preheat the oven to 350°F (175°C).

4. Place the coated apple balls on a silicone baking mat–lined sheet pan and bake until golden, 5 to 8 minutes. Cool completely.

ASSEMBLY

Dark chocolate "stems"

1. Dip a pastry brush into the Caramel Coulis and brush a swath of it on one side of each dessert plate. Top with some of the Crumble.

2. In a bowl, combine the Fried Apple with some of the Caramel Coulis. Fill the hollow core of each Poached Apple with the mixture.

3. Place a Poached Apple in the center of each plate and top with an Orange Tuile, then a square of the Light Cream, and then another tuile. Unmold the Green Apple Sorbet on top and garnish with a chocolate stem. Arrange a Crispy Apple Ball on a serving spoon on each plate.

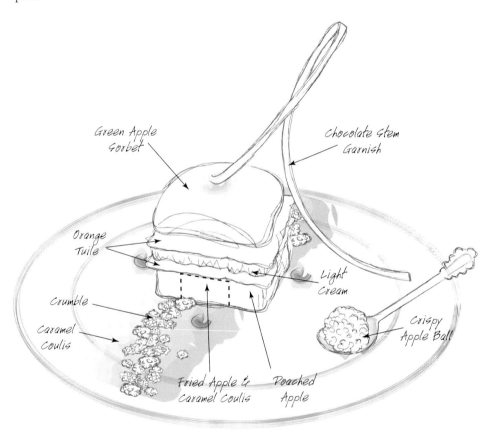

| Silvio Bessone |
| Lucio Forino |
| Roberto Rinaldini |

FRUIT EMOTIONS

Presented dramatically on a tiered black stand, Team Italy's plated dessert from the 2006 WPTC features a panoply of fruit flavors paired with dark chocolate. On the top tier is an Orange Jelly topped with a Fruit and Vegetable Soup made with fennel, celery, papaya, mango, and green apple and crowned with a flurry of Grated Coconut Gelato. The center tier features an orange biscuit cake paired with a saffron gelato and chocolate cream, while the lowest level holds an eggshell containing a Cocoa Bean Panna Cotta topped with a Mango and Ruby Peach Gelatin. **MAKES 14 SERVINGS**

Grated Coconut Gelato

200 g (7.1 oz/¾ cup plus 1 Tbsp) natural mineral water

70 g (2.5 oz/⅓ cup) granulated sugar

3 g (0.11 oz/¾ tsp) neutral stabilizer

600 g (21.2 oz/2⅔ cups) sweetened coconut pulp (10%)

1. In a medium saucepan over high heat, bring the water, sugar, and stabilizer to a boil. Remove from the heat and let cool.

2. When the sugar mixture cools to 104°F (39°C), add the coconut pulp and mix well. Pour the mixture into fourteen 3-oz (90-ml) round Flexipan molds and freeze until firm. (The Coconut Gelato will be grated on top of the Fruit and Vegetable Soup with Passion Fruit Syrup in the final assembly.)

Fruit and Vegetable Soup in Passion Fruit Syrup and Elderflower Infusion

PASSION FRUIT SYRUP

100 g (3.5 oz/⅓ cup plus 2 Tbsp) fresh passion fruit pulp

25 g (0.9 oz/2 Tbsp) superfine granulated sugar

25 g (0.9 oz/1 Tbsp plus 2 tsp) natural mineral water

1. In a medium saucepan, bring all of the ingredients to a boil over high heat. Remove from the heat and set aside.

ELDERFLOWER INFUSION

100 g (3.5 oz/⅓ cup plus 1 Tbsp plus 2 tsp) natural mineral water

50 g (1.8 oz/¼ cup) superfine granulated sugar

15 g (0.5 oz/⅓ cup plus 1 Tbsp) dried elderflowers

1. In a small saucepan, bring the water and sugar to a boil over high heat. Remove from the heat. When the mixture cools to 122°F (50°C), add the dried elderflowers and allow to infuse for 45 minutes. Strain and combine with the Passion Fruit Syrup.

FRUIT AND VEGETABLE SOUP

70 g (2.5 oz/⅔ cup) fresh mango, cut into brunoise

70 g (2.5 oz/⅔ cup) fresh papaya, cut into brunoise

70 g (2.5 oz/¼ of a medium bulb) fresh fennel, diced

50 g (1.8 oz/¼ of a medium apple) fresh green apple, diced

30 g (1.1 oz/¼ cup) fennel hearts, blanched in simple syrup (made with equal parts sugar and water), and diced

30 g (1.1 oz/about 2 stalks) fresh celery hearts, diced

1. Add all of the fruits and vegetables to the Passion Fruit Syrup.

Orange Jelly

125 g (4.4 oz/½ cup) fresh Sicilian orange pulp

37 g (1.3 oz/3 Tbsp) granulated sugar

2 g (0.07 oz/¾ tsp) pectin NH

1.5 g (0.05 oz/½ tsp) sodium alginate

1. In a medium saucepan, combine the orange pulp with 25 g (0.88 oz/2 Tbsp) of the sugar and cook over medium heat to 140°F (60°C). Remove from the heat and set aside.

2. In a medium bowl, combine the pectin, sodium alginate, and the remaining 12 g (0.42 oz/1 Tbsp) sugar. Add this to the orange mixture and bring the entire mixture to a boil.

3. Pour the jelly into serving glasses and chill.

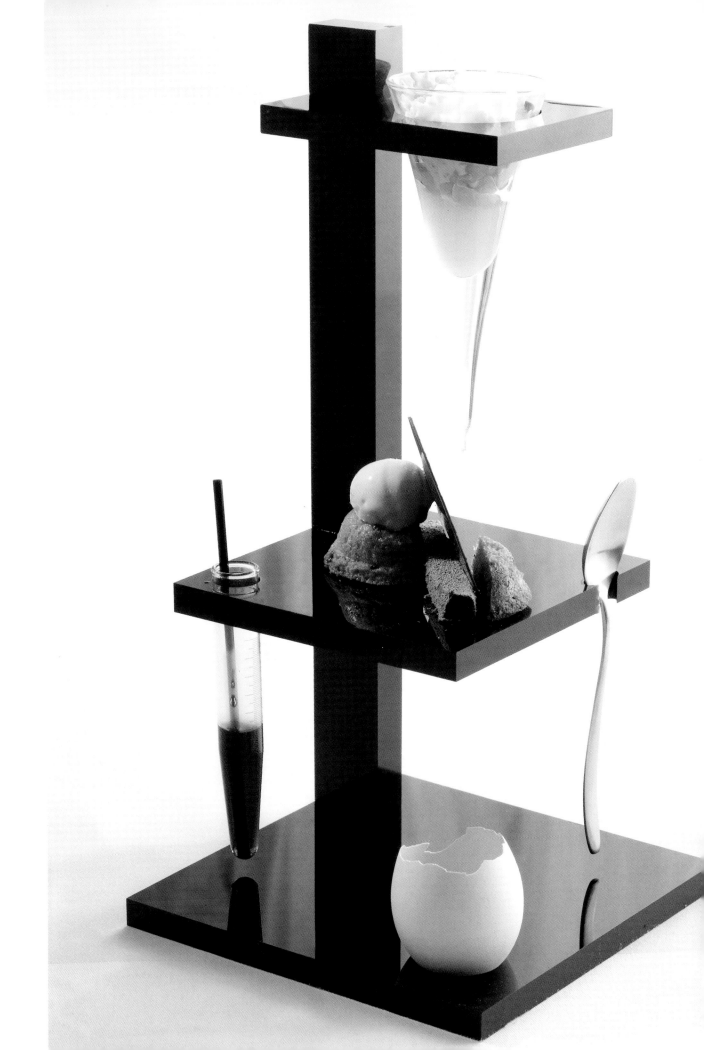

Chocolate Emotions

DARK CHOCOLATE CRÉMEUX

600 g (21.2 oz/2½ cups plus 1 Tbsp plus 1½ tsp) heavy cream (35% butterfat)

120 g (4.2 oz/½ cup) pasteurized egg yolks

60 g (2.1 oz/¼ cup plus 2 tsp) granulated sugar

270 g (9.5 oz) dark chocolate (66%), partially melted

1. In a medium saucepan, bring the cream to a gentle boil over medium-high heat. Meanwhile, in a bowl, whisk together the egg yolks and sugar. Whisk some of the hot cream into the egg yolk–sugar mixture to temper the eggs, then return the entire mixture to the saucepan and cook until slightly thickened, stirring constantly. Pass through a fine-mesh sieve.

2. While the custard is still warm, add the partially melted chocolate and mix well until smooth.

SOFT ORANGE-SCENTED BISCUIT

180 g (6.3 oz/3½) eggs

100 g (3.5 oz/scant ½ cup) extra-virgin olive oil

180 g (6.3 oz/1⅔ cups) pastry flour

90 g (3.2 oz/scant ½ cup) granulated sugar

60 g (2.1 oz/¼ cup plus 1½ tsp) cassonade sugar

5 g (0.2 oz/1¾ tsp) active dry yeast

0.5 g (0.9 oz/pinch) salt

Finely grated zest of ½ orange

1. Preheat the oven to 325°F (163°C).

2. In a food processor fitted with the steel blade, mix together all of the ingredients. Divide the mixture among 14 mignon Flexipan molds. Bake for 8 minutes. Cool completely.

SAFFRON GELATO

1 kg (35.5 oz/1 qt plus 2 Tbsp) whole milk

333 g (11.7 oz/1¼ cups plus 3 Tbsp) heavy cream (35% butterfat)

0.5 g (0.01 oz/½ tsp) Sicilian saffron pistils

350 g (12.3 oz/1¾ cups) granulated sugar

80 g (2.8 oz/¾ cup plus 1 Tbsp) dextrose powder

45 g (1.6 oz/scant ½ cup) nonfat dry milk

6 g (0.2 oz/2 tsp) neutral stabilizer

2 g (0.07 oz/1 tsp) fleur de sel

160 g (5.6 oz/½ cup plus 2 Tbsp) pasteurized egg yolks

40 g (1.4 oz/2 Tbsp) Acadia honey

1. In a large saucepan, combine the milk, cream, and saffron and bring to a boil over high heat. Remove from the heat and allow to infuse for 1 hour.

2. Add the remaining ingredients to the saucepan at 140°F (60°C) and then heat to 180°F (82°C), stirring constantly.

3. Cool the mixture in a polycarbonate container in a blast chiller. Transfer the cooled mixture to an ice cream maker and process according to the manufacturer's instructions.

4. Mold the gelato in 14¾-in (37.5-cm) demisphere molds and freeze until ready to use.

Egg Emotions

TONKA COCOA BEAN PANNA COTTA

400 g (14.1 oz/1¾ cups) heavy cream (35% butterfat)

1 Tonka cocoa bean, grated

200 g (7.1 oz) white chocolate, chopped

40 g (1.4 oz/3 ½ Tbsp) cocoa butter, softened

200 g (7.1 oz/¾ cup plus 1 Tbsp) whole milk

20 g (0.71 oz/1 Tbsp) glucose syrup

20 g (0.18 oz/10 sheets) gelatin (silver grade), bloomed and drained

1. In a small container, combine the cream with the grated Tonka cocoa bean, cover, and refrigerate for at least 24 hours. Strain through a fine-mesh sieve before using.

2. Place the white chocolate and cocoa butter in a large bowl. In a large saucepan, combine the milk and glucose and bring to a boil over medium heat. Add the drained gelatin and stir until melted. Pour the mixture slowly over the white chocolate and cocoa butter in the bowl and whisk until smooth. Whisk in the strained, chilled cocoa-infused cream.

3. Place the mixture in a polycarbonate container and cover the surface directly with plastic wrap. Allow to crystallize for 3 hours at 48°F (9°C).

MANGO AND RUBY PEACH GELATIN

120 g (4.2 oz/½ cup) sweetened ruby peach purée (10%)

100 g (3.5 oz/¼ cup plus 2 tsp) sweetened mango purée (10%)

60 g (2.1 oz/⅓ cup) granulated sugar

1.8 g (0.06 oz/¾ sheet) gelatin (silver grade), bloomed and drained

1. In a medium saucepan, combine the peach and mango purées, sugar, and drained gelatin. Cook over medium heat and bring to a temperature of 113°F (45°C). Mix until the gelatin is melted.

2. Pour into 14 mignon Flexipan demisphere molds and chill until set.

CHOCOWNIE

500 g (17.6 oz/2¼ cups) Italian white wine

150 g (5.3 oz/1½ cups plus 1 Tbsp) cacao nibs

15 g (0.53 oz/1 Tbsp plus 1 tsp) granulated sugar

1. In a medium saucepan, combine all of the ingredients and cook over medium heat to 140°F (60°C). Remove from the heat and allow to infuse for 2 hours.

2. Strain the Chocownie.

ASSEMBLY

1. Arrange a layer of Fruit and Vegetable Soup with Passion Fruit Syrup and Elderflower Infusion on top of the set Orange Jelly. Top this layer with a scoop of Grated Coconut Gelato and arrange on a serving plate (or, if using a tiered stand, on the top tier).

2. Arrange a Soft Orange-Scented Biscuit on each plate (or the middle tier of the stand), topped with the Saffron Gelato. Spoon some of the Dark Chocolate Crémeux alongside. Next to that (or on the lowest tier), place the Tonka Cocoa Bean Panna Cotta topped with the Mango and Ruby Peach Gelatin. Pour the Chocownie in a serving glass and serve alongside the panna cotta.

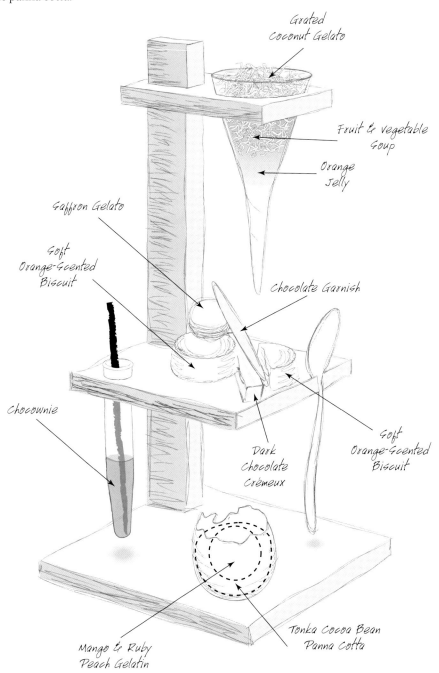

Grated Coconut Gelato

Fruit & Vegetable Soup

Orange Jelly

Saffron Gelato

Soft Orange-Scented Biscuit

Chocolate Garnish

Chocownie

Dark Chocolate Crémeux

Soft Orange-Scented Biscuit

Mango & Ruby Peach Gelatin

Tonka Cocoa Bean Panna Cotta

TEAM SWITZERLAND 2006

Rolf Mürner

Thomas Schwarzenberger

Gerald Saudan

FUSION

Team Switzerland's brightly colored plated dessert for the 2006 WPTC is a complex medley of flavors and textures. It features a Passion Fruit Mousse that has been sprayed red with tinted cocoa butter, a rich cheesecake paired with a tangy Raspberry Yogurt Sorbet, and a refreshing Mango Cocktail with Yogurt Foam. A Coconut Gelée and Raspberry Coulis add complementary flavors.

MAKES 14 SERVINGS

Passion Fruit Mousse

90 g (3.2 oz/⅓ cup plus 2 Tbsp plus ¾ tsp) granulated sugar

45 g (1.6 oz/3 Tbsp plus 1 tsp) unsalted butter

60 g (2.1 oz/1 extra-large) egg

180 g (5.4 oz/¾ cup) passion fruit juice

80 g (2.8 oz/⅔ cup plus 1 Tbsp) confectioners' sugar

180 g (6.3 oz/¾ cup) sour cream

12 g (0.42 oz/6 sheets) gelatin (gold grade), bloomed and drained

540 g (19 oz/4⅔ cups) whipped heavy cream

Red-tinted cocoa butter for spraying

1. In a medium saucepan, warm the granulated sugar, butter, egg, and 30 g (1.1 oz/about 2 Tbsp) of the passion fruit juice over low heat. Once warmed, add the remaining 150 g (4 oz/ ¼ cup plus 2 Tbsp) juice, confectioners' sugar, and sour cream. Mix until well blended.

2. Remove the mixture from the heat and add the drained gelatin. Gently fold in the whipped cream. Scrape the mousse into fourteen 2½-in- (6.3-cm-) square x 3-in- (7.6-cm-) high molds and freeze until firm.

3. Unmold and spray with red-tinted cocoa butter. Refrigerate until serving.

Raspberry Coulis

250 g (8.8 oz/1 cup plus 1 Tbsp plus 1 tsp) raspberry purée

50 g (1.8 oz/⅓ cup plus 2 Tbsp) confectioners' sugar

1. In a medium bowl, mix all of the ingredients together until well combined. Cover and refrigerate until ready to serve.

Chocolate Shortbread

200 g (7.1 oz/1½ cups plus 2 Tbsp plus 2¼ tsp) all-purpose flour

15 g (0.53 oz/2 Tbsp plus 1½ tsp) cocoa powder

2 g (0.07 oz/½ plus ⅛ tsp) baking powder

125 g (4.4 oz/1 stick plus 2¼ tsp) unsalted butter, softened

125 g (4.4 oz/⅔ cup) granulated sugar

25 g (0.88 oz/½ large) egg

10 g (0.35 oz/2½ tsp) rum

1. Preheat the oven to 320°F (160°C).

2. In a bowl, sift together the flour, cocoa powder, and baking powder. Whisk and set aside.

3. In the bowl of a stand mixer fitted with the paddle attachment, cream together the butter and sugar on high speed. Add the egg and rum and mix until well blended. Add the dry ingredients on low speed and mix just until combined.

4. Roll the dough out to a thickness of 0.08 in (2 mm) and blind bake in a 7.8-in (20-cm) square pan lined with a silicone baking mat. Cool.

5. Cut the shortbread into 2½-in (6.3-cm) squares.

Mango Gelée

200 g (7.1 oz/¾ cup) mango purée

50 g (1.8 oz/⅓ cup plus 2 Tbsp) confectioners' sugar

4 g (0.14 oz/2 sheets) gelatin (gold grade), bloomed and drained

133 g (4.7 oz/1 cup) diced mango

1. In a small saucepan, combine the mango purée and confectioners' sugar and bring to a gentle boil over medium-high heat. Remove from the heat and stir in the drained gelatin until dissolved. Stir in the diced mango, pour into a baking pan, and chill until set.

Cheesecake

200 g (7.1 oz/1 cup) fresh cream cheese

16 g (0.56 oz/2 Tbsp plus ½ tsp) cornstarch

10 g (0.35 oz/½ tsp plus ⅛ tsp) freshly squeezed lemon juice

100 g (3.5 oz/¾ stick plus 1 Tbsp) unsalted butter, softened

100 g (3.5 oz/½ cup) granulated sugar

60 g (2.1 oz/1 extra-large) egg

1. Preheat the oven to 320°F (160°C).

2. In a small bowl, combine the cream cheese, cornstarch, and lemon juice.

3. In the bowl of a stand mixer fitted with the paddle attachment, combine the butter and sugar. While mixing on medium speed, add the eggs and cheese mixture. Pour the batter into the shortbread crust and bake for 30 to 40 minutes.

4. Cool, chill, and cut into 1½ x 2½-in (3.8 x 6.3-cm) rectangles.

Caramel Tuile

175 g (6.2 oz/¾ cup plus 2 Tbsp) granulated sugar
150 g (5.3 oz/1 stick plus 2⅔ Tbsp plus 2 tsp) unsalted butter, softened
75 g (2.6 oz/⅓ cup) heavy cream
75 g (2.6 oz/3 Tbsp plus 1½ tsp) glucose syrup

1. Preheat the oven to 320°F (160°C).

2. In a large saucepan, combine all of the ingredients and bring to a boil over high heat. Spread out the mixture on a silicone baking mat–lined sheet pan and bake for 10 to 12 minutes. Let cool and cut into 2 x 3-in (5 x 7.6-cm) rectangles.

Raspberry Yogurt Sorbet

600 g (21.2 oz/2 cups) raspberry purée
180 g (6.3 oz/¾ cup) water
210 g (7.4 oz/¾ cup plus ¾ tsp) granulated sugar
250 g (8.8 oz/1 cup plus 1½ tsp) plain yogurt
6 g (0.21 oz/3 sheets) gelatin (gold grade), bloomed and drained

1. In a medium saucepan, combine the raspberry purée, water, and sugar and bring to a boil over high heat. Remove from the heat and let cool.

2. Add the yogurt and drained gelatin and stir until the gelatin is melted. Chill in an ice bath.

3. Process the sorbet base in an ice cream machine according to the manufacturer's instructions.

Mango Cocktail

200 g (7.1 oz/¾ cup plus 1 Tbsp) freshly squeezed orange juice
60 g (2.1 oz/¼ cup plus 2 tsp) granulated sugar
500 g (17.6 oz/1½ cups plus 1 Tbsp) mango purée
200 g (7.1 oz/1¾ cups) confectioners' sugar
70 g (2.5 oz/¼ cup plus 1½ tsp) coconut liqueur
400 g (14.1 oz/3 cups) cubed mango

1. In a medium saucepan, combine the orange juice and granulated sugar and bring to a boil over high heat. Reduce by half.

2. In a large bowl, combine the mango purée, confectioners' sugar, and coconut liqueur. Add the orange juice reduction and mango cubes and stir well. Cover and refrigerate until ready to serve.

Yogurt Foam

300 g (10.6 oz/1¼ cups) plain yogurt

80 g (2.8 oz/⅓ cup) heavy cream

80 g (2.8 oz/⅔ plus 2 tsp) confectioners' sugar

20 g (0.71 oz/1 Tbsp plus ¾ tsp) freshly squeezed lemon juice

1. Combine all of the ingredients in a N_2O-charged siphon to create a foam.

ASSEMBLY

Chocolate garnishes

1. Fill a small glass three-quarters of the way with the Mango Cocktail and top with Yogurt Foam and a chocolate garnish. Arrange on one side of a serving plate.

2. Arrange the Cheesecake rectangle next to the Mango Cocktail and top with a Caramel Tuile. Top with a quenelle of Raspberry Yogurt Sorbet.

3. Place the Passion Fruit Mousse on top of a Chocolate Shortbread square on the plate. Top with a dot of Raspberry Coulis.

4. Garnish the plate with Raspberry Coulis and a strip of Mango Gelée.

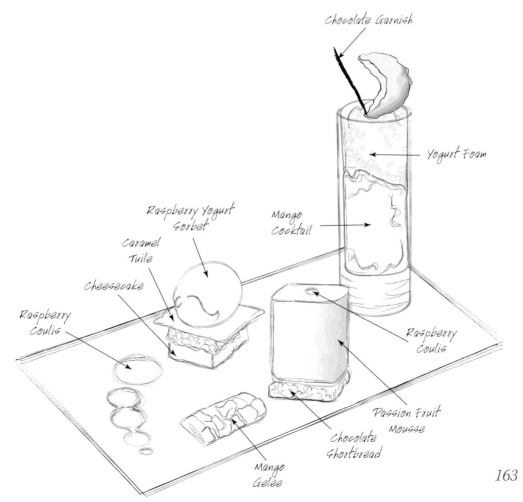

TEAM USA 2006

Laurent Lhuillier

David Ramirez

Jim Mullaney

YIN-YANG FLOURLESS CHOCOLATE CAKE

In creating this boat-shaped dessert, Team USA's goal was to choose flavors that would not overwhelm the judges' palates. Their key component, a flourless chocolate cake, is accompanied by a clean-tasting rice sorbet and an exotic fruit-flavored crémeux, and garnished creatively with a passion fruit–flavored tuile and foam. **MAKES 14 SERVINGS**

Exotic Drops

250 g (8.8 oz/1 cup) pineapple juice

1.3 g (0.04 oz/¼ tsp) Citras (see Sources page 310)

1.3 g (0.04 oz/¼ tsp) Algin (see Sources page 310)

75 g (2.64 oz/⅓ cup) banana purée

75 g (2.64 oz/⅓ cup) coconut purée

50 g (1.76 oz/3 Tbsp plus 1½ tsp) mango purée

50 g (1.76 oz/3 Tbsp plus 1½ tsp) passion fruit purée

1 kg (35.27 oz/4¼ cups) water

5 g (0.17 oz/1⅜ tsp) Calcic (see Sources page 310)

1. In a saucepan, combine the pineapple juice and Citras. Mix in the Algin and cook over medium heat to 180°F (82°C). Remove from the heat and cool.

2. Stir in the banana, coconut, mango, and passion fruit purées.

3. Combine the water with the Calcic. Fill a syringe with 2 to 3 g (0.035 to 0.1 oz) of the fruit purée mixture. Release drops into the water and Calcic mixture and allow to stand for 1 minute. Remove and set aside.

Passion Fruit Foam

275 g (9.7 oz/1 cup plus 2 Tbsp plus 1½ tsp) water

225 g (7.9 oz/¾ cup plus 3 Tbsp) passion fruit juice

1.5 g (0.05 oz/1 tsp) Lecite (see Sources page 310)

1. Combine all of the ingredients and store the mixture, covered, in the refrigerator until ready to serve. Immediately before serving, mix with an immersion blender for 1 minute.

Exotic Crémeux

200 g (7 oz/4 large) eggs

149 g (5.25 oz/8 large) egg yolks

106 g (3.7 oz/½ cup plus 1½ tsp) granulated sugar

80 g (2.8 oz/⅓ cup plus 1½ tsp) mango purée

80 g (2.8 oz/⅓ cup plus 1½ tsp) passion fruit purée

40 g (1.4 oz/2 Tbsp plus 2¼ tsp) coconut purée

28 g (1 oz/2 Tbsp) banana purée

8 g (0.28 oz/2½ tsp) powdered pectin

60 g (2.1 oz/½ stick plus ¾ tsp) unsalted butter

1. In a saucepan, whisk together the eggs, egg yolks, and sugar until blended. Add the mango, passion fruit, coconut, and banana purées, and the pectin and cook over medium heat, stirring frequently, until slightly thickened.

2. Add the butter and mix with an immersion blender until emulsified. Cover and refrigerate until ready to use.

Rice Pudding

120 g (4.2 oz/¾ cup) jasmine rice

640 g (22.5 oz/2⅔ cups) whole milk

160 g (5.64 oz/⅔ cup) coconut milk

2 vanilla beans, split lengthwise and seeds scraped

40 g (1.4 oz/3 Tbsp plus ¾ tsp) granulated sugar

1. In a saucepan, combine the rice with the milk, coconut milk, and vanilla bean seeds and pods and cook over medium-high heat until the mixture begins to simmer. Reduce the heat to low, cover, and cook just until the rice softens; begin checking it after 10 minutes, then continue to check it every 5 minutes. Stir in the sugar and cook just until the sugar dissolves. Remove from heat and cool. Remove the vanilla pods, cover, and refrigerate until ready to use.

Coconut Streusel

85 g (3 oz/¾ stick) unsalted butter, softened

28 g (1 oz/2 Tbsp plus ¾ tsp) granulated sugar

57 g (2 oz/⅔ cup) unsweetened desiccated coconut

87 g (3 oz/⅔ cup plus 1 Tbsp) all-purpose flour

1. Preheat the oven to 340°F (170°C).

2. In the bowl of a stand mixer fitted with the paddle attachment, cream together the butter and sugar on high speed. Add the coconut and flour and mix on low speed until combined. Pass the dough through a crosshatch-style wire rack or thick sieve and sprinkle onto a silicone baking mat–lined sheet pan.

3. Bake until golden. Cool completely and store in an airtight container at room temperature until ready to use.

Flourless Chocolate Cake

200 g (7 oz) bittersweet chocolate (64%), chopped

25 g (0.88 oz) cocoa paste

125 g (4.4 oz/1 stick plus 2¼ tsp) unsalted butter

160 g (5.64 oz/8½ large) egg yolks

115 g (4 oz/½ cup plus 1 Tbsp plus ¾ tsp) granulated sugar

240 g (8.46 oz/8 large) egg whites

1. Preheat the oven to 340°F (170°C).

2. Combine the chocolate with the cocoa paste and butter in a bowl and place the bowl over a saucepan of simmering water; the bottom of the bowl should not touch the water. Heat, stirring frequently, until melted. Remove from the heat and cool slightly.

3. In the bowl of a stand mixer fitted with the whisk attachment, whip the egg yolks and 60 g (2.1 oz/¼ cup plus 2 tsp) of the sugar on high speed until tripled in volume, about 5 minutes. Gently fold in the cooled chocolate mixture.

4. In a separate mixer bowl, using the whisk attachment, beat the egg whites on high speed until soft peaks begin to form. Gradually add the remaining 55 g (1.9 oz/¼ cup plus 1¾ tsp) sugar and beat until stiff and glossy. Gently fold the whites into the chocolate mixture. Scrape the batter onto a silicone baking mat–lined half-sheet pan and bake for 20 minutes, or until set. Cool completely.

5. Using a 4-in- (10.16-cm-) long barquette-shaped cutter, cut out 14 barquette shapes.

Rice Sorbet

400 g (14.1 oz/1¼ cups) jasmine rice

1 cinnamon stick

1.2 kg (42.33 oz/5 cups) whole milk

220 g (7.76 oz/1 cup plus 1 Tbsp plus 1½ tsp) granulated sugar

68 g (2.4 oz/⅓ cup plus 1 Tbsp plus 2½ tsp) glucose powder

68 g (2.4 oz/3 Tbsp plus 1¼ tsp) Trimoline (invert sugar)

1. Combine the rice, cinnamon stick, and milk in a medium saucepan and bring to a simmer over medium heat. Reduce the heat to low, cover, and cook for 15 minutes.

2. Measure out 800 g (28.2 oz/4 cups) of the rice infusion and combine in a saucepan with the sugar, glucose powder, and Trimoline. Cook, stirring frequently, until the sugar is dissolved. Cool in an ice bath.

3. Process the sorbet base in an ice cream machine according to the manufacturer's instructions.

Passion Fruit Tuile

450 g (15.87 oz/2¼ cups) granulated sugar

7 g (0.25 oz/2¼ tsp) powdered pectin

300 g (10.6 oz/2½ sticks plus 1 Tbsp plus ¾ tsp) unsalted butter

150 g (5.3 oz/⅓ cup plus 2 Tbsp plus 1 tsp) glucose syrup

150 g (5.3 oz/½ cup plus 2 Tbsp) passion fruit juice

30 g (1.05 oz/¼ cup) all-purpose flour

200 g (7 oz/2¼ cups plus 1 tsp) almond flour

1. Preheat the oven to 340°F (170°C).

2. Combine the sugar and pectin.

3. In a saucepan, heat the butter and glucose over medium heat until the butter is melted. Add the sugar-pectin mixture and cook over medium heat, stirring occasionally, until the sugar is dissolved. Stir in the passion fruit juice, then whisk in the all-purpose and almond flours and bring to a boil over high heat, whisking constantly. Allow to boil for 1 minute to cook the flour.

4. Spread the mixture onto a parchment paper–lined sheet pan and bake until golden brown, about 5 minutes. After baking and while still warm, use a rolling pin to roll the mixture between two pieces of parchment paper. Roll until thin. With the mixture still between the sheets of parchment, using a very sharp utility knife, cut out 4-in- (10.16-cm-) long barquette shapes from the tuiles (the same size and shape as you cut the chocolate cake). While warm, curve the tuiles over a 4-in (10.16-cm) diameter PVC pipe.

ASSEMBLY

Feuille de bric sheets, baked and cut into 4-in- (10.16-cm-) long barquette shapes

1. Arrange each Flourless Chocolate Cake barquette on a plate and cut out a 1½-in (4-cm) round from its center. Spoon some Rice Pudding in the center of each cake. Top with a baked feuille de bric sheet. Using a pastry bag fitted with a medium plain tip, pipe the Exotic Crémeux in dots around the edge of the cake, leaving room in the center for more Rice Pudding. Spoon some of the pudding in the center. Top with another one of the feuille de bric barquettes. Repeat the layering one more time.

2. Top each dessert with the Passion Fruit Tuile and a scoop of Rice Sorbet. Sprinkle with some Coconut Streusel. Spoon some of the Passion Fruit Foam at one end of the plate; dot with a few of the Exotic Drops.

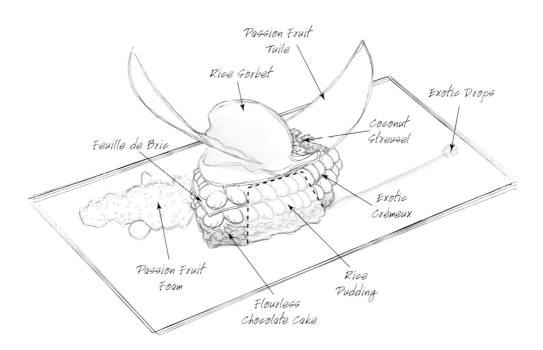

TEAM BRANLARD 2007

Laurent Branlard

Stéphane Tréand

Frédéric Monti

BROWN BUTTER FINANCIER

WITH FRESH MARINATED RASPBERRIES AND VANILLA DIPLOMAT CREAM, PINEAPPLE PASSION FRUIT CLOUD, BANANA PASSION BEIGNET, AND EXOTIC COULIS

Presented on a specially designed plate shaped like a guitar, Team Branlard's plated dessert from the 2007 WPTC celebrated that year's country music theme. But it was much more than a simple gimmick—this dessert is a sophisticated combination of flavors and textures. Raspberry and Lemon Tuiles, Coconut Streusel, a mango- and passion fruit–flavored Exotic Coulis, Yuzu Ice Cream, and a puff of pineapple–passion fruit sauce are artfully combined with a rich Brown Butter Financier in an extraordinary dessert that handily captured first place. **MAKES 12 SERVINGS**

Coconut Streusel

56 g (2 oz/⅔ cup) unsweetened shredded coconut

56 g (2 oz/⅔ cup) desiccated unsweetened coconut

142 g (5 oz/1 cup plus 3 Tbsp) all-purpose flour

112 g (4 oz/½ cup plus 1 Tbsp) superfine granulated sugar

3 g (0.1 oz/scant ½ tsp) salt

113 g (4 oz/1 stick) unsalted butter, cut into cubes

1. Preheat the oven to 350°F (175°C).

2. Toast the unsweetened and desiccated coconuts on a sheet pan for 8 minutes.

3. In the bowl of a stand mixer fitted with the paddle attachment, combine the toasted coconut, flour, sugar, and salt. Add the butter and mix on low speed to a crumbly texture. Spread onto a sheet pan and bake for 10 minutes, until golden. Cool and refrigerate until ready to use.

Exotic Coulis

180 g (6.3 oz/¾ cup) mango purée

180 g (6.3 oz/¾ cup) passion fruit purée

48 g (1.7 oz/3 Tbsp plus 2½ tsp) granulated sugar

9.6 g (0.31 oz/1 Tbsp) pectin powder

2.5 g (0.08 oz/1¼ sheets) gelatin (gold grade), bloomed and drained

1. In a saucepan, combine the mango and passion fruit purées and place over medium heat.

2. Combine the sugar with the pectin, add to the purées and bring to a boil, stirring. Remove from the heat, add the drained gelatin, and stir until dissolved. Strain the coulis through a fine-mesh sieve and reserve for plating.

Raspberry and Lemon Tuile

180 g (6.3 oz/1½ cups plus 1 Tbsp) confectioners' sugar

150 g (5.3 oz/⅓ cup plus 2 Tbsp) glucose

82 g (2.9 oz/⅓ cup) freshly squeezed lemon juice

82 g (2.9 oz/⅓ cup plus 1 Tbsp) raspberry juice

145 g (5.1 oz/1 stick plus 2 Tbsp plus ¾ tsp) unsalted butter, softened

2.25 g (0.07 oz/1 Tbsp) red food coloring

0.5 g (0.017 oz/¼ tsp) yellow food coloring

0.5 g (0.017 oz/¼ tsp) brown food coloring

2 g (0.07 oz/¾ tsp) raspberry compound

195 g (6.8 oz/1½ cups plus 2 Tbsp) all-purpose flour

1. Preheat the oven to 350°F (175°C).

2. In a bowl, combine the sugar, glucose, and lemon and raspberry juices. Add the softened butter, red, yellow, and brown food colorings, and the raspberry compound and mix until blended. Add the flour and mix just until combined.

3. Spread the batter out thinly in a parchment paper–lined sheet pan and bake for about 6 minutes.

4. Cut out 12 tuiles with a 3-in (7.6-cm) round cutter and reserve in an airtight container.

Passion Fruit Mousseline

100 g (3.5 oz/⅓ cup plus 2 Tbsp) passion fruit purée

100 g (3.5 oz/½ cup) superfine granulated sugar

100 g (3.5 oz/2 large) eggs

15 g (0.5 oz/2 Tbsp plus 1½ tsp) powdered heavy cream (available from Albert Uster Imports and WillPowder, see Sources page 310)

1 g (0.03 oz/½ tsp) neutral stabilizer

2 g (0.07 oz/1 sheet) gelatin (gold grade), bloomed and drained

120 g (4.2 oz/1 stick plus 1½ tsp) unsalted butter, softened

1. In a saucepan, heat the passion fruit purée with half of the sugar over medium-high heat, stirring to dissolve the sugar.

2. In a bowl, whisk together the eggs, powdered cream, stabilizer, and the remaining sugar. Pour the hot purée over the egg mixture and whisk to combine. Strain and return to the saucepan. Cook, whisking constantly, until the mixture boils and thickens. Remove from the heat and whisk in the drained gelatin. Scrape the mixture onto a sheet pan and cool.

3. Place the mixture in the bowl of a stand mixer fitted with the whisk attachment and mix on low speed, gradually adding the butter. Increase the speed and whip on high speed until light and fluffy. Cover and refrigerate until ready to use. (You will use this mixture for the beignet centers and also for the center of the brown butter cake.)

Passion Fruit Beignet Center

441 g (15.5 oz/3¾ cups) Passion Fruit Mousseline
24 slices fresh banana

1. Pipe Passion Fruit Mousseline into twelve ¾-in (2-cm) diameter silicone full sphere molds, filling only half of each sphere. Add 2 banana slices to each mold and fill with Passion Fruit Mousseline. Freeze until ready to use.

Vanilla Pastry Cream

375 g (13.2 oz/1½ cups plus 2 tsp) whole milk
41 g (1.4 oz/3 Tbsp) unsalted butter, cut into tablespoons
1 vanilla bean, split lengthwise
79 g (2.78 oz/6 Tbsp plus 1 tsp) superfine granulated sugar
65 g (2.3 oz/3½ large) egg yolks
32 g (1.1 oz/⅓ cup) powdered heavy cream
3.25 g (0.11 oz/1½ tsp) neutral stabilizer
2 g (0.07 oz/1 sheet) gelatin (gold grade), bloomed and drained

1. In a saucepan, combine the milk, butter, vanilla bean, and 19 g (0.67 oz/1 Tbsp plus 1½ tsp) of the sugar and cook over medium heat, stirring to dissolve the sugar.

2. Meanwhile, in a bowl, whisk together the egg yolks, powdered cream, stabilizer, and the remaining 60 g (2.1 oz/¼ cup plus 2¼ tsp) sugar. Pour the hot milk mixture over the egg yolk mixture, strain, and return to the pan. Place over medium-high heat and cook, whisking constantly, until the mixture boils and thickens. Remove from the heat, add the drained gelatin, and stir until dissolved. Scrape the pastry cream out onto a sheet pan and cool.

Vanilla Diplomat

200 g (7 oz/¾ cup plus 1 Tbsp) heavy cream

500 g (17.6 oz/2 cups plus 1 Tbsp) Vanilla Pastry Cream

20 g (0.7 oz/1 Tbsp plus 1½ tsp) coconut rum

1. In the bowl of a stand mixer fitted with the whisk attachment, whip the cream on high speed to soft peaks.

2. In a separate mixer bowl, using the paddle attachment, mix the pastry cream with the coconut rum on medium speed until smooth. Fold in the whipped cream. Transfer to a pastry bag fitted with an Inox #5 tip and reserve.

Marinated Raspberries

300 g (10.6 oz/1¼ cups) water

240 g (8.5 oz/1 cup plus 3 Tbsp) superfine granulated sugar

5 g (0.17 oz/2 tsp) grated fresh ginger

4.5 g (0.15 oz/2¼ tsp) finely grated lemon zest

38 g (1.3 oz/2 Tbsp plus 1 tsp) raspberry liqueur

360 g (12.7 oz/3¼ cups) fresh raspberries

1. In a saucepan, heat the water and sugar over medium-high heat, stirring until the sugar is dissolved. Add the ginger and lemon zest and let infuse for 20 minutes. Add the raspberry liqueur.

2. Strain the liquid over the raspberries. Cover and refrigerate until ready to use.

Yuzu Ice Cream

240 g (8.5 oz/1 cup plus 3 Tbsp) superfine granulated sugar

80 g (2.8 oz/½ cup) glucose powder

74 g (2.6/¾ cup) nonfat dry milk

4 g (0.14 oz/1¾ tsp) ice cream stabilizer

4 g (0.14 oz/2 tsp) glycerol monostearate

950 g (33.5 oz/3¾ cups plus 3 Tbsp) whole milk

95 g (3.3 oz/1 cup) fresh yuzu zest

40 g (1.4 oz/2 Tbsp) invert sugar

60 g (2.1 oz/3 extra-large) egg yolks

380 g (13.4 oz/1½ cups plus 2 Tbsp) heavy cream (35% butterfat)

340 g (12 oz/1⅓ cups plus 1 Tbsp plus 1½ tsp) yuzu juice

85 g (3 oz/⅓ cup plus 1¼ tsp) freshly squeezed lemon juice

2 g (0.07 oz/2 tsp) green food coloring

1. In a small bowl, mix together half of the superfine granulated sugar with the glucose powder and dry milk and set aside.

2. In another small bowl, combine the remaining superfine granulated sugar with the ice cream stabilizer and glycerol monostearate and set aside.

3. In a saucepan, combine the milk, yuzu zest, and invert sugar and cook over medium heat until the mixture reaches 68°F (20°C). When at temperature, add the sugar and glucose mixture and whisk to combine. Continue to cook, and when the mixture reaches 95°F (34°C), add the sugar and stabilizer mixture and whisk to combine. Increase the heat to high and bring the mixture to 185°F (85°C), stirring constantly.

4. Meanwhile, in a large bowl, whisk together the egg yolks and cream. When the milk mixture reaches 185°F (85°C), strain it over the egg yolk mixture, whisking to combine. Whisk in the yuzu and lemon juices and the green food coloring. Chill in an ice bath.

5. Process the mixture in an ice cream machine according to the manufacturer's instructions.

Beignet Batter

300 g (10.5 oz/1 cup plus 3 Tbsp) beer
4.5 g (0.15 oz/1½ tsp) active dry yeast
210 g (7.4 oz/1¾ cups) all-purpose flour
56 g (1.9 oz/3 large) egg yolks
50 g (1.7 oz/3 Tbsp plus 2¼ tsp) grapeseed oil
¾ vanilla bean, split lengthwise and seeds scraped
90 g (3.17 oz/3 large) egg whites
2 g (0.07 oz/rounded ¼ tsp) salt
140 g (5 oz/⅔ cup plus 1 Tbsp plus ¾ tsp) superfine granulated sugar

1. In a saucepan over medium heat, heat the beer to 112°F (45°C) and sprinkle over the yeast. Remove from the heat and let stand for 5 minutes.

2. In a stand mixer fitted with the paddle attachment, mix the flour on low speed and gradually add the beer mixture, egg yolks, oil, and vanilla bean seeds and mix until blended.

3. In a separate mixer bowl, using the whisk attachment, beat the egg whites and salt on high speed to soft peaks. Gradually add the sugar and beat on high speed until whites are glossy and form stiff peaks. Fold the meringue into the beer batter. Transfer the batter to a pastry bag fitted with a medium, plain tip. Pipe the batter into twelve 2-in (5-cm) silicone full spheres until half full. Add a Passion Fruit Beignet Center to each sphere and fill completely with beignet batter. Freeze until ready to use.

Brown Butter Financier

98 g (3.4 oz/½ cup) butter

116 g (4.1 oz/1 cup plus ½ tsp) confectioners' sugar

92 g (3.2 oz/1 cup plus 2¼ tsp) almond flour

36 g (1.3 oz/2 Tbsp 1½ tsp) muscovado sugar

38 g (1.3 oz/1 Tbsp plus 2½ tsp) invert sugar

108 g (3.8 oz/⅓ cup plus 2 Tbsp plus 1½ tsp) heavy cream (35% butterfat)

90 g (3.17 oz/3 large) egg whites

60 g (2.1 oz/⅔ whole banana) ripe banana flesh

6 g (0.21 oz/1½ tsp) pure vanilla extract

6 g (0.21 oz/1 Tbsp) finely grated lime zest

78 g (2.75 oz/⅔ cup) all-purpose flour

5 g (0.17 oz/1 tsp) baking powder

120 g (4.2 oz/4 large) egg whites

3 g (0.1 oz/scant ½ tsp) salt

24 g (0.85 oz/2 Tbsp) superfine granulated sugar

1. Preheat the oven to 350°F (175°C).

2. In a saucepan over medium heat, heat the butter until it is melted. Continue to cook the butter until the solids at the bottom of the pan begin to turn brown and the butter is fragrant, about 5 minutes.

3. In a food processor fitted with the steel blade, process together the confectioners' sugar, almond flour, muscovado sugar, invert sugar, heavy cream, brown butter, egg whites, banana, vanilla, and lime zest until blended. Scrape the mixture into a large bowl. Combine the flour and baking powder and fold the mixture into the batter.

4. In the bowl of a stand mixer fitted with the whisk attachment, beat the egg whites with the salt on high speed until soft peaks form. Gradually add the superfine granulated sugar and beat on high speed until a stiff and glossy meringue forms. Fold the meringue into the batter. Pipe the batter into twelve 3-in (7.6-cm) round silicone savarin molds and top with Coconut Streusel. Bake for about 18 minutes, until golden. Unmold and cool completely.

Pineapple Passion Fruit Cloud

200 g (7 oz/¾ cup plus 1 Tbsp) pineapple juice

80 g (2.8 oz/⅓ cup plus 1½ tsp) passion fruit purée

50 g (1.76 oz/2 Tbsp plus 1¼ tsp) glucose syrup

¾ vanilla bean, split lengthwise and seeds scraped

60 g (2.1 oz/¼ cup plus 2¾ tsp) superfine granulated sugar

2.5 g (0.08 oz/1 tsp) methylcellulose f50 (available from Albert Uster Imports, amazon.com or WillPowder; see Sources page 310)

2 g (0.07 oz/1 tsp) finely grated lime zest

1 g (0.03 oz/spritz) lime zest spray (available from Amoretti; see Sources page 310)

1. In a saucepan, combine the pineapple juice, passion fruit purée, glucose, vanilla bean seeds and pod, and half of the sugar and place over medium heat.

2. In a bowl, combine the remaining half of the sugar with the methylcellulose f50. Whisk into the purée mixture and heat to 185°F (85°C).

3. Transfer the mixture to the bowl of a stand mixer fitted with the whisk attachment and beat on high speed until tripled in volume. Fold in the lime zest and spray right before using.

ASSEMBLY

858 g (30.36 oz/4 cups) vegetable oil
Bittersweet chocolate note garnishes

1. In a deep saucepan or vegetable fryer, heat the oil to 360°F. Line a sheet pan with paper towels. Fry the beignets, a few at a time, in the hot oil until brown, 2 to 3 minutes. Spoon a circle of Pineapple Passion Fruit Cloud on a plate, off center, and place a beignet on top. Using a plastic squeeze bottle, pipe a few dots of Exotic Coulis on each plate, off center, near the beignet.

2. Place the Marinated Raspberries and Passion Fruit Mousseline inside the Brown Butter Financiers. Place one in the center of each plate.

3. Place a circle of Raspberry and Lemon Tuile on top of each financier. Top with Vanilla Diplomat cream. Place a second Tuile on top, and top with Vanilla Diplomat cream. Top with a third Tuile. Place a small amount of Coconut Streusel on top of the tuiles. Place a quenelle of Yuzu Ice Cream on top of the streusel and garnish with chocolate décor.

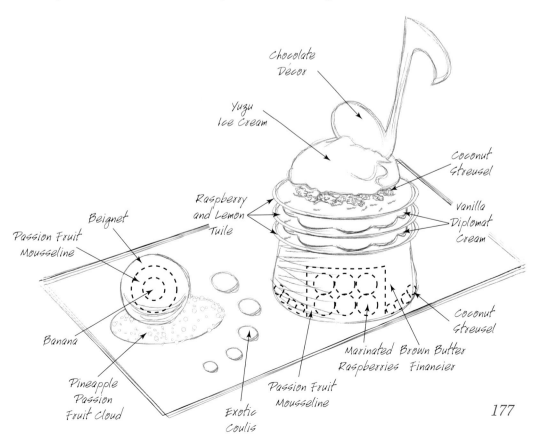

| Jin Caldwell |
| Kristina Karlicki |
| Sally Camacho |

GEORGIA (PEACHES AND CREAM)

The theme for the 2007 National Pastry Team Championship was country music and Team Caldwell chose "The Devil Went Down to Georgia" as the inspiration for their plated dessert. The dessert is a sophisticated version of the classic pairing of peaches and cream, featuring a Georgia Peach Compote surrounding a rich almond cake, an orange-scented Chantilly cream and a Spiced Peach Sauce. A quenelle of vanilla ice cream completes the classic flavor profile.

MAKES 12 SERVINGS

Peach Compote

90 g (3.17 oz/¾ stick plus ⅓ tsp) unsalted butter

1 kg (35.27 oz/about 8 medium) peaches, peeled and cut into large dice

2 vanilla beans, split lengthwise and seeds scraped

1.5 g (0.05 oz/¼ tsp) sea salt

80 g (2.8 oz/⅓ cup) orange liqueur

1. Melt the butter in a sauté pan over medium-high heat. Add the peaches, vanilla bean seeds and pods, and salt and sauté for 1 minute. Add the orange liqueur and flambé, letting the flame burn off the alcohol. Strain out the liquid and reserve it for the Peach Sauce. Place the sauce and peaches in separate covered containers and refrigerate until ready to use.

Orange Chantilly Cream

150 g (5.3 oz/⅔ cup) heavy cream

1 vanilla bean, split lengthwise and seeds scraped

10 g (0.35 oz/2½ tsp) granulated sugar

15 g (0.53 oz/1 Tbsp) orange liqueur

1. In the bowl of a stand mixer fitted with the whisk attachment, beat the cream and vanilla bean seeds on high speed to soft peaks. Add the sugar and orange liqueur and whip to stiff peaks. Cover and refrigerate until ready to use.

Spiced Peach Sauce

600 g (21.16 oz/about 5 medium) peaches, peeled and cut into large dice

300 g (10.5 oz/about 4 medium) red plums, peeled and cut into large dice

300 g (10.5 oz/1¼ cups plus 1 tsp) water

120 g (4.2 oz/½ cups) reserved sauce from Peach Compote

100 g (3.5 oz/⅓ cup plus 1 Tbsp plus 1½ tsp) orange liqueur

40 g (1.4 oz/2 Tbsp plus 1½ tsp) freshly squeezed orange juice

40 g (1.4 oz/2 Tbsp plus 2½ tsp) dry white wine

10 g (0.35 oz/2¼ tsp) granulated sugar

8 g (0.28 oz/¾-in piece) peeled fresh ginger, sliced

2 cinnamon sticks

3 whole cardamom seeds

6 whole black peppercorns

1.5 g (0.05 oz/¼ tsp) sea salt

1. Combine all of the ingredients in a saucepan and bring to a boil over high heat. Reduce the heat to low and simmer for 10 minutes.

2. Using an immersion blender, process the mixture until smooth. Pass through a chinois. Cover and refrigerate until ready to use.

Honey Tuile

70 g (2.5 oz/½ stick plus 1 Tbsp) unsalted butter, cut into tablespoons

50 g (1.76 oz/2 Tbsp plus 1 tsp) glucose syrup

10 g (0.35 oz/1½ tsp) honey

70 g (2.5 oz/rounded ⅓ cup) granulated sugar

2 g (0.07 oz/¼ tsp) glazing pectin

1. Preheat the oven to 338°F (170°C).

2. In a small saucepan, combine the butter, glucose, and honey and cook over medium heat until the butter is melted.

3. In a small bowl, combine the sugar and pectin and gradually add it to the honey mixture in the pan. Increase the heat to high and cook until the mixture registers 245°F (173°F) on a thermometer. Remove from the heat and spread over a 3-in (7.6-cm) round stencil, placed on a silicone baking mat–lined sheet pan, to form 12 tuiles. Bake until golden brown, about 4 minutes. Cool completely.

Petits Beurres

71 g (2.5 oz/⅔ cup) pastry flour

34 g (1.2 oz/¼ cup plus 2½ tsp) confectioners' sugar

30 g (1.05 oz/⅓ cup) almond flour

10 g (0.35 oz/1 Tbsp plus 1 tsp) oatmeal flour

1 g (0.03 oz/pinch) sea salt

0.25 g (0.008 oz/¼ tsp) ground cinnamon

95 g (3.35 oz/¾ stick plus 2¼ tsp) unsalted butter, softened

1. Preheat the oven to 325°F (163°C).

2. In the bowl of a stand mixer fitted with the paddle attachment, combine the pastry flour, sugar, almond flour, oatmeal flour, sea salt, cinnamon, and 55 g (1.9 oz/¼ cup) of the softened butter, mixing on low speed until it forms a sandy-textured mixture, 2 to 3 minutes. Spread the mixture onto a silicone baking mat–lined sheet pan and bake until pale brown, 6 to 8 minutes. Cool.

3. Return the mixture to the mixing bowl, add the remaining 40 g (1.4 oz/2 Tbsp plus 2¼ tsp) softened butter, and mix until blended. Press into the bottom of twelve 2½-in (6.3-cm) rings and bake on a silicone baking mat–lined sheet pan for 4 to 6 minutes until golden brown. Remove the rings and cool completely.

Pain de Gênes

75 g (2.6 oz/¼ cup plus ¾ tsp) almond paste (100%)

17 g (0.6 oz/1 Tbsp plus 1 tsp) granulated sugar

62 g (2.18 oz/1¼ large) eggs

15 g (0.53 oz/2 Tbsp) pastry flour, sifted

4 g (0.14 oz/¾ tsp) orange liqueur

90 g (3.17 oz/¾ stick plus ⅓ tsp) unsalted butter, melted

1 g (0.03 oz/pinch) sea salt

1. Preheat the oven to 350°F (175°C).

2. In the bowl of a stand mixer fitted with the paddle attachment, cream the almond paste and sugar on high speed for 2 minutes, then gradually add the eggs and mix until smooth. Add the pastry flour and orange liqueur and mix on low speed until smooth. Add the melted butter and salt and mix until blended.

3. Pipe the batter into twelve 3-in (7.6-cm) savarin molds and bake for 6 to 8 minutes until golden brown. Cool for 5 minutes, then unmold and cool completely.

Vanilla Bean Ice Cream

946 g (33.3 oz/3¾ cups plus 2 Tbsp plus 1½ tsp) whole milk

473 g (16.7 oz/2 cups plus 2 tsp) heavy cream

200 g (7 oz/1 cup) granulated sugar

100 g (3.5 oz/⅓ cup) Trimoline (invert sugar)

1 g (0.03 oz/pinch) salt

4 vanilla beans, split lengthwise and seeds scraped

240 g (8.4 oz/13 large) egg yolks

1. In a saucepan, combine the milk, cream, 100 g (3.5 oz/½ cup) of the granulated sugar, the invert sugar, salt, and vanilla bean seeds and pods and bring to a boil over medium-high heat. Remove from the heat and let stand for 5 minutes.

2. Meanwhile, in a bowl, by hand, whisk together the egg yolks and the remaining granulated sugar. Mix some of the hot milk mixture into the egg yolks to temper the eggs, then return the mixture to the saucepan and cook over medium heat, stirring constantly, until the mixture reaches 185°F (85°C). Strain the mixture into a bowl and cool in an ice bath.

Cigarette Tuile

50 g (1.76 oz/3 Tbsp plus 1½ tsp) unsalted butter

50 g (1.76 oz/⅓ cup plus 2 Tbsp) confectioners' sugar

50 g (1.76 oz/1⅔ large) egg whites

40 g (1.4 oz/⅓ cup) all-purpose flour

½ vanilla bean, split lengthwise and seeds scraped

1. Preheat the oven to 350°F (175°C).

2. In the bowl of a stand mixer fitted with the paddle attachment, combine all of the ingredients, adding only the seeds from the vanilla bean, and mix on medium speed until smooth.

3. Spread the batter out onto a silicone baking mat–lined sheet pan and bake for 6 to 8 minutes until golden brown. Break off shards of the tuile and, while still warm, curve over a dowel. Reserve for garnish.

ASSEMBLY

1. Spoon some Peach Compote in the center of each of twelve shallow bowls, and place a Pain de Gênes on top. Pipe some Orange Chantilly Cream into the center of the Pain de Gênes and top with a Honey Tuile, then a Petit Beurre. Spoon a quenelle of Vanilla Bean Ice Cream on top, then garnish with a shard of Cigarette Tuile. Spoon some of the Spiced Peach Sauce around the Peach Compote.

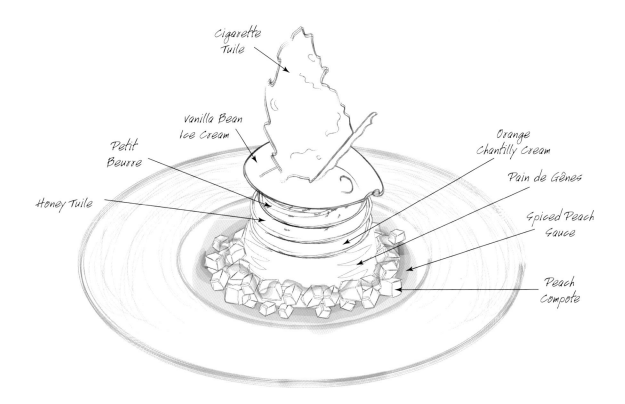

A TASTE OF HONEY

CORNMEAL ALMOND CAKE FILLED WITH VANILLA BEAN CUSTARD, SERVED WITH THYME-SCENTED CANDIED CITRUS ZEST AND HONEY GELATO

To reflect the country music theme of the 2007 National Pastry Team Championship, Team Danks chose to honor the Chet Atkins song "A Taste of Honey" in their plated dessert. It features a pastry cream–filled Cornmeal Almond Cake, Honey Gelato, Candied Citrus Zest, a delicate Citrus-Thyme Tuile Cookie, and flakes of crushed caramelized honey. **MAKES 12 SERVINGS**

Honey Gelato

19 g (0.67 oz/2 Tbsp) glucose powder

5 g (0.17 oz/2½ tsp) ice cream stabilizer

500 g (17.6 oz/2 cups plus 1 Tbsp) whole milk

19 g (0.67 oz/3 Tbsp) nonfat dry milk

77 g (2.7 oz/⅓ cup) heavy cream (40% butterfat)

175 g (6.17 oz/½ cup) orange blossom honey

60 g (2.1 oz/3 Tbsp plus 2 tsp) pasteurized egg yolks

1. In a bowl, combine the glucose powder and ice cream stabilizer and set aside.

2. In a saucepan, heat the milk and dry milk over low heat to 95°F (34°C). Add the heavy cream. Heat to 99°F (37°C) and whisk in the honey. Heat to 104°F (39°C) and whisk in the egg yolks. Continue to heat to 113°F (45°C) and whisk in the stabilizer mixture. Heat to 170°F (77°C), stirring constantly. Place the saucepan in an ice bath and cool rapidly to 40°F (4°C). Cover and refrigerate for at least 4 hours.

3. Blend the mixture with an immersion blender, and then process in an ice cream machine according to the manufacturer's instructions.

Candied Citrus Zest

1500 g (53 oz/6⅓ cups) cold water

6 g (0.21 oz/scant 1 tsp) salt

100 g (3.5 oz/1½ cups) blood orange peel

40 g (1.4 oz/⅔ cup) grapefruit peel

200 g (7 oz/1 cup) granulated sugar

150 g (5.3 oz/⅔ cup) freshly squeezed blood orange juice

50 g (1.76 oz/3 Tbsp plus 1 tsp) freshly squeezed grapefruit juice

25 g (0.88 oz/1 Tbsp plus 1 tsp) invert sugar

½ vanilla bean, split lengthwise and seeds scraped

4 g (0.14 oz/1 small bunch) fresh thyme

25 g (0.88 oz/1 Tbsp plus ¾ tsp) glucose syrup

1. Preheat the oven to 350°F (175°C).

2. Divide the water and salt among three saucepans. Bring one of the saucepans of water to a boil over high heat with the blood orange and grapefruit peels. Strain and shock the peels in ice water. Repeat the process two more times using the remaining saucepans of salted water.

3. In an ovenproof saucepan, combine the granulated sugar, citrus juices, invert sugar, and vanilla bean seeds and pod to a boil over high heat. Add the blanched citrus peels and thyme. Cover and bake until the mixture thickens and the peels are tender; this can take anywhere from 20 to 45 minutes, depending on the softness of the peels. Strain the peels, reserving the syrup in a saucepan. Leave the oven preheated to 350°F (175°C).

4. Bring the syrup to a boil over medium-high heat and reduce slightly. Stir in the glucose and citrus peel. Cool completely, then cover and refrigerate until ready to use.

Bee Sting Mixture

60 g (2.1 oz/½ stick plus 1 tsp) unsalted butter

60 g (2.1 oz/¼ cup plus 2¾ tsp) granulated sugar

48 g (1.7 oz/½ cup plus 1 Tbsp) blanched sliced almonds

48 g (1.7 oz/3 Tbsp plus 1 tsp) heavy cream (40% butterfat)

18 g (0.63 oz/2¾ tsp) honey

1. Combine all of the ingredients in a saucepan and cook over medium-high heat, stirring frequently, until the mixture leaves the sides of the pan. Remove from the heat.

2. When the Cornmeal Almond Cake (see below) is partially baked, place a little of the Bee Sting Mixture on top of the cake and bake until caramelized, as directed below.

3. Spread any extra Bee Sting Mixture onto a silicone baking mat and bake at 350°F (175°C) until caramelized. Allow to cool until hardened, then crush into pieces. This will be placed under the Honey Gelato.

Cornmeal Almond Cake

50 g (1.76 oz/¼ cup plus 1½ tsp) finely ground cornmeal

42 g (1.48 oz/⅓ cup plus 2¾ tsp) cake flour

3 g (0.1 oz/rounded ½ tsp) baking powder

90 g (3.17 oz/¾ stick plus ⅓ tsp) unsalted butter

100 g (3.5 oz/¾ cup plus 2 Tbsp) confectioners' sugar

5 g (0.17 oz/2½ tsp) orange zest

48 g (1.7 oz/½ cup plus 2¼ tsp) almond flour

75 g (2.6 oz/1½ large) whole eggs

68 g (2.4 oz/3½ large) egg yolks

45 g (1.58 oz/3 Tbsp) sour cream

1. Preheat the oven to 350°F (175°C).

2. Sift together the cornmeal, cake flour, and baking powder.

3. In the bowl of a stand mixer fitted with the paddle attachment, beat the butter, sugar, and orange zest on high speed until light, about 3 minutes. Add the almond flour and mix until blended. Add the whole eggs and egg yolks, mixing well after each addition. Reduce the speed to low, add the dry ingredients, and mix until blended. Add the sour cream and mix until blended. Scrape the batter into twelve 3-in (7.6-cm) ring molds that are placed on a form to create a hollow center in the bottom. Bake until just beginning to set. Top each mold off with the Bee Sting Mixture and bake until it caramelizes, about 5 minutes longer. Cool and unmold.

Citrus-Thyme Tuile Cookie

25 g (0.88 oz/2 Tbsp) granulated sugar

25 g (0.88 oz/1 Tbsp plus 2¼ tsp packed) light brown sugar

18 g (0.63 oz/2 Tbsp plus ¾ tsp) high-gluten flour

25 g (0.88 oz/1 Tbsp plus 1½ tsp) freshly squeezed orange juice

25 g (0.88 oz/1 Tbsp plus 2¼ tsp) unsalted butter, melted

1 g (0.03 oz/1 tsp) fresh thyme leaves

1. Preheat the oven to 350°F (175°C).

2. In a bowl, combine the granulated and light brown sugars and flour. Stir in the orange juice, then the melted butter. Stir in the thyme leaves. Cover the bowl and chill until firm, about 2 hours.

3. Spread the batter thinly over a 4-in (10.16-cm) round stencil, placed on a silicone baking mat–lined sheet pan, to make 12 tuiles. Bake until golden and set, about 4 minutes. Cool completely.

Pastry Cream

180 g (6.3 oz/¾ cup) whole milk

1 vanilla bean, split lengthwise and seeds scraped

50 g (1.76 oz/¼ cup) granulated sugar

12 g (0.42 oz/1 Tbsp plus 1½ tsp) cake flour

35 g (1.2 oz/2 Tbsp plus ½ tsp) pasteurized egg yolks

15 g (0.53 oz/1 Tbsp plus ¾ tsp) unsalted butter

1. In a saucepan, bring the milk and vanilla bean seeds and pod to a gentle boil over medium-high heat. Remove from the heat.

2. In a bowl, combine the sugar, flour, and egg yolks. Add some of the hot milk to the egg yolk–sugar mixture to temper the eggs, and return the mixture to the saucepan. Bring to a boil, whisking constantly. Remove from the heat and whisk in the butter. Strain into a bowl, cover, and chill.

ASSEMBLY

Pulled sugar rings (see page 308)

1. Fill the hollow at the bottom of each Cornmeal Almond Cake with the Pastry Cream and place each on a dessert plate. Arrange a small amount of Candied Citrus Zest beside the cake and drizzle some of the cooking syrup around the front of the plate. Spoon some of the crushed Bee Sting Mixture on the plate and top with a quenelle of Honey Gelato. Place a Citrus-Thyme Tuile Cookie, upright and leaning against the cake, between the gelato and the cake. Garnish with a pulled sugar "ring of fire."

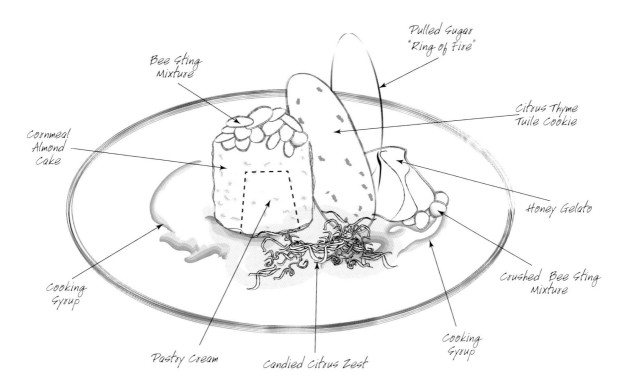

TEAM HOLDEN 2007

Roger Holden

Eric Voigt

Scott Hunter

OLD EL PASO

Having grown up in the Southwest, Pastry Chef Scott Hunter has always loved the brilliant color and flavor of the cactus pear, so Team Holden decided to feature it in their plated dessert at the 2007 NPTC. Accented with strawberry, tequila, and lime juice, a frozen Cactus Pear Sorbet is flanked on one side by a Mango Cake, and on the other by an unusual Hot Mango Soup flavored with cilantro.

MAKES 12 SERVINGS

Mango Cake

234 g (8.25 oz/1¾ cups plus 3 Tbsp plus ¾ tsp) all-purpose flour

13 g (0.45 oz/2½ tsp) baking powder

1 g (0.03 oz/pinch) salt

120 g (4.2 oz/6½ large) egg yolks

250 g (8.8 oz/1¼ cups) granulated sugar

200 g (7 oz/¾ cup plus 1 Tbsp) mango juice

180 g (6.3 oz/6 large) egg whites

51 g (1.8 oz/1¼ cups) diced mango flesh

1. Preheat the oven to 375°F (175°C).

2. Sift together the flour, baking powder, and salt.

3. In a stand mixer fitted with the whisk attachment, whip the egg yolks and 100 g (3.5 oz/½ cup) of the sugar on high speed to the ribbon stage. Reduce the speed to low and mix in the mango juice.

4. In a separate mixer bowl, using the whisk attachment, beat the egg whites on high speed to soft peaks. Gradually add the remaining 150 g (5.3 oz/¾ cup) sugar and beat to medium peaks to form a meringue. Alternately fold the dry ingredients, egg yolks, and diced mango into the meringue. Scrape the batter into twelve 3-in (7.6-cm) silicone demisphere molds and bake until golden brown. Unmold and cool.

Mango Cream

400 g (14.1 oz/1⅔ cups plus 1 Tbsp plus 1½ tsp) heavy cream

160 g (5.6 oz/⅔ cup) mango purée

80 g (2.8 oz/⅔ cup plus 1 Tbsp plus ½ tsp) confectioners' sugar

7 g (0.24 oz/2 tsp) stabilizer

15 g (0.5 oz/1 Tbsp) tequila

10 g (0.35 oz/2 tsp) freshly squeezed lemon juice

1. Combine all of the ingredients and process the mixture in a Pacojet twice.

2. Transfer to a disposable pastry bag and chill until needed.

Cilantro Syrup

90 g (3.17 oz/2 bunches) cilantro leaves

15 g (0.5 oz/1 cup) fresh mint leaves

150 g (5.3 oz/⅓ cup plus 2 Tbsp plus 1 tsp) corn syrup

25 g (0.88 oz/1 Tbsp plus ¾ tsp) simple syrup (made with equal parts sugar and water)

1. Blanch the cilantro and mint in boiling water for a few seconds, shock in an ice water bath, and squeeze out the excess water. Place the herbs in the jar of a blender.

2. In a small saucepan, bring the corn and simple syrup to a boil over high heat and process in the blender with the herbs until smooth. Strain through a chinois and reserve until needed.

Mango Foam

250 g (8.7 oz/1 cup plus 1 Tbsp plus 1 tsp) mango purée

30 g (1.05 oz/2 Tbsp plus 1¼ tsp) granulated sugar

0.625 g (0.02 oz/⅓ sheet) gelatin (gold grade), bloomed and drained

15 g (0.5 oz/1 Tbsp) freshly squeezed lime juice

1. In a saucepan, combine the mango purée and sugar and bring to a boil over high heat. Add the drained gelatin and lime juice and stir until the gelatin is dissolved. Pour into a whipped cream canister and chill until ready to use.

Cactus Pear Sorbet

1 kg (2.2 lb/4¼ cups) water

100 g (3.5 oz/¼ cup plus 2½ tsp) glucose syrup

500 g (17.6 oz/2½ cups) granulated sugar

1365 g (48.1 oz/6 cups) cactus pear purée

150 g (5.3 oz/⅔ cup) strawberry purée

55 g (1.9 oz/3 Tbsp plus 1½ tsp) freshly squeezed lime juice

8 g (0.28 oz/1½ tsp) tequila

1. In a large saucepan, bring the water, glucose, and sugar to a boil over medium-high heat, stirring to dissolve the sugar. Add the cactus pear and strawberry purées and the lime juice and stir to combine. Cool the mixture, then process in an ice cream machine according to the manufacturer's instructions. Top with a sprinkling of tequila and freeze until ready to serve.

Hot Mango Soup

500 g (17.6 oz/2 cups plus 3 Tbsp) mango purée

80 g (2.8 oz/⅓ cup) freshly squeezed orange juice

50 g (1.76 oz/3 Tbsp plus 1 tsp) passion fruit juice

65 g (2.3 oz/¼ cup plus 1 tsp) half-and-half

22 g (0.77 oz/1½ tsp) water

6 g (0.21 oz/1 Tbsp) lime zest

10 g (0.35 oz/2 tsp) freshly squeezed lime juice

22 g (0.77 oz/1 Tbsp plus 2½ tsp) granulated sugar

1 vanilla bean, split lengthwise and seeds scraped

1. In a saucepan, combine all of the ingredients and bring to a boil over high heat. Remove from the heat and let infuse for 15 minutes.

2. Discard the vanilla pod and process the soup in a blender until smooth, then strain. When ready to use, reheat.

Milk Foam

20 g (0.7 oz/1 Tbsp plus 2 tsp) granulated sugar

10 g (0.35 oz/1 Tbsp plus 2 tsp) lecithin

454 g (1 lb/1¾ cups plus 2 Tbsp) skim milk

1. In a bowl, combine the sugar and lecithin. Add the milk and, when ready to serve, mix with an immersion blender until foamy.

Pecan Streusel

216 g (7.6 oz/1½ sticks plus 3 Tbsp plus 1 tsp) unsalted butter (82% butterfat)

216 g (7.6 oz/1 cup plus 1 Tbsp plus 1¾ tsp) granulated sugar

216 g (7.6 oz/1¾ cups plus 2 Tbsp) pastry flour

240 g (8.46 oz/2¾ cups) pecan flour

100 g (3.5 oz/1 cup) pecans, chopped

3 g (0.1 oz/pinch) fleur de sel

1. In the bowl of a stand mixer fitted with the paddle attachment, mix all of the ingredients together on low speed until crumbly. Refrigerate for 1 hour.

2. Preheat a convection oven to 325°F (108°C).

3. Place twelve 3-in (7.6-cm) ring molds on a silicone baking mat–lined sheet pan and pat the streusel into the bottom of each ring. Bake in the convection oven until browned, 8 to 12 minutes. Cool in the rings, then unmold.

Mango Chips

55 g (1.9 oz/¼ cup plus 1¼ tsp) granulated sugar

55 g (1.9 oz/3 Tbsp plus 2½ tsp) water

12 thin slices mango

12 g (0.42 oz/2 Tbsp) lime zest

6 g (0.21 oz/1½ tsp) fleur de sel

1. Preheat the oven to 225°F (108°C).

2. In a large saucepan, combine the sugar and water and bring to a boil over high heat. Add the mango slices and poach for 1 to 2 minutes.

3. Arrange the mango slices on a silicone baking mat–lined sheet pan and bake until dry, 2 to 3 hours. Sprinkle with lime zest and fleur de sel. Store in an airtight container with desiccant at room temperature until ready to use.

Mango Soaking Syrup

216 g (7.6 oz/1 cup plus 1 Tbsp plus ¾ tsp) granulated sugar

216 g (7.6 oz/¾ cup plus 2 Tbsp plus 2 tsp) water

216 g (7.6 oz/¾ cup plus 2 Tbsp) mango juice

1. In a saucepan, combine the sugar and water and cook over medium-high heat, stirring until the sugar is dissolved. Add the mango juice, cool, and refrigerate for at least 1 hour.

ASSEMBLY

Micro cilantro

Chocolate curls

1 g (0.03 oz/pinch) whole allspice for grinding on soup

1. Arrange a piece of Pecan Streusel at one end of each plate. Brush a Mango Cake with the Mango Soaking Syrup and place on top of the streusel. Pipe some Mango Cream on top of the cake and top with a Mango Chip. Spoon some Hot Mango Soup next to the cake.

2. Place a scoop of Cactus Pear Sorbet in the center of each plate next to the cake.

3. Pour some Hot Mango Soup into a small glass and place it next to the sorbet. Spoon some Milk Foam on top of the soup, and then some Mango Foam. Using a pepper mill, grind some allspice on top. Garnish with micro cilantro and chocolate curls. Dot the plate with Cilantro Syrup.

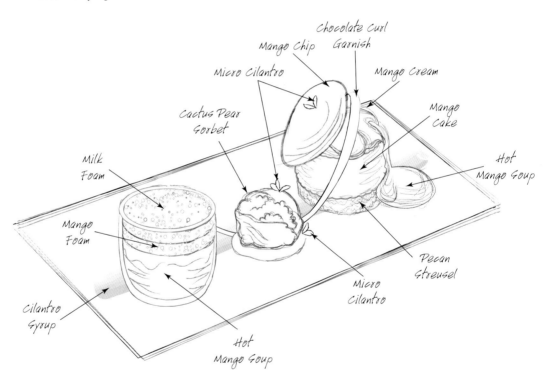

TEAM KNUDSEN 2007

Niels Knudsen

Josué Alvarado

Kaushik Chowdhury

DOLLY'S DUO CHOCOLATE NAPOLEON WITH TWO MOUSSES

Team Knudsen presented a dessert at the 2007 NPTC that combined a tart cranberry sauce and mousse with a Milk Chocolate Jack Daniel's Mousse layered between ultrathin rectangles of dark, white, and milk chocolate. This faux napoleon is crowned with a quenelle of White Chocolate Whipped Cream, while a mango and pineapple compote adds a pleasant acidity. **MAKES 12 SERVINGS**

Almond Nougatine

100 g (3.5 oz/¾ cup plus 1 Tbsp) blanched almonds

100 g (3.5 oz/½ cup) granulated sugar

100 g (3.5 oz/¼ cup plus 2¾ tsp) light corn syrup

½ vanilla bean, split lengthwise and seeds scraped

1. Spread out the almonds on a sheet pan and warm in a 350°F (175°C) oven.

2. In a saucepan, combine the sugar and corn syrup and cook over medium-high heat. Just before the syrup starts to caramelize, stir in the almonds. Add the vanilla bean and continue cooking until the sugar and almonds take on a deep, golden brown color.

3. Carefully remove the vanilla pod, spread the mixture onto a silicone baking mat, and let cool.

Milk Chocolate Jack Daniel's Mousse

200 g (7 oz/¾ cup plus 1 Tbsp) whole milk

60 g (2.1 oz/¼ cup plus 2¾ tsp) granulated sugar

1 vanilla bean, split lengthwise and seeds scraped

46 g (1.6 oz/2½ large) egg yolks

150 g (5.3 oz) milk chocolate, chopped

10 g (0.35 oz/5 sheets) gelatin (silver grade), bloomed and drained

50 g (1.76 oz/3 Tbsp plus 1½ tsp) Jack Daniel's whiskey

400 g (14.1 oz/3⅓ cups plus 2 Tbsp) whipped heavy cream

1. In a saucepan, combine the milk, sugar, and vanilla bean seeds and pod and cook over medium-high heat until it registers 194°F (90°C) on a thermometer. In a bowl, whisk together the egg yolks and whisk in some of the hot milk mixture to temper the eggs. Return the entire mixture to the saucepan and cook until the mixture is thickened and coats the back of the spoon, forming a crème anglaise. Remove the vanilla pod.

2. Place the chocolate in a bowl and pour over the hot crème anglaise. Add the drained gelatin and whisk until the chocolate is melted and the gelatin is dissolved. Whisk in the whiskey. Set aside to cool.

3. When the chocolate base is completely cool, fold in the whipped cream. Chill until firm enough to pipe out.

Cranberry Mousse

200 g (7 oz/1¾ cups) fresh cranberries

Zest of ¼ orange

Juice of 2 oranges

100 g (3.5 oz/½ cup) granulated sugar

5 g (0.18 oz/1 tsp) Triple Sec

8 g (0.28 oz/4 sheets) gelatin (silver grade), bloomed and drained

116 g (4 oz/½ cup) heavy cream, whipped

1. In a saucepan, combine the cranberries, orange zest, orange juice, and sugar and cook over medium-high heat. Just before the sugar caramelizes, add the Triple Sec and remove the pan from the heat. Add the drained gelatin and purée the mixture in a blender. Pass through a fine-mesh sieve and set aside to cool completely.

2. When cool, fold the cream into the cranberry mixture. Chill until firm enough to pipe.

White Chocolate Whipped Cream

70 g (2.5 oz) white chocolate, chopped

250 g (8.8 oz/1 cup plus 1 Tbsp plus ¾ tsp) heavy cream

1 vanilla bean, split lengthwise and seeds scraped

1. Place the chopped white chocolate in a bowl and set aside.

2. In a saucepan, bring the cream and vanilla bean seeds and pod to a gentle boil over medium-high heat. Pour the hot cream over the chocolate in the bowl. Whisk until smooth. Chill for at least 4 hours.

3. Remove the vanilla pod and whip the mixture on high speed in a stand mixer fitted with the whisk attachment to medium peaks. Cover and store in the refrigerator until ready to use.

Macerated Fruit Compote

100 g (3.5 oz/⅓ cup plus 1 Tbsp plus 2 tsp) passion fruit juice

50 g (1.76 oz/¼ cup) granulated sugar

½ vanilla bean, split lengthwise and seeds scraped

0.5 g (0.017 oz/pinch) ground cardamom

0.5 g (0.017 oz/2) cinnamon sticks

56 g (1.9 oz/½ cup) diced mango

56 g (1.9 oz/½ cup) diced pineapple

1. In a saucepan, bring the passion fruit juice, sugar, vanilla bean seeds and pod, cardamom, and cinnamon sticks to a boil over medium-high heat. Remove from the heat and remove the vanilla pod and cinnamon sticks. Stir in the mango and pineapple. Transfer to a container, cover, and chill for at least 1 hour.

Cranberry Sauce

200 g (7 oz/1¾ cups) frozen cranberries

0.5 g (0.017 oz/¼ tsp) finely grated orange zest

100 g (3.5 oz/⅓ cup plus 1 Tbsp plus 2 tsp) freshly squeezed orange juice

20 g (0.7 oz/2 Tbsp plus 2 tsp) cornstarch

50 g (1.76 oz/3 Tbsp plus 1 tsp) Grand Marnier

1. In a saucepan, combine the cranberries, orange zest, and orange juice and bring to a boil over high heat. Reduce the heat and simmer for 5 to 7 minutes until some of the cranberries burst.

2. Mix the cornstarch with a small amount of water and add it to the sauce. Bring to a boil and let boil for 1 minute, until thickened. Remove from the heat and strain through a fine-mesh sieve. Stir in the Grand Marnier and set aside to cool.

ASSEMBLY

2 x 4½-in (5 x 11.4-cm) rectangles of tempered bittersweet, white, and milk chocolate (12 each)

Chopped toasted almonds

Pulled sugar garnish (see page 308)

1. Place a dark chocolate rectangle in the center of each plate. Using a pastry bag fitted with a medium, plain tip, pipe dollops of Cranberry Mousse in lines down the length of the rectangle, covering it completely. Top with a white chocolate rectangle. Using a pastry bag fitted with a medium, plain tip, pipe dollops of Milk Chocolate Jack Daniel's Mousse on top of the rectangle, covering it completely. Top with a milk chocolate rectangle.

2. Top the chocolate with a quenelle of White Chocolate Whipped Cream and some chopped toasted almonds. Garnish each plate with a spoonful of Macerated Fruit Compote and dots of the Cranberry Sauce.

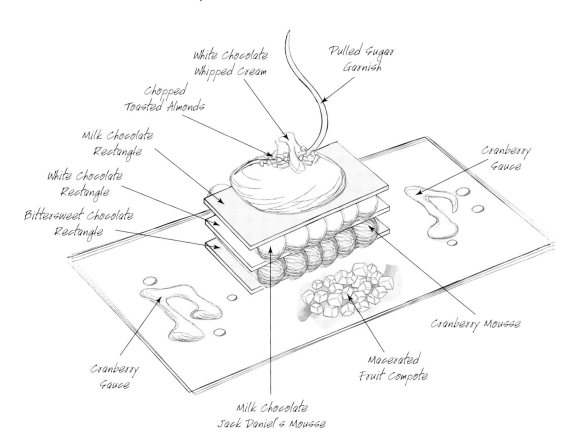

White Chocolate Whipped Cream

Pulled Sugar Garnish

Chopped Toasted Almonds

Milk Chocolate Rectangle

White Chocolate Rectangle

Bittersweet Chocolate Rectangle

Cranberry Sauce

Cranberry Mousse

Macerated Fruit Compote

Cranberry Sauce

Milk Chocolate Jack Daniel's Mousse

TEAM PAGANO 2007

Chad Pagano

Rebecca Millican

Nicole Kaplan

GINGERED HONEY PANNA COTTA

WITH LEMONGRASS CONSOMMÉ, MANGO GELÉE, AND LACE TUILE

Timing is a key factor in the competition, so as part of their strategy, Team Pagano developed a relatively simple dessert that could be plated in a minimal amount of time. They also avoided chocolate or anything that would be sweet and heavy. Their Gingered Honey Panna Cotta is paired with a citrusy Lemongrass Consommé, rounds of Mango Gelée, and cubes of refreshing kiwi and pineapple.

MAKES 12 SERVINGS

Gingered Honey Panna Cotta

980 g (34.56 oz/4 cups plus 3 Tbsp plus 1½ tsp) heavy cream

380 g (13.4 oz/1½ cups plus 1 Tbsp) whole milk

154 g (5.4 oz/⅓ cup plus 2 Tbsp plus 1 tsp) honey

120 g (4.2 oz/½ cup plus 1 Tbsp plus 2 tsp) granulated sugar

45 g (1.58 oz/4-in piece) peeled, fresh ginger, thinly sliced

1 vanilla bean, split lengthwise and seeds scraped

28 g (1 oz/14 sheets) gelatin (silver grade), bloomed and drained

45 g (1.58 oz/3 Tbsp) crème fraîche

1. In a saucepan, combine all of the ingredients, except for the gelatin and crème fraîche, and bring to a boil over medium-high heat. Remove from the heat and let infuse for 30 minutes.

2. Reheat and add the drained gelatin and crème fraîche. Whisk until smooth. Strain through a fine-mesh sieve and chill in an ice water bath.

3. Pour the mixture into twelve 3-in (7.6-cm) round silicone molds and chill until set, at least 3 hours.

Lemongrass Consommé

1375 g (48.5 oz/5¾ cups plus 1 Tbsp plus ¾ tsp) water

500 g (17.6 oz/2½ cups) granulated sugar

150 g (5.3 oz/about 2 medium stalks) lemongrass

70 g (2.46 oz/6-in piece) peeled, fresh ginger, thinly sliced

10 g (0.35 oz/1 Tbsp plus 2 tsp) finely grated lime zest

12 g (0.42 oz/⅓ cup) star anise

2½ vanilla beans, split lengthwise and seeds scraped

25 whole coriander seeds

18 whole black peppercorns

63 g (2.2 oz/¼ cup plus 1 tsp) passion fruit purée

16 g (0.56 oz/1 Tbsp) freshly squeezed orange juice

13 g (0.45 oz/2¾ tsp) freshly squeezed lime juice

1. In a saucepan, combine the water, sugar, lemongrass, ginger, lime zest, star anise, vanilla bean seeds and pods, coriander seeds, and peppercorns and bring to a boil over high heat. Remove from the heat, cover, and let infuse for 15 minutes.

2. Strain the mixture through a fine-mesh sieve and cool in an ice bath. Stir in the passion fruit purée, orange juice, and lime juice. Cover and refrigerate until ready to serve.

Coconut Rocher Disks

80 g (2.8 oz) white chocolate, chopped

30 g (1.05 oz/2 Tbsp plus 2 ½ tsp) cocoa butter

110 g (3.8 oz/1¾ cups) feuilletine

50 g (1.76 oz/⅔ cup) unsweetened desiccated coconut

1. In a bowl set over a saucepan of barely simmering water, melt the white chocolate with the cocoa butter, stirring frequently. Fold in the feuilletine and the coconut.

2. Spread the mixture out onto a piece of parchment paper, cover with another piece of parchment paper, and roll out into a thin ⅛-in (3.17-mm) layer. Let set.

3. Cut into twelve 3-in (7.6-cm) disks. Store in an airtight container at room temperature until ready to use.

Mango Gelée

200 g (7 oz/¾ cup plus 2 Tbsp) mango purée

50 g (1.76 oz/3 Tbsp plus 1½ tsp) passion fruit purée

125 g (4.4 oz/½ cup plus 2 Tbsp) granulated sugar

50 g (1.76 oz/2 Tbsp plus 1 tsp) glucose syrup

10 g (0.35 oz/1 Tbsp) powdered pectin

30 g (1.05 oz/2 Tbsp) freshly squeezed lemon juice

1. In a saucepan, combine all of the ingredients except for the lemon juice and bring to a boil over high heat. Boil for 3 minutes, then add the lemon juice. Pour the mixture into twelve 1-in (2.54-cm) round silicone molds and chill to set.

Lace Tuile

40 g (1.4 oz/2 Tbsp plus 2¼ tsp) unsalted butter, melted

56 g (1.9 oz/¼ cup plus 1½ tsp) granulated sugar

10 g (0.35 oz/1 Tbsp plus 1 tsp) all-purpose flour

12 g (0.42 oz/2 tsp) freshly squeezed lime juice

4 g (0.14 oz/1 tsp) passion fruit purée

1. Place the melted butter in a bowl, then stir in the sugar, flour, lime juice, and passion fruit purée. Refrigerate until thickened, about 1 hour.

2. Preheat the oven to 300°F (150°C).

3. Spread the batter over a 2 x 4-in (5 x 10-cm) rectangular stencil, placed on a silicone baking mat–lined sheet pan, to form 12 tuiles. Bake until crisp, about 12 minutes. While still warm, curve each tuile into a wave shape.

ASSEMBLY

Cubed pineapple and kiwi

1. Arrange each Gingered Honey Panna Cotta on a Coconut Rocher Disk. Garnish the top of each panna cotta with a Lace Tuile. Spoon some pineapple and kiwi cubes next to the panna cotta, and place the Mango Gelée next to the fruit.

2. Serve the Lemongrass Consommé in a small bowl next to the Mango Gelée.

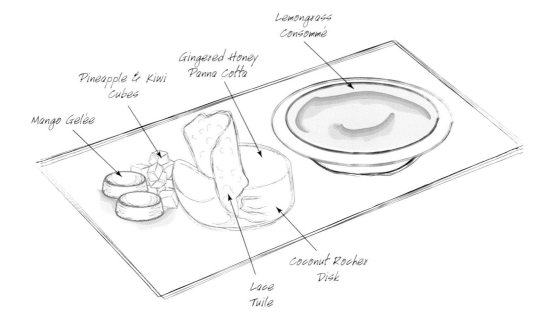

TEAM RUSKELL 2007

Richard Ruskell

Stephen Durfee

Louise Chien

CREOLE

Tying into the 2007 competition's theme of country music, the heart of this dessert is a riff on the Southern American classic, banana pudding cake. Team Ruskell chose the dessert because it was quick and reliable to make, had easily recognizable flavors and a firm, custardy texture that they could serve warm, à la minute. *According to team member Stephen Durfee, the key to the success of this dessert is its "eatability"—you can cut through the entire thing with a spoon without ruining its appearance.*   **MAKES 12 SERVINGS**

Soft Banana Cake

Butter and granulated sugar for the molds

55 g (1.94 oz/½ stick plus 1½ tsp) unsalted butter

105 g (3.7 oz/½ cup plus 1 Tbsp plus ¾ tsp) granulated sugar

40 g (1.4 oz/¼ cup) demerara sugar, finely ground

56 g (1.9 oz/3 large) egg yolks

50 g (1.76 oz/⅓ cup plus 1 Tbsp plus 2 tsp) all-purpose flour

Pinch of freshly grated nutmeg

2 g (0.07 oz/¼ tsp) salt

200 g (7 oz/¾ cup plus 1 Tbsp plus ¾ tsp) whole milk

140 g (4.9 oz/⅔ cup) banana purée

40 g (1.4 oz/2 Tbsp plus 2 tsp) sour cream

25 g (0.88 oz/1 Tbsp plus 2 tsp) freshly squeezed lemon juice

90 g (3.17 oz/3 large) egg whites

Pinch of cream of tartar

1. Preheat the oven to 300°F (150°C). Butter and sugar 12 ramekins.

2. In the bowl of a stand mixer fitted with the paddle attachment, cream together the butter, 75 g (2.6 oz/⅓ cup plus 1 Tbsp) of the granulated sugar, and the demerara sugar on high speed. Add the egg yolks alternately with the flour, nutmeg, and salt. Add the milk, banana purée, sour cream, and lemon juice, mixing just until blended.

3. In a separate mixer bowl, using the whisk attachment, beat the egg whites on high speed until foamy. Add the cream of tartar and beat, gradually adding the remaining 30 g (1.05 oz/2 Tbsp plus 1¼ tsp) granulated sugar. Beat on high speed to soft peaks. Fold into the banana mixture.

4. Pour the mixture into the prepared ramekins and bake, uncovered, in a water bath for 30 minutes. Carefully unmold the cakes and cool.

Yogurt Sorbet

400 g (14 oz/1½ cups plus 2 Tbsp plus 1½ tsp) Greek yogurt

300 g (10.58 oz/1 cup) simple syrup (made with equal parts sugar and water)

40 g (1.4 oz/2 Tbsp plus 2¼ tsp) banana purée

25 g (0.88 oz/1 Tbsp plus 2 tsp) freshly squeezed lemon juice

1. Combine all of the ingredients in a bowl with an immersion blender. Process the mixture in an ice cream machine according to the manufacturer's instructions.

Pecan Dentelle

30 g (1.05 oz/2⅛ Tbsp plus ⅓ tsp) unsalted butter, melted and cooled

10 g (0.35 oz/1½ tsp) light corn syrup

40 g (1.4 oz/3 Tbsp plus ¾ tsp) granulated sugar

40 g (1.4 oz/⅓ cup) pecans, chopped

1. Combine all of the ingredients and refrigerate for at least 2 hours.

2. Preheat the oven to 350°F (175°C).

3. Pipe out ½-in (1.27-cm) diameter drops into 12 shallow 3-in (7.6-cm) tart pans. Bake until golden, about 10 minutes. Cool and remove from the pans.

Chicory Brown Sugar Sauce

120 g (4.2 oz/½ cup) heavy cream

24 g (0.8 oz/⅓ cup) chicory coffee

40 g (1.4 oz/3 Tbsp packed) light brown sugar

0.8 g (0.03 oz/⅛ tsp) salt

30 g (1.05 oz/2 Tbsp) unsalted butter

2 g (0.07 oz/½ tsp) pure vanilla extract

1. In a saucepan, combine the cream and chicory coffee and bring to a boil over medium-high heat. Remove from the heat, cover, and let infuse for 30 minutes. Strain through a fine-mesh sieve.

2. Measure out 60 g (2.1 oz/¼ cup) of the infused cream and return it to the saucepan along with the sugar and salt. Bring to a simmer, then whisk in the cold butter and vanilla. Cover and refrigerate until ready to serve. Reheat in the microwave before using.

Tuile Cookie

25 g (0.88 oz/1 Tbsp plus 2½ tsp) unsalted butter

50 g (1.76 oz/⅓ cup plus 2 Tbsp) confectioners' sugar

30 g (1.05 oz/¼ cup) all-purpose flour

28 g (1 oz/1 large) egg white

1. In the bowl of a stand mixer fitted with the paddle attachment, cream together the butter and sugar on high speed. Remove the bowl from the mixer stand and alternately stir in the flour and egg white to make a smooth paste. Chill for about 30 minutes before using.

2. Preheat the oven to 350°F (175°C).

3. Spread the batter over a long, wedge-shaped stencil, about 10 in (25.4 cm), placed on a silicone baking mat–lined sheet pan. Bake until browned around the edges, about 5 minutes. While still hot, curve each tuile until it is almost a circle. Repeat to make a total of 12 cookies.

ASSEMBLY

1. Spoon a line of Chicory Brown Sugar Sauce down the center of each rectangular plate. Place a Soft Banana Cake in the center of each plate and top with a Pecan Dentelle, then a scoop of Yogurt Sorbet. Tuck the wide end of a Tuile Cookie under the cake, letting it arch over the dessert.

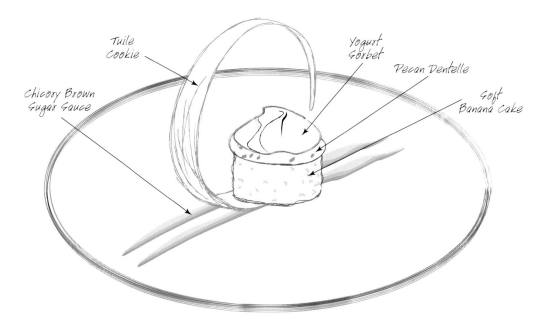

TEAM CHINA 2008

| Anthony Qin |
| Anson Zhang |
| Alen Yan |

LITCHI CREAM

WITH RED FRUIT COMPOTE

This pretty dessert, with its green and red color scheme, was done by Team China for the 2008 WPTC. It combines the flavors of pistachio, almond, litchi, and red berries in a layered parfait with a Strawberry-Mint Sorbet and Strawberry Jus as refreshing accompaniments. The Litchi Cream has a hint of rose water in it, giving this dessert a floral undertone. **MAKES 14 SERVINGS**

Red Fruit Compote

180 g (6.34 oz/¾ cup) red berry purée

90 g (3.17 oz/⅓ cup plus 2 Tbsp plus ¾ tsp) granulated sugar

1. Combine the red berry purée and sugar in a saucepan over high heat and cook until the mixture registers 65° Brix on a refractometer. Transfer to an airtight container and refrigerate until ready to use.

Litchi Cream

6 g (0.21 oz/3 sheets) gelatin (silver), bloomed and drained

200 g (7 oz/¾ cup plus 2 Tbsp) litchi purée

100 g (3.5 oz/½ cup) granulated sugar

300 g (10.6 oz/1¼ cups) heavy cream, whipped

A few drops of rose water

1. Place the drained gelatin in a bowl set over a saucepan of barely simmering water, or place it in a small heatproof cup and place the container in the saucepan of barely simmering water. Heat, stirring frequently, until the gelatin is melted.

2. In a saucepan, combine the litchi purée, sugar, and gelatin and place over medium heat until hot. Cool completely.

3. Fold in the whipped cream and rose water and refrigerate, covered, until ready to use.

Almond Pistachio Sponge

345 g (12.16 oz/1¼ cups) raw almond paste
320 g (11.28 oz/6½ large) eggs
60 g (2.1 oz/½ cup plus 1¼ tsp) cake flour
2 g (0.07 oz/¼ tsp plus ⅛ tsp) baking powder
100 g (3.5 oz/¾ stick) unsalted butter, melted and hot

1. Preheat the oven to 355°F (124°C).

2. In the bowl of a stand mixer fitted with the paddle attachment, beat the almond paste on medium speed, gradually adding half of the eggs. Change to the whisk attachment and gradually add the remaining eggs, beating on high speed until light and foamy.

3. In a bowl, sift together the flour and baking powder and fold in the almond batter. Fold in the hot melted butter.

4. Scrape the batter onto a silicone baking mat–lined sheet pan and bake until set, about 20 minutes. Cool.

Strawberry-Mint Sorbet

130 g (4.58 oz/⅔ cup) granulated sugar
8 g (0.28 oz/2½ tsp) sorbet stabilizer
100 g (3.5 oz/⅓ cup plus 1 Tbsp plus 2¼ tsp) water
75 g (2.64 oz/⅓ cup plus 2 Tbsp plus 1½ tsp) glucose powder
1 kg (35.27 oz/4⅓ cups) strawberry-mint purée

1. In a bowl, combine 13 g (0.45 oz/1 Tbsp) of the sugar with the stabilizer and set aside.

2. In a saucepan, combine the water, the remaining 117 g (4.12 oz/½ cup plus 1 Tbsp plus 2 tsp) sugar, stabilizer mixture, and glucose powder and bring to a boil over medium-high heat. Remove from the heat and chill for at least 3 hours.

3. Stir the strawberry-mint purée into the sorbet base and process in an ice cream machine according to the manufacturer's instructions.

Pistachio Crumble

100 g (3.5 oz/1 stick) unsalted butter

100 g (3.5 oz/⅓ cup plus 2 Tbsp plus 1¼ tsp packed) light brown sugar

100 g (3.5 oz/¾ cup plus 2 Tbsp) cake flour

100 g (3.5 oz/1 cup plus 2 Tbsp) pistachio flour

1. In the bowl of a stand mixer fitted with the paddle attachment, mix all of the ingredients together on low speed until blended. Refrigerate until firm, about 1 hour.

2. Preheat the oven to 355°F (124°C).

3. Pass the dough through a wire cooling rack to form small pieces. Place the crumble on a silicone baking mat–lined sheet pan and bake until lightly browned, about 12 minutes. Cool completely.

Strawberry Jus

2 kg (4.4 lb/4½ pints) fresh strawberries, cleaned, hulled, and quartered

25 g (0.88 oz/2 Tbsp) granulated sugar

1. Place the strawberries in a large, stainless steel bowl and sprinkle with the sugar. Place the bowl over a pot of barely simmering water. Place a piece of plastic wrap over the bowl and let it sit over the simmering water for 30 to 40 minutes, keeping an eye on the water and adding more if needed, until the berries exude their juices. Remove from the heat and cool.

2. Cover the bowl and refrigerate the jus for at least 3 hours.

3. Before serving, pour the strawberry juice into a sieve set over a bowl and allow it to drip through; don't rub the pulp.

Red Berry Tuile

265 g (9.34 oz/2⅓ cups) fresh raspberries

60 g (2.1 oz/½ cup) confectioners' sugar

80 g (2.82 oz/⅓ cup plus 1 Tbsp plus 1¼ tsp) Isomalt

45 g (1.58 oz/½ cup) maltodextrin (see Sources, 310)

35 g (1.23 oz/3 Tbsp) dried whole raspberries

1. Combine all of the ingredients in the bowl of a food processor fitted with the steel blade and process until smooth. Strain through a fine-mesh sieve.

2. Spread the mixture over a 2-in (5-cm) square stencil, placed on a silicone baking mat–lined sheet pan, to form 14 tuiles, and dry overnight at 175°F (80°C) in a food dehydrator.

ASSEMBLY

Fresh strawberries
Finely chopped pistachios
Strawberry powder
Pulled sugar sticks (see page 308)

1. Cut a 2-in (5-cm) round of Almond Pistachio Sponge cake and place it in the bottom of a 2-in (5-cm) diameter x 3-in- (7.6-cm-) high ring mold. Top with a layer of Red Fruit Compote, then a layer of the Pistachio Crumble. Top with another round of Almond Pistachio Sponge, then fill the mold with Litchi Cream. Repeat to make 14 desserts. Freeze until the Litchi Cream is firm.

2. Unmold each dessert and place on a plate. Top with a strawberry and a Red Berry Tuile. Arrange a small circle of chopped pistachio nuts next to each dessert, and place a quenelle of the Strawberry-Mint Sorbet on top.

3. Fill a small bowl halfway with Strawberry Jus and place it next to the sorbet. Garnish each plate with a pulled sugar stick and a line of strawberry powder.

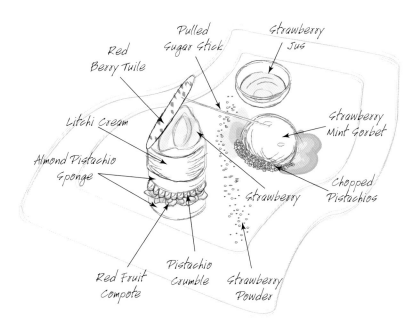

| Roberto Rinaldini |
| Fabrizio Galla |
| Rossano Vinciarelli |

IMAGINATION BOX

Known for its dramatic dessert presentations, Team Italy did not disappoint at the WPTC in 2008. Their plated dessert was served in a large, custom-made box with a small container of dry ice in it, which created a foggy, dreamlike effect. The dessert itself was composed of three separate elements: the first was an Iced Infusion of Sicilian Orange paired with a Hot Apple Cider; the second a red fruit foam topped with a Tonka Bean Panna Cotta and Mint Coulis; and the third a radical riff on classic Italian tiramisu. **MAKES 14 SERVINGS**

Dessert No. 1

ICED INFUSION OF SICILIAN ORANGE

35 g (1.23 oz/2 Tbsp plus 1 tsp) water

65 g (2.3 oz/⅓ cup) granulated sugar

45 g (1.58 oz/2 Tbsp plus ½ tsp) glucose, syrup

Zest of 2 oranges, cut off in strips and white pith removed

200 g (7 oz/¾ cup plus 1 Tbsp plus ¾ tsp) freshly squeezed Sicilian orange juice

1. In a saucepan, combine the water, sugar, glucose, and orange zest and bring to a boil over high heat. Remove from the heat and cool.

2. Stir in the orange juice. Pour the mixture into small serving glasses, filling them one-third full, and freeze until ready to serve.

HOT APPLE CIDER

300 g (10.58 oz/1¼ cups) apple pulp

20 g (0.7 oz/1 Tbsp) simple syrup (made with equal parts sugar and water)

1. In a saucepan, combine the apple pulp and simple syrup and cook over low heat until the mixture registers 115°F (46°C) on a thermometer. Pass through a cheesecloth-lined sieve. Reserve, covered, in the refrigerator; this will be heated and poured over the Iced Infusion of Sicilian Orange at serving time.

Dessert No. 2

LEMON-SCENTED RED FRUIT AIR

162 g (5.71 oz/⅔ cup) water

138 g (4.86 oz/⅔ cup) superfine granulated sugar

0.8 g (0.028 oz/½ tsp) finely grated lemon zest

130 g (4.58 oz/½ cup plus 1 Tbsp) strawberry pulp

90 g (3.17 oz/⅓ cup plus 1 Tbsp) raspberry pulp

12 g (0.42 oz/6 sheets) gelatin (silver grade), bloomed and drained

1. In a saucepan, combine the water, sugar, and lemon zest and bring just to a boil over medium-high heat. Remove from the heat and cool. Stir in the strawberry and raspberry pulps.

2. Melt the drained gelatin over hot water and stir into the fruit mixture. Chill.

3. In a stand mixer fitted with the whisk attachment, whip the mixture on high speed until light. Transfer to a pastry bag fitted with a medium, plain tip. Pipe into small glasses, filling them one-fifth of the way. Freeze until firm.

TONKA BEAN PANNA COTTA

100 g (3.5 oz/⅓ cup plus 1 Tbsp plus 2 tsp) whole milk

10 g (0.35 oz/1½ tsp) glucose syrup

0.35 g (0.012 oz/2) tonka beans

4 g (0.14 oz/1¼ sheets) gelatin (bronze grade), bloomed and drained

100 g (3.5 oz) white chocolate, chopped

20 g (0.7 oz/2 Tbsp) cocoa butter

200 g (7 oz/¾ cup plus 1 Tbsp plus 2¼ tsp) heavy cream (35% butterfat)

1. In a saucepan, combine the milk, glucose, and tonka beans and place over medium heat until the mixture registers 150°F (65°C) on a thermometer. Add the drained gelatin and stir to dissolve. Pour over the white chocolate and cocoa butter and emulsify slowly with a whisk. Gradually add the cream and continue to whisk until smooth. Cool completely.

2. Pour over the Lemon-Scented Red Fruit Air, filling the glasses three-quarters of the way. Chill until ready to serve.

RASPBERRY AND BLUEBERRY SALAD IN VANILLA INFUSION

100 g (3.5 oz/⅓ cup plus 1 Tbsp plus 2¼ tsp) water

120 g (4.23 oz/½ cup plus 1 Tbsp plus 2 tsp) granulated sugar

1 vanilla bean, split lengthwise and seeds scraped

100 g (3.5 oz/1 scant cup) fresh raspberries (preferably from Trentino)

100 g (3.5 oz/¾ cup) fresh blueberries

1. In a saucepan, combine the water, sugar, and vanilla bean seeds and pod and bring to a boil over high heat, stirring to dissolve the sugar. Cool, then remove the vanilla pod. Add the raspberries and blueberries and refrigerate, covered, until ready to use.

MINT COULIS

50 g (1.76 oz/3 Tbsp plus 1 tsp) water

15 g (0.53 oz/⅓ cup packed) fresh mint leaves

100 g (3.5 oz/¼ cup 2¼ tsp) glucose syrup

2 g (0.07 oz/a few drops) green food coloring

1. In a small saucepan, combine the water and mint leaves and bring to a boil over medium-high heat. Add the glucose and cook to 63° Brix. Cool and then chill.

2. When cold, stir in the food coloring and pass through a fine-mesh sieve. Pour into a squeeze bottle and chill until ready to serve.

ASSEMBLY FOR DESSERT NO. 2

Pulled sugar spirals (see page 308)

1. At serving time, top the Tonka Bean Panna Cotta layer in each glass with a little Raspberry and Blueberry Salad and a few drops of Mint Coulis. Garnish each with a pulled sugar spiral.

Dessert No. 3

SAVOY SPONGE CAKE

250 g (8.8 oz/8⅓ large) egg whites, room temperature

250 g (8.8 oz/1¼ cups) granulated sugar

170 g (6 oz/9 large) egg yolks

200 g (7 oz/1½ cups plus 2 Tbsp plus 2 tsp) all-purpose flour

50 g (1.76 oz/⅓ cup plus 1 Tbsp plus 2 tsp) cornstarch

1. Preheat the oven to 355°F (180°C).

2. In the bowl of a stand mixer fitted with the whisk attachment, beat the egg whites, gradually adding the sugar, on medium-high speed to soft peaks. Beat in the egg yolks.

3. Sift together the flour and cornstarch. Remove the bowl containing the eggs from the mixer stand and gently fold in the flour mixture. Spread out the batter in a silicone baking mat lined sheet pan and bake for about 12 minutes, until golden and baked through. Cool for 10 minutes, then unmold the cake and cool completely.

MASCARPONE FOAM AND BOURBON VANILLA

140 g (4.9 oz/½ cup plus Tbsp plus ¾ tsp) whole milk

½ bourbon vanilla bean, split lengthwise and seeds scraped

100 g (3.5 oz/⅓ cup plus 1 Tbsp plus ¾ tsp) pasteurized egg yolks

95 g (3.35 oz/⅓ cup plus 2 Tbsp plus 2 tsp) granulated sugar

8 g (0.28 oz/4 sheets) gelatin (silver grade), bloomed and drained

50 g (1.76 oz/3 Tbsp plus 1¼ tsp) heavy cream (35% butterfat)

200 g (7 oz/¾ cup plus 1 Tbsp) mascarpone cheese

1. In a saucepan, combine the milk and vanilla bean seeds and pod and bring to a gentle boil.

2. Meanwhile, whisk together the egg yolks and sugar. Add some of the hot milk to the egg yolk–sugar mixture to temper the eggs, then return the entire mixture to the saucepan. Cook over medium heat, stirring constantly with a wooden spoon, until the mixture thickens and coats the back of the spoon and reaches 175°F (80°C). Remove from the heat, add the drained gelatin, and stir until dissolved. Cool to 97°F (35°C), then remove the vanilla pod.

3. Meanwhile, in the bowl of a stand mixer fitted with the whisk attachment, whip the cream with the mascarpone on medium-high speed to medium peaks. When the egg base has cooled to 97°F (35°C), gently fold in the whipped cream mixture. Cover and refrigerate until ready to use.

ESPRESSO SYRUP

200 g (7 oz/¾ cup plus 1 Tbsp plus 1½ tsp) hot brewed espresso

70 g (2.46 oz/⅓ cup plus 2 tsp) granulated sugar

1. Add the sugar to the hot espresso and stir to dissolve.

ASSEMBLY FOR DESSERT NO. 3

Cocoa powder

1. Cut rounds out of the Savoy Sponge Cake that fit the inside of your serving glasses; you will use one round per serving. Dip each round into the Espresso Syrup.

2. Spoon or pipe a layer of Mascarpone Foam and Bourbon Vanilla into each glass. Top with a round of cake and another layer of the foam. Dust with cocoa powder.

FINAL ASSEMBLY

1. Arrange the three desserts on a plate alongside a small container of dry ice.

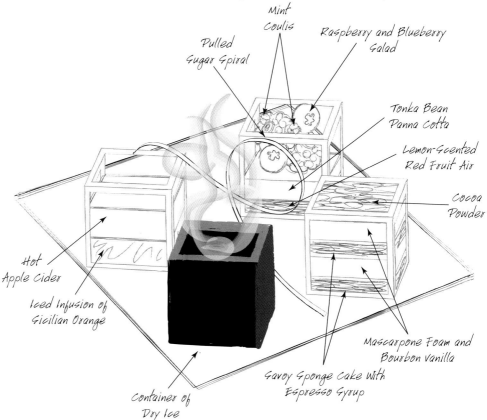

| Hideki Kawamura |
| Koji Fujita |
| Koichi Izumi |

AURORA

While strawberry and almond were the dominant flavors in Team Japan's plated dessert from the 2008 WPTC, lemon, lime, coconut, honey, caramel, and balsamic vinegar added interesting background notes. The base of the dessert is an Almond Biscuit, which is topped with components of various textures: a crunchy Coconut Meringue, creamy White Chocolate Lime Cream, Caramel White Chocolate Tuile, and a quenelle of frozen Strawberry Balsamic Sorbet. A vibrant shard of Raspberry Paper crowns the dessert, which is surrounded by a warm Strawberry Balsamic Ragout, lime anglaise, and Lemon Honey Jelly.

MAKES 12 SERVINGS

Almond Biscuit

56 g (1.97 oz/½ cup) rice flour

36 g (1.26 oz/⅓ cup plus 1 Tbsp plus 1½ tsp) almond flour

128 g (4.5 oz/1 stick plus 1 Tbsp) unsalted butter

64 g (2.25 oz/3½ large) egg yolks

Pinch of salt

128 g (4.5 oz/4 extra-large) egg whites

72 g (2.53 oz/⅓ cup plus 2¼ tsp) granulated sugar

1. Preheat the oven to 355°F (124°C).

2. In a food processor fitted with the steel blade, blend together the rice and almond flour, butter, egg yolks, and salt. Transfer the mixture to a bowl.

3. In the bowl of a stand mixer fitted with the whisk attachment, beat the egg whites on high speed to soft peaks. Gradually add the sugar and beat until a stiff and glossy meringue forms. Fold the meringue into the rice flour mixture.

4. Transfer the batter to a pastry bag fitted with a medium, plain tip and pipe into twelve 3-in (7.6-cm) ring molds. Bake for about 8 minutes, or until a tester comes out clean. Cool completely, then store in an airtight container until ready to use.

Coconut Meringue

104 g (3.6 oz/3½ large) egg whites

58 g (2.04 oz/¼ cup plus 2 tsp) granulated sugar

104 g (3.66 oz/¾ cup plus 2 Tbsp plus 1½ tsp) confectioners' sugar

34 g (1.2 oz/⅓ cup plus 1 Tbsp) almond flour

26 g (0.9 oz/⅓ cup) unsweetened desiccated coconut

1. Preheat the oven to 248°F (120°C).

2. In the bowl of a stand mixer fitted with the whisk attachment, whip the egg whites on high speed with 12 g (0.42 oz/1 Tbsp) of the granulated sugar. Gradually add the remaining 46 g (1.6 oz/3 Tbsp plus 2 tsp) granulated sugar and whip until a stiff and glossy meringue forms. Fold in 76 g (2.68 oz/⅔ cup) of the confectioners' sugar. Fold in the remaining 28 g (1 oz/¼ cup) confectioners' sugar, the almond flour, and the desiccated coconut.

3. Pipe twelve 3-in (7.6-cm) rounds of the meringue onto a silicone baking mat–lined sheet pan and bake until dry, about 80 minutes.

Lemon Honey Jelly

100 g (3.5 oz/¼ cup plus 2½ tsp) honey

100 g (3.5 oz/⅓ cup plus 1 Tbsp plus 2½ tsp) water

20 g (0.7 oz/1 Tbsp plus 1 tsp) freshly squeezed lemon juice

3 g (0.1 oz/1½ sheets) gelatin (silver grade), bloomed and drained

1. In a saucepan, combine the honey and water and place over low heat just until warm. Add the lemon juice and drained gelatin and stir to dissolve the gelatin.

2. Pour the jelly into twelve 1-in (2.54-cm) square flexible silicone molds and freeze until set.

Caramel White Chocolate Tuile

112 g (3.95 oz/⅓ cup plus 2 tsp) fondant

75 g (2.6 oz/3 Tbsp plus 1½ tsp) glucose syrup

75 g (2.6 oz) white chocolate, chopped

1. In a saucepan, heat the fondant and glucose over high heat to 320°F (160°C). Pour over the chocolate and emulsify with an immersion blender. Pour onto a silicone baking mat and roll into an even layer. Let set completely.

2. Preheat the oven to 355°F (180°C). Break the tuile mixture into chunks and grind finely in a food processor. Sift over a 4-in (10-cm) round stencil, or *chablon,* placed on a silicone baking mat–lined sheet pan, to form 12 tuiles. Bake for a few seconds. While still warm, shape the tuiles around a PVC tube to curl slightly.

White Chocolate Lime Cream

288 g (10.16 oz) white chocolate, chopped

54 g (1.9 oz/3 Tbsp plus 1½ tsp) whole milk

93 g (3.28 oz/⅓ cup plus 1 Tbsp) freshly squeezed lime juice

15 g (0.53 oz/1 Tbsp) freshly squeezed orange juice

3 g (0.1 oz/1½ tsp) finely grated lime zest

4.5 g (0.16 oz/2¼ sheets) gelatin (silver grade), bloomed and drained

360 g (12.7 oz/1½ cups) heavy cream

1. Place the chopped chocolate in a large bowl and set aside.

2. In a small saucepan, combine the milk, lime and orange juices, and lime zest and place over medium-high heat until hot to the touch. Add the drained gelatin and stir until dissolved. Pour the mixture over the white chocolate and emulsify with an immersion blender. Cool until tepid.

3. In the bowl of a stand mixer fitted with the whisk attachment, whip the cream on high speed to soft peaks. Fold into the cooled white chocolate mixture. Transfer to a pastry bag fitted with a medium, plain tip and pipe the cream into twelve 2¾-in (7-cm) flexible, silicone demisphere molds. Freeze until firm.

Lime Anglaise Sauce

225 g (8 oz/¾ cup plus 2 Tbsp plus 2¼ tsp) whole milk

150 g (5.3 oz/⅔ cup) heavy cream

6 g (0.21 oz/1 Tbsp) lime zest

75 g (2.6 oz/1½ large) eggs

51 g (1.8 oz/¼ cup) granulated sugar

1.5 g (0.05 oz/⅔ sheet) gelatin (silver grade), bloomed and drained

1. Combine the milk, cream, and lime zest in a small saucepan and cook over medium-high heat until just beginning to boil. Remove from the heat, cover, and allow to infuse for 30 minutes.

2. In a bowl, whisk together the eggs and sugar. Pour half of the hot cream mixture into the egg-sugar mixture to temper the eggs, then return the entire mixture to the saucepan. Cook, stirring constantly, until the mixture thickens, coats the back of the spoon and reaches 175°F (80°C). Add the drained gelatin and stir until dissolved. Cool completely. Transfer to an airtight container and refrigerate until ready to use.

Strawberry Balsamic Sorbet

74 g (2.6 oz/⅓ cup) water

40 g (1.4 oz/3 Tbsp plus ¾ tsp) granulated sugar

8 g (0.28 oz/2½ tsp) sorbet stabilizer

480 g (16.9 oz/2 cups plus 1 Tbsp plus 1½ tsp) strawberry purée

480 g (16.9 oz/2 cups plus 1 Tbsp plus 1½ tsp) wild strawberry purée

66 g (2.3 oz/3 Tbsp plus 1½ tsp) Trimoline (invert sugar)

60 g (2.1 oz/¼ cup) balsamic vinegar

34 g (1.19 oz/2 Tbsp) freshly squeezed lemon juice

38 g (1.3 oz/⅓ cup) confectioners' sugar

1. Combine the water, granulated sugar, and sorbet stabilizer in a saucepan over medium-high heat and cook, stirring, to dissolve the sugar.

2. In another saucepan, combine the purées, invert sugar, balsamic vinegar, lemon juice, and confectioners' sugar and place over medium heat until warm. Add the sugar syrup. Cool. Refrigerate the sorbet base for 1 hour.

3. Process the chilled sorbet base in an ice cream machine according to the manufacturer's instructions. Pipe the sorbet into 12 flexible, silicone quenelle molds and freeze until firm.

Strawberry Balsamic Ragout

84 g (2.96 oz/⅓ cup plus 1 Tbsp) strawberry purée

80 g (2.82 oz/⅓ cup plus 1 Tbsp plus 1¼ tsp) granulated sugar

20 g (0.7 oz/1 Tbsp plus 1 tsp) freshly squeezed lemon juice

15 g (0.5 oz/1 Tbsp) balsamic vinegar

240 g (8.46 oz/2 cups) fresh strawberries, washed, hulled, and chopped

1. In a saucepan, combine the strawberry purée, sugar, lemon juice, and balsamic vinegar and bring just to a boil over medium-high heat. Add the chopped strawberries. Cool.

2. Refrigerate the ragout, covered, until ready to serve.

Raspberry Paper

100 g (3.5 oz/⅓ cup plus 2 Tbsp) raspberry purée

10 g (0.35 oz/1 Tbsp plus 1½ tsp) methylcellulose f50 (see Sources, page 310)

35 g (1.23 oz/2 Tbsp plus 2¼ tsp) granulated sugar

1. Preheat the oven to 250°F (122°C).

2. Combine all of the ingredients in a microwave-safe container and heat on high power, stirring every 30 seconds, until the mixture comes to a boil. Spread onto a silicone baking mat–lined sheet pan and bake for 15 minutes. Cool.

3. Tear off irregular pieces of the raspberry paper to use as a garnish.

ASSEMBLY

1. Warm up the Almond Biscuits and place one on each plate. Place a Coconut Meringue on top of each biscuit, then unmold a White Chocolate Lime Cream on top. Arrange a Caramel White Chocolate Tuile on top of the cream, then unmold a quenelle of Strawberry Balsamic Sorbet on top. Garnish with a piece of Raspberry Paper.

2. Spoon some warm Strawberry Balsamic Ragout on one side of each dessert and some Lime Anglaise Sauce on the opposite side. Place a Lemon Honey Jelly on each plate.

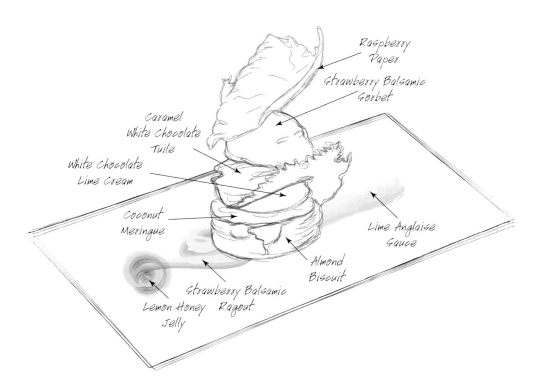

TEAM SWITZERLAND 2008

Giuliano Sargenti

Fabian Rimann

Elias Läderach

STRAWBERRY SOUP, VANILLA PANNA COTTA NAPOLEON, AND ALMOND TARTLET

Created by Team Switzerland for the World Pastry Team Championship in 2008 in Nashville, this dessert symbolizes the harmony of the elements. The Sparkling Wine–Yogurt Espuma represents air, the Strawberry Marmalade the earth, and the Key Lime Cream the water.

MAKES 14 SERVINGS

Almond Streusel

100 g (3.5 oz/¾ stick plus 1 Tbsp) unsalted butter

100 g (3.5 oz/½ cup) granulated sugar

100 g (3.5 oz/1 cup plus 2 Tbsp) almond flour

60 g (2.1 oz/½ cup) all-purpose flour

1. Preheat the oven to 320°F (160°F).

2. Combine all of the ingredients in the bowl of a stand mixer fitted with the paddle attachment. Mix on low speed until the mixture forms a dough.

3. Transfer the dough to a work surface and shape into a disk. Roll out to a thickness of ⅛ in (3 mm). Transfer to a silicone baking mat–lined baking sheet and bake just until lightly browned. Cool and cut into 2½-in (6.3-cm) squares.

Lemon Jaconde

150 g (5.3 oz/3 large) whole eggs

90 g (3.2 oz/1 cup) almond flour

90 g (3.2 oz/scant ½ cup) granulated sugar

30 g (1.1 oz/¼ cup) all-purpose flour

15 g (0.5 oz/2¼ tsp) invert sugar

8 g (0.3 oz/1 Tbsp plus 1 tsp) finely grated lemon zest

90 g (3.2 oz/3 large) egg whites

45 g (1.6 oz/3 Tbsp plus ¾ tsp) unsalted butter, melted

1. Preheat the oven to 350°F (175°C).

2. Combine the whole eggs, almond flour, 30 g (1.1 oz/2 Tbsp plus 1½ tsp) of the granulated sugar, the flour, invert sugar, and lemon zest and process in a food processor fitted with the steel blade.

3. In a stand mixer fitted with the whisk attachment, whip the egg whites with the remaining 60 g (2.1 oz/¼ cup plus 2¾ tsp) granulated sugar on high speed to form a meringue. Fold the meringue into the almond flour mixture. Fold in the melted butter.

4. Spread out the batter in a sheet pan and bake for 8 minutes, or until set. Cool.

Sparkling Wine–Yogurt Espuma

80 g (2.8 oz/4⅓ large) egg yolks

100 g (3.5 oz/½ cup) granulated sugar

120 g (4.2 oz/½ cup) sparkling wine

30 g (1.1 oz/2 Tbsp) freshly squeezed lemon juice

20 g (0.7 oz/1 Tbsp plus ¾ tsp) freshly squeezed Key lime juice

1 vanilla bean, split lengthwise and seeds scraped

200 g (7.1 oz/¾ cup plus 1 Tbsp) plain full-fat yogurt

3 g (0.1 oz/1½ sheets) gelatin (silver grade), bloomed and drained

1. Fill a saucepan halfway with water and bring it to a simmer over medium-low heat. Whisk the egg yolks and sugar in a stainless steel bowl to blend. Whisk in the wine, lemon juice, lime juice, and vanilla bean seeds. Place the bowl over the saucepan of simmering water. Whisk constantly for 4 to 5 minutes or more to cook the sauce, until it has the consistency of lightly whipped cream. Clear the bottom of the bowl constantly with the whisk so that the eggs do not scramble, and adjust the heat as needed. When thick, foamy, and tripled in volume, remove from the heat.

2. Whisk in the yogurt and drained gelatin. Refrigerate the espuma, covered, until ready to use.

Strawberry Soup

300 g (10.6 oz/1¼ cups) strawberry purée

15 g (0.5 oz/2 Tbsp) confectioners' sugar

30 g (1.1 oz/2 Tbsp) sparkling wine

1 vanilla bean, split lengthwise and seeds scraped

1. Blend together the strawberry purée, sugar, wine, and vanilla bean seeds. Cover and refrigerate until ready to use.

Vanilla Panna Cotta

615 g (1 lb, 6 oz/2⅔ cups) heavy cream

90 g (3.2 oz/⅓ cup plus 1 Tbsp) whole milk

45 g (1.6 oz/3 Tbsp plus 2 tsp) granulated sugar

1 vanilla bean, split lengthwise and seeds scraped

6 g (0.21 oz/3 sheets) gelatin (silver grade), bloomed and drained

1. In a saucepan, cook 450 g (15.8 oz/1¾ cups plus 2 Tbsp) of the heavy cream, the milk, sugar, and vanilla bean seeds over medium-high heat, stirring until the sugar dissolves.

2. Add the drained gelatin and stir to dissolve. Cool down the mixture.

3. Gently mix with the remaining 165 g (6.2 oz/⅔ cup) heavy cream. Place in a covered container and hold at cool room temperature until assembly.

Key Lime Cream

40 g (1.4 oz/3 Tbsp plus ¾ tsp) granulated sugar

1 g (0.03 oz/½ tsp) Key lime zest

50 g (1.8 oz/3 Tbsp plus ¾ tsp) freshly squeezed Key lime juice

600 g (1 lb, 5 oz/2½ cups) heavy cream

1. In a saucepan, bring the sugar, lime zest, and lime juice to a simmer over low heat; continue to simmer over the lowest heat for an hour. Cool.

2. Add the heavy cream to the lime reduction and chill.

3. In the bowl of a stand mixer fitted with the wire whisk, whip the chilled mixture on high speed to medium peaks. Cover and refrigerate until ready to use.

Strawberry Marmalade

260 g (9.2 oz/2⅓ cups) fresh strawberries, washed, hulled, and diced

260 g (9.2 oz/1¼ cups plus 2 tsp) granulated sugar

20 g (0.7 oz/2 Tbsp) Key lime suprêmes

1 g (0.03 oz/½ tsp) lemon zest

15 g (0.5 oz/1 Tbsp) freshly squeezed lemon juice

60 g (2.1 oz/¼ cup) sparkling wine

3 g (0.1 oz/1 tsp) powdered pectin

4 g (0.14 oz/2 tsp) citric acid

1. In a saucepan, cook the strawberries with 220 g (7.8 oz/1 cup plus 1 Tbsp plus 2 tsp) of the sugar, the Key lime segments, lemon zest and juice, and the wine over medium heat for 5 minutes, until the sugar is dissolved.

2. Combine the remaining 40 g (1.4 oz/3 Tbsp) sugar and the pectin. Add to the strawberry mixture and bring to a boil over medium-high heat.

3. Stir in the citric acid and cool. Refrigerate, covered, until ready to use.

Strawberry Ragout

300 g (10.6 oz/2⅔ cups) strawberry purée

15 g (0.5 oz/2 Tbsp) confectioners' sugar

30 g (1.1 oz/2 Tbsp) sparkling wine

1 vanilla bean, split lengthwise and seeds scraped

150 g (5.3 oz/1⅓ cups) fresh strawberries, washed, hulled, and diced

1. Mix the strawberry purée with the sugar, wine, and vanilla bean seeds.

2. Stir in the strawberries. Cover and refrigerate until ready to use.

Almond Tartlet

80 g (2.8 oz/⅓ cup plus 1 tsp) unsalted butter

72 g (2.5 oz/⅔ cup) confectioners' sugar

50 g (1.76 oz/1 large) egg

80 g (2.8 oz/¾ cup plus 2 Tbsp plus 1½ tsp) almond flour

90 g (3.2 oz/⅓ cup plus 1 Tbsp) heavy cream

35 g (1.2 oz/¼ cup plus 2 tsp) all-purpose flour

10 g (0.4 oz/1 Tbsp plus 1 tsp) cornstarch

2 g (0.07 oz/½ tsp) finely grated lemon zest

0.5 g (0.02 oz/pinch) salt

1. Preheat the oven to 320°F (160°C).

2. In a stand mixer fitted with the paddle attachment, cream together the butter and sugar on high speed. Add the egg slowly, mixing until blended. Add the almond flour and mix until combined. Add the remaining ingredients and mix just until blended.

3. Spoon a layer of Strawberry Marmalade in the bottom of each of fourteen 2¾-in (7-cm) diameter ovenproof ramekins. Top with the Almond Tartlet batter and bake until golden, about 12 minutes. Cool completely.

Strawberry Sorbet

575 g (1 lb, 4 oz/2½ cups) strawberry purée

465 g (1 lb, 0.4 oz/scant 2 cups) water

170 g (6 oz/¾ cup plus ⅔ tsp) granulated sugar

78 g (2.8 oz/3 Tbsp plus 2½ tsp) glucose syrup

2 g (0.07 oz/½ plus ⅛ tsp) sorbet stabilizer

1. Combine all of the ingredients in a saucepan and bring to a boil over medium-high heat. Cool down rapidly then chill.

2. Process the chilled sorbet base in an ice cream machine according to the manufacturer's instructions.

Strawberry Tuile

100 g (3.5 oz/¾ stick plus 1 Tbsp) unsalted butter

50 g (1.8 oz/2 Tbsp plus 1 tsp) glucose syrup

30 g (1.1 oz/2 Tbsp) strawberry juice

150 g (5.3 oz/¾ cup) granulated sugar

10 g (0.4 oz/1 Tbsp plus 1½ tsp) all-purpose flour

5 g (0.18 oz/2½ tsp) strawberry powder

2.5 g (0.09 oz/1½ tsp) powdered pectin

1. Preheat the oven to 320°F (160°C).

2. In a saucepan, combine the butter, glucose, and strawberry juice and cook over medium-high heat, stirring frequently, to dissolve the glucose and melt the butter. Add the remaining ingredients and mix to combine.

3. Spread out the batter in a silicone baking mat–lined sheet pan over a 3-in (7.6-cm) round stencil to form 14 tuiles. Bake until set, 5 to 7 minutes. Cool completely.

ASSEMBLY

Fourteen 2½-in (6.3-cm) thin, bittersweet chocolate squares

1. Layer the Lemon Jaconde in the bottom of a terrine pan. Top with a layer of the Strawberry Marmalade, then the Vanilla Panna Cotta. Chill until firm. Cut into ½-in (1.27-cm) slices.

2. Pour some Strawberry Soup into each serving glass. Top with Sparkling Wine–Yogurt Espuma.

3. Top each Almond Streusel square with a panna cotta slice. Top with a thin chocolate square, then a layer of Key Lime Cream. Top with a Strawberry Tuile, then a small spoonful of Strawberry Ragout.

4. Place each Almond Tartlet in a small serving dish and top with Almond Streusel and a quenelle of Strawberry Sorbet.

5. On each plate, arrange a glass of soup, then a panna cotta dessert, then an Almond Tartlet.

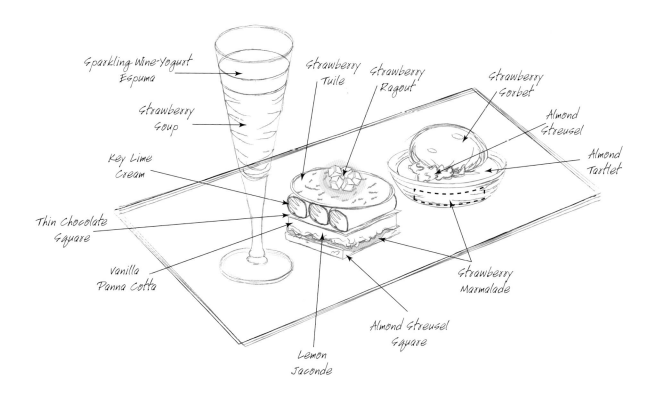

TEAM CHOWDHURY 2009

Kaushik Chowdhury

Melynda Gilmore

Keith Taylor

PINEAPPLE RUM CAKE,

RASPBERRY FLORENTINE, COCONUT SORBET, PINEAPPLE COMPOTE, AND RUM ANGLAISE

Kaushik Chowdhury knew that the refreshing combination of pineapple and coconut was sure to please the judges at the 2009 NPTC, so his team designed a dessert featuring these tropical flavors, along with a generous shot of rum. Here a comforting Pineapple Rum Cake is accompanied by a bright Pineapple Compote, Coconut Sorbet, a crunchy Raspberry Florentine, and a Rum Anglaise sauce.

MAKES 12 SERVINGS

Pineapple Rum Cake

304 g (10.72 oz/2⅔ cups) cake flour

318 g (11.21 oz/1½ cups plus 1¼ tsp) granulated sugar

106 g (3.73 oz/⅓ cup plus 2 Tbsp plus 2¼ tsp packed) brown sugar

8 g (0.28 oz/1½ slightly rounded tsp) baking soda

6 g (0.21 oz/1 tsp) salt

3 g (0.1 oz/1 tsp) ground ginger

1.5 g (0.05 oz/1½ tsp) ground cinnamon

305 g (10.75 oz/1⅓ cups plus 1 Tbsp plus 2¼ tsp) vegetable oil

267 g (9.41 oz/5⅓ large) eggs

10 g (0.35 oz/2½ tsp) rum

2 g (0.07 oz/2 tsp) pure vanilla extract

120 g (4.23 oz/1 cup) chopped fresh pineapple

1. Preheat the oven to 350°F (175°C).

2. In the bowl of a stand mixer fitted with the paddle attachment, mix together the flour, granulated and brown sugars, baking soda, salt, ginger, and cinnamon on low speed. Add the oil, eggs, rum, and vanilla and mix until well blended. Add the chopped pineapple and mix until blended.

3. Scrape the batter into twelve 4 x 1-in (10 x 2.54-cm) flexible, silicone, mini loaf pans and bake for 15 minutes, or until baked through. Unmold and cool.

Pineapple Compote

75 g (2.64 oz/⅓ cup plus 1 Tbsp) granulated sugar

30 g (1.05 oz/2 Tbsp) water

425 g (15 oz/about ⅓ medium pineapple) cored and peeled pineapple, cut into small dice

50 g (1.76 oz/3 Tbsp plus ¾ tsp) freshly squeezed lemon juice

16 g (0.56 oz/1 Tbsp plus ½ tsp) rum

8 g (0.28 oz/1 Tbsp) cornstarch

1. In a saucepan, combine the sugar and water and cook over medium-high heat to the caramel stage (see page 10). Add the diced pineapple and cook for a few minutes.

2. In a small bowl, stir together the lemon juice, rum, and cornstarch. Add to the pineapple mixture and bring to a boil, stirring constantly. Cool.

Coconut Sorbet

454 g (1 lb/1¾ cups plus 2 Tbsp plus 2¼ tsp) water

454 g (1 lb/2¼ cups plus 1 tsp) granulated sugar

3.3 g (0.12 oz/1 tsp) sorbet stabilizer

454 g (1 lb/2 cups) coconut milk

142 g (5 oz/½ cup plus 1 Tbsp plus 1 tsp) whole milk

1. In a saucepan, bring the water to a boil over high heat and stir in the sugar and sorbet stabilizer. Add the coconut milk and milk to the mixture and stir to combine. Chill in an ice bath.

2. Process the sorbet base in an ice cream machine according to the manufacturer's instructions.

3. Using a pastry bag fitted with a medium, plain tip, pipe the sorbet into 12 cylindrical molds, ¾ in (2 cm) in diameter and 4 in (10 cm) long, and freeze.

Rum Anglaise

113 g (4 oz/⅓ cup plus 2 Tbsp plus 2¼ tsp) heavy cream

113 g (4 oz/⅓ cup plus 2 Tbsp plus 1½ tsp) whole milk

14 g (0.5 oz/1 Tbsp) rum

2 vanilla beans, split lengthwise and seeds scraped

113 g (4 oz/½ cup plus 1 Tbsp) granulated sugar

113 g (4 oz/6 large) egg yolks

1. In a saucepan, combine the cream, milk, rum, vanilla bean seeds and pods, and half of the sugar and bring to a gentle boil over medium-high heat, stirring to dissolve the sugar.

2. Meanwhile, whisk the egg yolks with the remaining sugar until light. Add half of the hot cream mixture to the egg yolk–sugar mixture to temper the eggs, then return the entire mixture to the saucepan. Cook over medium heat, stirring constantly with a wooden spoon, until the sauce is thickened, coats the back of the spoon and reaches 175°F (80°C). Remove from the heat and pass through a fine-mesh sieve. Cool, then chill until ready to use.

Raspberry Florentine

225 g (7.9 oz/scant 2 cups) confectioners' sugar

180 g (6.3 oz/1½ sticks plus 2¼ tsp) unsalted butter

75 g (2.64 oz/3 Tbsp plus 1½ tsp) honey

75 g (2.64 oz/⅓ cup) water

75 g (2.64 oz/⅔ cup) all-purpose flour

20 g (0.7 oz/3 Tbsp plus 1 tsp) raspberry powder

1. Preheat the oven to 350°F (175°C).

2. Combine the sugar and butter in the bowl of a food processor fitted with the steel blade and process until smooth. Add the honey and water and process until blended. Add the flour and raspberry powder and process until combined.

3. Spread out the batter in a silicone baking mat–lined sheet pan and bake for about 5 minutes. Remove from the oven and immediately cut into 2½ x 4-in (6.3 x 10-cm) rectangles. While still warm, roll one of the long ends once around to form a tight tube shape. Repeat to form 12 tubes.

Tuile

85 g (3 oz/¾ stick) unsalted butter

156 g (5.5 oz/1⅓ cups plus 2¼ tsp) confectioners' sugar

100 g (3.5 oz/3⅓ large) egg whites

113 g (4 oz/¾ cup plus 3 Tbsp plus ½ tsp) all-purpose flour

1. In the bowl of a stand mixer fitted with the paddle attachment, cream together the butter and sugar on high speed until smooth and light. Slowly add the egg whites and flour and mix until blended. Cover and refrigerate the batter for at least 2 hours.

2. Preheat the oven to 350°F (175°C).

3. Place a 6 x ½-in (15.25 x 1.27-cm) stencil in the shape of clock hands (see photo on page 232) onto a silicone baking mat–lined sheet pan. Spread the batter over the stencil to form 12 tuiles. Bake until just beginning to turn golden around the edges. While still warm, curve into a loop shape.

ASSEMBLY

1. Spoon a line of Rum Anglaise down the length of each rectangular plate. Drag a spoon through the center of the line. Pipe a few dots of the sauce at one end of the line.

2. Place a Pineapple Rum Cake in the center of each plate. Top with a Raspberry Florentine, then balance the looped end of a Tuile on top, and lay one of the Coconut Sorbet tubes on top of the tuile to hold it in place. Spoon a line of the Pineapple Compote next to each cake.

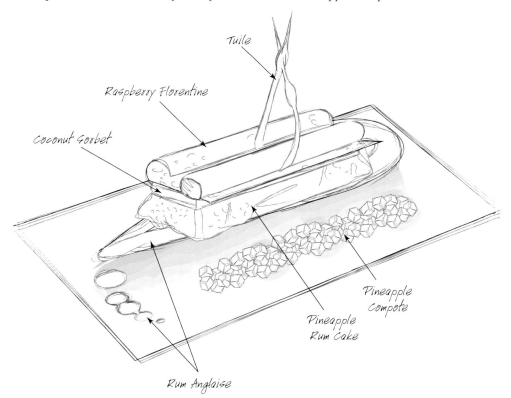

Tuile

Raspberry Florentine

Coconut Sorbet

Pineapple Compote

Pineapple Rum Cake

Rum Anglaise

Loan Co

Paul John Padua

Panida Garrett

TROPICAL NAPOLEON

This dessert combines a plucky lemon cake with smooth, melt-in-your-mouth, exotic fruit crémeux. A sweet blueberry sauce, Grapefruit Sorbet, and an aromatic Rosemary Tuile complete the flavor profile.

MAKES 12 SERVINGS

Lemon Chiffon Cake

396 g (14 oz/2 cups) granulated sugar

135 g (4.76 oz/1 cup plus 3 Tbsp) cake flour

3.5 g (0.12 oz/½ tsp) salt

12 g (0.42 oz/2 Tbsp) finely grated lemon zest

1.504 kg (53 oz/1 pt plus 2 cups plus 3 Tbsp plus 1½ tsp) whole milk

270 g (9.5 oz/1 cup plus 1 Tbsp plus 1 tsp) freshly squeezed lemon juice

260 g (9.18 oz/14 large) egg yolks

6 g (0.21 oz/1½ tsp) pure vanilla extract

420 g (14.81 oz/14 large) egg whites

1. Preheat the oven to at 320°F (160°C).

2. In a large bowl, combine 198 g (7 oz/1 cup) of the sugar with the cake flour, salt, and lemon zest. Stir in 482 g (17 oz/2 cups) of the milk, then whisk in the remaining milk, lemon juice, egg yolks, and vanilla.

3. In the bowl of a stand mixer fitted with the whisk attachment, whip the egg whites on high speed to soft peaks. Gradually add the remaining 198 g (7 oz/1 cup) sugar and whip to stiff peaks to form a meringue. Gently fold the meringue into the batter.

4. Scrape the batter into twelve 3-in (7.6-cm) flexible, silicone cylinder molds and bake in a water bath until golden, 10 to 15 minutes. Unmold and cool completely.

Tropical Crémeux

200 g (7 oz/¾ cup plus 2 Tbsp) exotic purée

150 g (5.3 oz/⅔ cup plus 1 tsp) heavy cream

30 g (1.05 oz/2 Tbsp) whole milk

37 g (1.3 oz/2 large) egg yolks

50 g (1.76 oz/1 large) whole egg

50 g (1.76 oz/¼ cup) granulated sugar

4 g (0.14 oz/2 sheets) gelatin (gold grade), bloomed and drained

1. In a saucepan, bring the exotic purée, cream, and milk to a gentle boil over medium-high heat.

2. Meanwhile, in a bowl, whisk together the egg yolks, whole egg, and sugar. Add half of the hot cream mixture to the egg yolk–sugar mixture to temper the eggs, then return the entire mixture to the saucepan. Cook over medium heat, stirring constantly, until thickened. Add the drained gelatin and stir until dissolved. Divide the crémeux among twelve 3-in (7.6-cm) flexible, silicone cylinder molds and six 2-in (5-cm) oval, flexible, silicone molds and freeze until ready to use.

Blueberry Sauce

454 g (1 lb/3¼ cups) fresh blueberries

240 g (8.46 oz/1 cup plus 3 Tbsp plus ¾ tsp) granulated sugar

59 g (2 oz/¼ cup) water

3 vanilla beans, split lengthwise and seeds scraped

1. In a saucepan, bring all of the ingredients to a boil over medium-high heat, then lower the heat and let simmer for a few minutes. Add some water if the sauce is too thick.

2. Strain the sauce through a fine-mesh sieve. Discard the vanilla pods. Cool, then cover and refrigerate until ready to use.

Grapefruit Sorbet

53 g (1.87 oz/¼ cup plus ¾ tsp) granulated sugar

13 g (0.45 oz/2 Tbsp plus ½ tsp) dextrose powder

2 g (0.07 oz/½ tsp plus ⅛ tsp) sorbet stabilizer

59 g (2 oz/¼ cup) water

500 g (17.6 oz/2 cups plus 2 Tbsp plus 2¼ tsp) pink grapefruit purée

40 g (1.4 oz/2 Tbsp) glucose syrup

1. In a bowl, combine the sugar, dextrose powder and sorbet stabilizer.

2. In a saucepan over low heat, heat the water to 104°F (39°C), then whisk in the dry ingredients. Continue whisking and bring the mixture to 185°F (85°C). Remove from the heat. Fold in the grapefruit purée and glucose. Chill in an ice bath, then process in an ice cream machine according to the manufacturer's instructions.

Grapefruit Jelly

454 g (1 lb/1¾ cups plus 2 Tbsp plus 2¼ tsp) cold water
6.9 g (0.24 oz/1 Tbsp) agar agar
1.9 lt (63.27 fl oz/2 qt) freshly squeezed pink grapefruit juice

1. In a saucepan, mix the water and agar agar powder. Gently bring to a boil over medium-high heat, then reduce the heat to low and simmer for 2 to 3 minutes. Remove from the heat and whisk in the pink grapefruit juice.

2. Pour the jelly onto a sheet pan and let set in the refrigerator.

3. Cut into ½-in (1-cm) cubes. Refrigerate, covered, until ready to use.

Rosemary Tuile

56 g (1.97 oz/½ cup) pastry flour

52 g (1.83 oz/⅓ cup plus 2 Tbsp plus ¾ tsp) confectioners' sugar

28 g (1 oz/1 large) egg white

42 g (1.5 oz/3 Tbsp) unsalted butter, melted

2 g (0.07 oz/1 tsp) finely chopped fresh rosemary

1. Preheat the oven to 350°F (175°C).

2. In a bowl, mix together the flour, sugar, and egg white to a paste. Stir in the melted butter. Mix well, then stir in the chopped rosemary.

3. Spread the mixture over a sunburst stencil (see photo on page 239) placed on a silicone baking mat–lined sheet pan to create 12 tuiles. Bake until just beginning to brown around the edges, about 5 minutes. Cool completely.

ASSEMBLY

Pulled sugar loops (see page 308)

1. Cut each Lemon Chiffon Cake in half horizontally. Unmold the Tropical Crémeux and arrange one on top of the bottom half of each cake. Top with the other half of the cake. Unmold the 2-in (5-cm) oval molds of Tropical Crémeux and cut each in half. Arrange one half on top of each cake and place the cake on a plate.

2. Lean a Rosemary Tuile against each cake. Spoon some Blueberry Sauce next to the cakes on each plate. Place a quenelle of Grapefruit Sorbet on each plate and some cubes of Grapefruit Jelly next to it. Garnish with a pulled sugar loop.

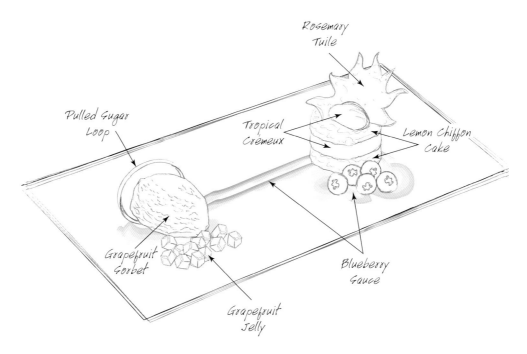

Ebow Dadzie
Anthony Smith
Bill Foltz

BANANA WALNUT FINANCIER

PINEAPPLE JELLY CENTER, CRUNCHY PASSION TUILE, COCONUT CREAM, AND LEMON–CRÈME FRAÎCHE ICE CREAM

Team Dadzie did some research before deciding on the flavors for their plated dessert at the 2009 National Pastry Team Championship, and found that pineapple had not been a featured flavor in years prior. So they combined sautéed pineapple cubes with coconut milk and vanilla beans and paired them with a Banana Walnut Financier with a Pineapple Jelly center and a tangy Lemon–Crème Fraîche Ice Cream to create a unique tropical dessert.

MAKES 12 SERVINGS

Banana Walnut Financier

215 g (7.58 oz/1½ sticks plus 3 Tbsp plus ¾ tsp) unsalted butter

112 g (3.95 oz/½ cup plus 1 tsp packed) brown sugar

85 g (3 oz/⅓ cup plus 1 Tbsp plus 2½ tsp) granulated sugar

425 g (15 oz/2½ medium) perfectly ripe bananas

125 g (4.4 oz/2½ large) eggs

191 g 6.73 oz/1½ cups plus 1 Tbsp plus 1½ tsp) all-purpose flour

4 g (0.14 oz/¾ tsp) baking soda

2 g (0.07 oz/scant ¼ tsp) salt

0.5 g (0.017 oz/⅛ tsp) freshly grated nutmeg

32 g (1.12 oz/2 Tbsp plus ½ tsp) buttermilk

2.5 g (0.088 oz/½ tsp) pure vanilla extract

64 g (2.25 oz/⅔ cup) walnut halves, toasted and chopped

1. Preheat the oven to 350°F (175°C).

2. In the bowl of a stand mixer fitted with the paddle attachment, cream together the butter and brown and granulated sugars on high speed. Peel the bananas and add them in large chunks, mixing on medium speed until blended. Add the eggs, one at a time, mixing well after each addition.

3. In a separate bowl, whisk together the flour, baking soda, salt, and nutmeg and add it alternately to the batter with the buttermilk and vanilla. Add the walnuts and mix just until blended.

4. Spoon or pipe the batter into twelve 3-in (7.6-cm) round, flexible, silicone baking molds and bake until golden brown, about 12 minutes. Unmold and cool completely.

Pineapple Jelly

50 g (1.76 oz/2 Tbsp plus 1 tsp) glucose syrup

300 g (10.5 oz/1¼ cups) pineapple purée

50 g (1.76 oz/¼ cup) granulated sugar

5 g (0.17 oz/1½ tsp) powdered pectin

1.5 g (0.05 oz/¾ tsp) citric acid

1. In a saucepan, heat the glucose over medium-high heat until hot. Add the pineapple purée and continue to heat until hot. Add the sugar and pectin and bring to a boil. Stir in the citric acid.

2. Pour the jelly into the small center depressions on the back of silicone savarin molds and chill until firm.

Classic Coconut Crème

18.6 g (0.65 oz/2 Tbsp) powdered gelatin

112 g (3.95 oz/⅓ cup plus 2 Tbsp plus 1½ tsp) water

340 g (12 oz/1⅓ cups plus 1 Tbsp plus 1½ tsp) cream of coconut

149 g (5.25 oz/8 large) egg yolks

227 g (8 oz/1 cup plus 2 Tbsp plus ½ tsp) granulated sugar

454 g (16 oz/scant 2 cups) heavy cream

1. Sprinkle the gelatin over the water and let stand to bloom for 5 minutes.

2. In a saucepan, heat the cream of coconut over medium-high heat until almost at a boil. Meanwhile in a bowl, whisk together the egg yolks and sugar. Whisk half of the hot cream of coconut into the egg yolk–sugar mixture, then return the entire mixture to the saucepan. Cook, stirring constantly, until slightly thickened. Remove from the heat and whisk in the gelatin until dissolved. Cool completely.

3. In the bowl of a stand mixer fitted with the whisk attachment, whip the cream to medium peaks on high speed. Fold in the cooled coconut mixture. Refrigerate until ready to use.

Passion Fruit Tuile

113 g (4 oz/⅓ cup) glucose syrup

113 g (4 oz/⅓ cup plus 1½ tsp) light corn syrup

113 g (4 oz/½ cup plus 1 Tbsp) granulated sugar

113 g (4 oz/½ cup) passion fruit paste

113 g (4 oz/1 stick) unsalted butter

2 g (0.07 oz/1 tsp) finely grated orange zest

0.5 g (0.01 oz/¼ tsp) ground cinnamon

1 g (0.03 oz/½ tsp) citric acid

40 g (1.42 oz/⅓ cup) all-purpose flour

0.75 g (0.026 oz/½ tsp) orange food coloring

1. Preheat the oven to 315°F (157°C).

2. In a saucepan, combine the glucose and corn syrup over medium heat until warm. Stir in the sugar. Add the passion fruit paste, butter, orange zest, cinnamon, and citric acid and bring to a boil, stirring. Remove from the heat and stir in the flour. Stir in the food coloring. Cool.

3. Spread the batter over a 3-in (7.6-cm) round stencil, placed on a silicone baking mat–lined sheet pan, to form 12 tuiles. Bake until set, about 7 minutes. Cool completely.

Lemon–Crème Fraîche Ice Cream

150 g (5.3 oz/3 large) eggs

250 g (8.8 oz/1¼ cups) granulated sugar

500 g (17.63 oz/2 cups plus 1 Tbsp) whole milk

726 g (25.6 oz/3 cups) crème fraîche

18.2 g (0.64 oz/3½ tsp) freshly squeezed lemon juice

1. In a bowl, whisk together the eggs with half of the sugar until pale.

2. In a saucepan, combine the milk with the remaining sugar and bring to a boil over high heat, stirring to dissolve the sugar. Whisk half of the hot milk into the egg-sugar mixture to temper the eggs, then return the entire mixture to the saucepan. Cook over medium heat, stirring constantly with a wooden spoon, until the sauce thickens and reaches 185°F (85°C). Cool, and then chill in an ice bath.

3. Stir in the crème fraîche and lemon juice and process in an ice cream machine according to the manufacturer's instructions. Freeze in an airtight container until ready to serve.

Sautéed Pineapple and Vanilla

350 g (12.34 oz/1¾ cups) granulated sugar

50 g (1.76 oz/3 Tbsp plus 1½ tsp) unsalted butter

2 vanilla beans, split lengthwise

200 g (7 oz/¾ cup plus 1 Tbsp) pineapple juice

75 g (2.6 oz/⅓ cup) coconut milk

10 g (0.35 oz/1 Tbsp plus 1 tsp) cornstarch

350 g (12.34 oz/3⅓ cups) cubed fresh pineapple

6 g (0.21 oz/1½ tsp) rum

1. In a saucepan, combine the sugar and butter and place over medium heat, stirring to dissolve the sugar. Add the vanilla beans. Add the pineapple juice, coconut milk, and cornstarch and bring to a boil, whisking constantly. Remove from the heat and stir in the cubed pineapple and rum. Remove the vanilla pod.

ASSEMBLY

Pulled sugar spirals (see page 308)

1. Cut a round out from the top of each Banana Walnut Financier and insert a circle of Pineapple Jelly. Top with a Passion Fruit Tuile. Pipe a layer of Classic Coconut Crème on top of the tuile and top with another tuile. Top with a quenelle of Lemon–Crème Fraîche Ice Cream. Spoon some of the Sautéed Pineapple and Vanilla around each dessert, and garnish the top with a pulled sugar spiral.

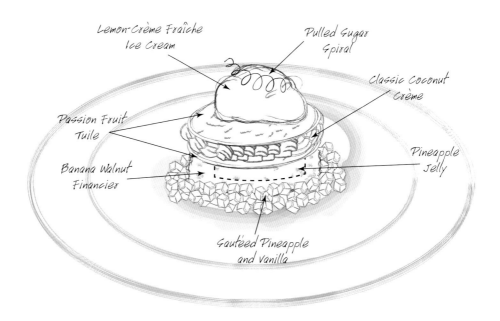

Tracy DeWitt

David Smoake

Dan Boman

ORANGE SAVARIN

ORANGE CHIBOUST, BANANA CROUSTILLANT, BLOOD ORANGE SORBET, AND ORANGE CARAMEL SAUCE

The members of Team DeWitt, husband and wife Tracy DeWitt and David Smoake and their colleague Dan Boman, are all instructors at the Scottsdale Culinary Institute, and they relish a challenge. The dessert they created for the 2009 NPTC featured an orange savarin, a risky choice because it's made with a fickle, yeast-based dough. Happily for them, the dough rose as it was supposed to on the day of the competition, and the dessert was a success. A pool of Orange Caramel Sauce surrounds the savarin, which is topped with a bright Pomegranate Sauce, Orange Chiboust, and a Banana Croustillant. A quenelle of sweet-tart Blood Orange Sorbet pulls together the citrus flavor profile. In a nod to the time theme, the hands of a clock are represented in chocolate, while a loop of pulled sugar outlines the clock's face. **MAKES 12 SERVINGS**

Orange Chiboust

200 g (7 oz/¾ cup plus 1 Tbsp plus ¾ tsp) freshly squeezed orange juice

20 g (0.7 oz/1 Tbsp plus 1 tsp) freshly squeezed lemon juice

50 g (1.76 oz/1 large) whole egg

20 g (0.7 oz/2 Tbsp plus 2 tsp) cornstarch

130 g (4.58 oz/1 cup plus 2 Tbsp plus 1¼ tsp) granulated sugar

5 g (0.17 oz/2½ sheets) gelatin (silver grade), bloomed and drained

25 g (0.88 oz/1 Tbsp plus 2 tsp) water

50 g (1.76 oz/3 Tbsp plus 1 tsp) egg whites

100 g (3.5 oz/⅓ cup plus 2 Tbsp) heavy cream, whipped to soft peaks

1. In a saucepan, combine the orange and lemon juice and bring to a boil over high heat. Meanwhile, in a bowl, whisk together the egg, cornstarch, and 30 g (1.05 oz/2 Tbsp plus 1¼ tsp) of the sugar until smooth. Whisk half of the hot orange juice mixture into the egg-sugar mixture to temper the eggs and continue to whisk until smooth. Return the entire mixture

to the saucepan and cook, whisking constantly, until it comes to a boil and thickens. Remove from the heat and whisk in the drained gelatin. Transfer the pastry cream to a large bowl.

2. In another saucepan, cook the remaining 100 g (3.5 oz/1 cup) sugar with the water over medium heat. Meanwhile, in the bowl of a stand mixer fitted with the whisk attachment, begin beating the egg whites on medium speed. When the sugar syrup reaches 238°F (114°C), slowly add the syrup to the beating whites. Beat on high speed until the whites are cool, stiff, and glossy and have formed a meringue. Fold the meringue into the pastry cream. Fold in the whipped cream. Cover and refrigerate until ready to use.

Orange Syrup

1 kg (35.27 oz/1 qt plus 3 Tbsp plus 2¼ tsp) water

400 g (14.1 oz/2 cups) granulated sugar

2 large strips orange zest, white pith removed

2 large strips lemon zest, white pith removed

2 cinnamon sticks

200 g (7 oz/¾ cup plus 1 Tbsp plus ¾ tsp) freshly squeezed orange juice

100 g (3.5 oz/⅓ cup plus 1 Tbsp plus 1½ tsp) orange liqueur

1. In a saucepan, combine the water, sugar, orange and lemon zests, and cinnamon sticks and bring to a boil over high heat, stirring to dissolve the sugar. Remove from the heat and allow to infuse, covered, for 30 minutes. Stir in the orange juice and orange liqueur. Cover and refrigerate until ready to use.

Savarin

168 g (6 oz/1¼ cups plus 2 tsp) bread flour

168 g (6 oz/1¼ cups plus 3 Tbsp plus 1½ tsp) cake flour

30 g (1.05 oz/2 Tbsp plus 1¼ tsp) granulated sugar

10 g (0.35 oz/1 Tbsp plus ¾ tsp) dry instant yeast

7.5 g (0.26 oz/1⅛ tsp) salt

356 g (12.55 oz/7 large) eggs

150 g (5.3 oz/1 stick plus 2⅔ Tbsp plus 2 tsp) unsalted butter, cut into tablespoons and softened

1. In the bowl of a stand mixer fitted with the paddle attachment, mix together the flours, sugar, yeast, salt, and eggs. Continue to mix on medium-low speed for 8 to 10 minutes until the dough is well developed. Add the softened butter 1 tablespoon at a time, mixing until well blended. Divide the dough among twelve 3-in (7.6-cm) flexible, silicone savarin molds and set aside to proof until doubled in volume.

2. Preheat the oven to 375°F (190°C).

3. Bake the savarins until light golden brown on top. Remove from the molds and place on a sheet pan. Bake for 5 to 6 minutes longer, or until golden brown. Transfer them to a wire rack placed over a sheet pan.

4. While they are still warm, brush the savarins generously with the Orange Syrup. Cool.

Orange Caramel Sauce

225 g (7.93 oz/1 cup plus 2 Tbsp) granulated sugar

80 g (2.82 oz/⅓ cup plus 1¼ tsp) water

2 vanilla beans, split lengthwise and seeds scraped

12 g (0.42 oz/2 Tbsp) finely grated orange zest

100 g (3.5 oz/⅓ cup plus 1 Tbsp plus 2 tsp) freshly squeezed orange juice

40 g (1.41 oz/2 Tbsp plus 2¼ tsp) orange juice concentrate

3 g (0.1 oz/½ tsp) salt

1. In a saucepan, combine the sugar with 50 g (1.76 oz/3 Tbsp plus 1 tsp) of the water and the vanilla bean seeds and pods and cook over medium-high heat to a light caramel. Deglaze with the remaining 30 g (1.05 oz/2 Tbsp) water, the orange zest, orange juice, and orange juice concentrate. Add the salt and strain through a fine-mesh sieve. Cool, then cover and refrigerate until ready to use.

Banana Croustillant

100 g (3.5 oz/1 medium) peeled ripe banana

60 g (2.1 oz/½ cup plus 1½ tsp) pastry flour

1. Preheat the oven to 400°F (205°C).

2. Mash the banana, then stir in the flour. Spread out the batter in a thin layer over a 7 x 1½-in (17¾ x 3.8-cm) rectangular stencil, placed on a silicone baking mat–lined sheet pan, to make 12 croustillants. Bake until golden brown, 4 to 6 minutes. While still warm, shape each croustillant into a spiral.

Pomegranate Sauce

94 g (3.31 oz/⅓ cup plus 2 Tbsp plus 1½ tsp) granulated sugar

3 g (0.1 oz/1 tsp) pectin NH

94 g (3.31 oz/⅓ cup plus 1 Tbsp plus 1½ tsp) pomegranate purée

1 g (0.03 oz/a few drops) freshly squeezed lemon juice

1. In a bowl, mix together the sugar and pectin. Place the pomegranate purée in a saucepan and add the sugar mixture. Bring to a boil over medium-high heat, stirring frequently. Cool and stir in the lemon juice. Cover and refrigerate until ready to use.

Blood Orange Sorbet

333 g (11.74 oz/1 cup plus 3 Tbsp) blood orange pulp

93 g (3.28 oz/⅓ cup plus 2 Tbsp plus 1½ tsp) granulated sugar

40 g (1.41 oz/¼ cup) glucose powder

3.3 g (0.11 oz/1 tsp) sorbet stabilizer

83 g (2.92 oz/⅓ cup plus 2 tsp) water

1. In a saucepan, combine 83 g (2.92 oz/⅓ cup plus 2¼ tsp) of the blood orange pulp with the sugar, glucose, sorbet stabilizer, and water and cook over medium heat to 185°F (85°C), stirring frequently. Remove from the heat and cool.

2. Stir in the remaining 250 g (8.8 oz/⅔ cup plus 2 Tbsp plus ¾ tsp) blood orange pulp. Chill the sorbet base in an ice bath, then process in an ice cream machine according to the manufacturer's instructions.

ASSEMBLY

Pulled sugar loops (see page 308)
Chocolate clock hands garnishes

1. Place each Savarin in the center of a shallow bowl and spoon some Pomegranate Sauce in its center. Top with a large spoonful of Orange Chiboust. Arrange a pulled sugar loop in the chiboust, along with the chocolate clock hands. Arrange one end of a Banana Croustillant spiral on each savarin and the other end on the edge of the plate. Place a quenelle of Blood Orange Sorbet on the croustillant at the edge of each plate. Spoon some Orange Caramel Sauce around each savarin.

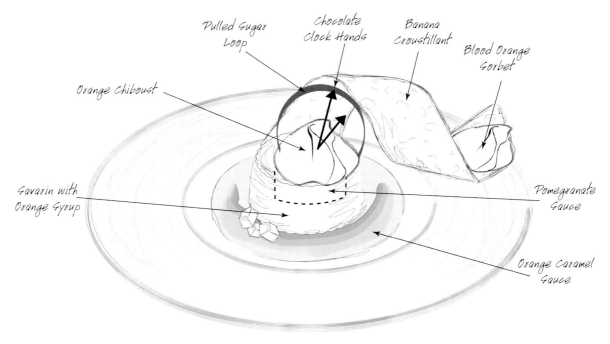

| Rebecca Millican |
| Zac Young |
| Thierry Aujard |

PASSION FRUIT– BANANA PARFAIT

Team Millican's objective in creating this dessert for the 2009 NPTC was to use familiar flavors in a sophisticated and creative way. They chose a Passion Fruit–Banana Parfait as their main element, and complemented it with Salted Caramel, a Hazelnut Sablé, Sour Cherry Granité, and Four-Cherry Compote. A miniature Lemon Madeleine adds contrasting texture to this colorful dessert.

MAKES 12 SERVINGS

Passion Fruit–Banana Parfait

300 g (10.58 oz/6 large) eggs

240 g (8.46 oz/1 cup plus 3 Tbsp plus ¾ tsp) granulated sugar

240 g (8.46 oz/1 cup) passion fruit purée

90 g (3.17 oz/⅓ cup plus 1 Tbsp) banana purée

60 g (2.11 oz/3 Tbsp plus 2¾ tsp) freshly squeezed lime juice

150 g (5.3 oz/1 stick plus 2 Tbsp plus 2 tsp) unsalted butter, cut into tablespoons

200 g (7 oz/¾ cup plus 1 Tbsp plus 2½ tsp) heavy cream, whipped to soft peaks

1. In a saucepan, whisk together the eggs, sugar, passion fruit and banana purées, and lime juice. Add the butter pieces and cook over medium heat, whisking constantly, until the mixture thickens and coats the back of a spoon; do not let it boil or it will curdle. Remove from the heat and pass through a fine-mesh sieve. Chill in an ice bath.

2. Gently fold in the whipped cream. Scrape into twelve 2½-in (6.3-cm) square silicone molds with a half-sphere depression at the edge of one side of the mold. Insert a 1-in (2.5-cm) diameter demisphere mold into the top of each parfait to create a depression (the Salted Caramel will be piped into this space), and freeze the parfaits until set.

Chocolate Streusel Base

300 g (10.58 oz/2½ sticks plus 1 Tbsp plus 1 tsp) unsalted butter

300 g (10.58 oz/1½ cups) granulated sugar

300 g (10.58 oz/3⅓ cups plus 1 Tbsp plus 1½ tsp) toasted hazelnut flour

225 g (7.9 oz/1¾ cups plus 2 Tbsp) all-purpose flour

75 g (2.64 oz/¾ cup plus 1 Tbsp) cocoa powder

1. In the bowl of a stand mixer fitted with the paddle attachment, cream together the butter and sugar on high speed. Gradually add the flours and cocoa powder and mix until combined. Shape the dough into a cylinder, wrap in plastic wrap and freeze until firm, about 2 hours.

2. Preheat the oven to 325°F (163°C).

3. Using a box grater, coarsely grate the dough onto a silicone baking mat–lined sheet pan. Spread the grated dough out evenly and bake for 20 minutes. Cool.

Caramelized Hazelnuts

100 g (3.5 oz/½ cup) granulated sugar

30 g (1.05 oz/2 Tbsp) water

250 g (8.8 oz/2⅓ cups) granulated hazelnuts

12 g (0.42 oz/2¾ tsp) unsalted butter

1. In a saucepan, combine the sugar and water and cook over medium-high heat until the sugar is dissolved. Add the hazelnuts and stir until sandy. Stir in the butter and mix until melted. Spread out the nuts on a silicone baking mat–lined sheet pan and cool completely.

Praline à l'Ancienne

77 g (2.7 oz/⅓ cup plus 1 Tbsp plus 1 tsp) granulated sugar

115 g (4 oz/⅓ cup plus 1½ tsp) liquid glucose

300 g (10.58 oz/2 cups) whole blanched almonds, toasted and warm

200 g (7 oz/1¼ cups plus 3 Tbsp) whole skinned hazelnuts, toasted and warm

½ vanilla bean, split lengthwise and seeds scraped

1. Preheat the oven to 350°F (175°C).

2. In a saucepan, combine the sugar and glucose and cook over high heat to the caramel stage (see page 10). Add the warm almonds and hazelnuts and the vanilla bean seeds and toss to coat. Spread onto a parchment paper–lined sheet pan and place in the oven. Heat until the caramel nut mixture is flat and nicely colored. Cool completely.

3. Chop the praline into chunks and grind in a food processor. Store in an airtight container at room temperature until ready to use.

Chocolate Streusel

50 g (1.76 oz/1/4 cup plus 2 ¼ tsp) cocoa butter

35 g (1.23 oz/2 Tbsp plus 1½ tsp) unsalted butter

100 g (3.5 oz/⅔ cup) toasted hazelnuts

90 g (3.17 oz/⅔ cup) Caramelized Hazelnuts

135 g (4.76 oz/⅓ cup plus 2 Tbsp) Praline à l'Ancienne

285 g (10 oz/2 cups) Chocolate Streusel Base

150 g (5.3 oz/1½ cups) cacao nibs

1. In a saucepan, melt the cocoa butter with the butter over low heat.

2. Process the toasted and caramelized hazelnuts to a paste and add them, along with the Praline à l'Ancienne, to the cocoa butter mixture, stirring to combine. Gently fold in the Chocolate Streusel Base and cacao nibs. Roll out thinly, to a thickness of about ⅛ in (3.17 mm), on a silicone baking mat and freeze until firm.

3. Cut the Chocolate Streusel into 3-in (7.6-cm) squares and freeze until ready to use.

Hazelnut Sablé

185 g (6.52 oz/1½ sticks plus 1 Tbsp plus ⅓ tsp) unsalted butter

110 g (3.88 oz/1¼ cups) hazelnut flour

105 g (3.7 oz/¾ cup plus 2 Tbsp plus 2 tsp) confectioners' sugar

200 g (7 oz/1½ cups plus 2 Tbsp plus 2 tsp) all-purpose flour

3 g (0.1 oz/¾ tsp) fleur de sel

1. In the bowl of a stand mixer fitted with the paddle attachment, mix together the butter, hazelnut flour, and sugar on medium speed until blended. Reduce the speed to low, add the all-purpose flour and salt, and mix until blended. Shape into a disk, wrap, and refrigerate for at least 1 hour.

2. Preheat the oven to 350°F (175°C).

3. Roll the dough out on a silicone baking mat to a thickness of ⅛ in (3.17 cm). Transfer the dough and mat to a sheet pan and bake until golden, about 12 minutes. While warm, cut into 1-in (2.54-cm) rounds. Cool.

Salted Caramel

200 g (7 oz/1 cup) granulated sugar

140 g (4.93 oz/⅓ cup plus 1 Tbsp plus 2 tsp) liquid glucose

2 g (0.07 oz/scant ¼ tsp) salt

230 g (8.11 oz/1 cup) heavy cream

120 g (4.23 oz/1 stick plus 1½ tsp) unsalted butter

7 g (0.24 oz/3½ sheets) gelatin (silver grade), bloomed and drained

1. In a saucepan, combine the sugar and glucose and cook over high heat to the caramel stage (see page 10). Stir in the salt and let cool for 2 minutes. Add the cream and butter and stir

until the butter is melted. If necessary, return the pan to the heat to dissolve any bits of hardened caramel. Remove from the heat, add the drained gelatin, and stir until dissolved.

2. When the Passion Fruit–Banana Parfaits are frozen, remove the 1-in (2.5-cm) demisphere molds and pipe or spoon the caramel into the depressions. Refrigerate until ready to serve.

Sour Cherry Granité

500 g (17.6 oz/2 cups plus 2 Tbsp plus 2¼ tsp) sour cherry purée

1. Freeze the purée in a blast freezer. Scrape to form flakes. Keep frozen until plating.

Four-Cherry Compote

75 g (2.6 oz/½ cup) Bing cherries, pitted and diced
70 g (2.46 oz/scant ½ cup) IQF sour cherries, diced
65 g (2.3 oz/½ cup plus 2 Tbsp) dried sour cherries, diced
120 g (4.23 oz/½ cup) cherry juice
30 g (1.05 oz/2 Tbsp plus 1¼ tsp) granulated sugar
10 g (0.35 oz/1½ tsp) liquid glucose
1 vanilla bean, split lengthwise

1. In a bowl, combine the Bing, sour, and dried cherries with the cherry juice.

2. In a saucepan, combine the sugar and glucose and cook over high heat to a light caramel. Add the vanilla bean and reduce until thick. Cool and add to the cherries. Remove the vanilla pod, cover, and refrigerate until ready to use.

Lemon Madeleines

200 g (7 oz/1¾ cups) confectioners' sugar
82 g (2.9 oz/⅔ cup plus 1 Tbsp) all-purpose flour
68 g (2.4 oz/¾ cup plus 1 tsp) almond flour
180 g (6.34 oz/¾ cup plus 2 Tbsp plus 2¼ tsp) butter
170 g (6 oz/5½ large) egg whites
20 g (0.7 oz/1 Tbsp) honey
2 g (0.07 oz/1 tsp) lemon zest
78 g (2.75 oz/⅓ cup) freshly squeezed lemon juice

1. In a bowl, sift together the sugar, all-purpose flour, and almond flour and whisk to combine.

2. In a saucepan over medium heat, heat the butter until it is melted. Continue to cook the butter until the solids at the bottom of the pan begin to turn brown and the butter is fragrant, about 5 minutes.

3. In another bowl, whisk the egg whites until frothy, then stir into the dry ingredients. Stir in the brown butter, honey, lemon zest, and juice.

4. Scrape into 12 small madeleine molds and chill for 1 hour.

5. Preheat the oven to 375°F (190°C).

6. Bake the madeleines until golden, about 20 minutes. Unmold and cool completely.

ASSEMBLY

Blown sugar cherries that are open at bottom (see page 308)
Gold leaf for garnish

1. Place each Chocolate Streusel Base on a plate and place a Hazelnut Sablé on top. Next place a Passion Fruit–Banana Parfait on top.

2. Fill each blown sugar cherry with some Sour Cherry Granité and place it on top of the parfait. Garnish each cherry stem with a piece of gold leaf. Spoon some Four-Cherry Compote onto each plate and top with a Lemon Madeleine.

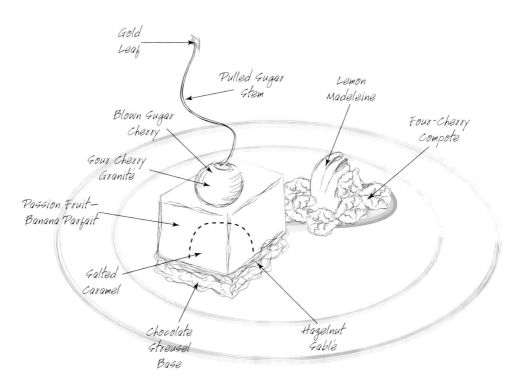

| Carlos Salazar |
| Yoni Mora |
| Marco Cossio |

PEACH MELBA MODERN

Team Salazar's goal with this dessert from the 2009 NPTC was to put a modern twist on an American classic, the Peach Melba. Their sleek-looking version features hibiscus-infused peaches, a Coconut Dacquoise and a Peach Yogurt Mousse. The dessert ended up being a real challenge for the team, as the main components needed to be assembled à la minute, *but they managed to pull it off in the final frenzied minutes before judging.*　　**MAKES 12 SERVINGS**

Light Citrus Cake

300 g (10.58 oz/6 large) eggs

280 g (9.87 oz/1¼ cups plus 2 Tbsp plus 1¼ tsp) granulated sugar

300 g (10.58 oz/3⅓ cups plus 1 Tbsp plus 1½ tsp) almond flour

80 g (2.8 oz/⅓ cup plus 1 Tbsp plus ¾ tsp) cake flour

2 g (0.07 oz/scant ¼ tsp) sea salt

6 g (0.21 oz/1 Tbsp) finely grated orange zest

2 g (0.07 oz/1 tsp) finely grated lemon zest

10 g (0.35 oz/2½ tsp) pure vanilla extract

190 g (6.7 oz/1 scant cup) clarified butter

1. Preheat the oven to 375°F (190°C).

2. In the bowl of a stand mixer fitted with the whisk attachment, beat the eggs with the sugar on high speed until light.

3. In a bowl, sift together the almond flour and cake flour. Reduce the speed to medium, add the salt, orange and lemon zests, vanilla, and butter to the egg mixture, and mix for 10 minutes. Spread out the batter in a silicone baking mat–lined sheet pan and bake until set, about 7 minutes. Cool completely.

4. Cut out twelve 4-in- (10-cm-) long barquette shapes from the cake. Store in an airtight container at room temperature until ready to use.

Praline Sablé

250 g (8.81 oz/2 sticks plus 1 Tbsp plus 2¼ tsp) unsalted butter

130 g (4.58 oz/1 cup plus 2 Tbsp) confectioners' sugar

60 g (2.1 oz/3 Tbsp) hazelnut paste

230 g (8.11 oz/1 cup) cake flour

130 g (4.58 oz/1½ cups) almond flour

1 g (0.03 oz/⅛ tsp) baking powder

60 g (2.1 oz/1 cup) feuilletine

1. In the bowl of a stand mixer fitted with the paddle attachment, cream together the butter and sugar on high speed. Add the hazelnut paste and mix until blended.

2. In a bowl, sift together the cake flour, almond flour, and baking powder. Add the dry ingredients to the batter and mix until blended. Add the feuilletine and blend. Shape the dough into a disk, wrap in plastic wrap, and refrigerate the dough for 2 hours.

3. Preheat the oven to 325°F (163°C).

4. Roll the dough out to thickness of ⅓ in (8.5 mm) on a silicone baking mat–lined sheet pan. Bake for 6 minutes. Remove the pan from the oven and cut into twelve 4-in- (10-cm-) long barquette shapes. Return to the oven and bake for 6 minutes more. Cut again to smooth the edges. Cool.

Peach Yogurt Mousse

200 g (7 oz/¾ cup plus 2 Tbsp) peach purée

70 g (2.46 oz/⅔ cup) confectioners' sugar

10 g (0.35 oz/2¼ tsp) peach liqueur

4 g (0.14 oz/2 sheets) gelatin (gold grade), bloomed and drained

125 g (4.4 oz/½ cup) plain full-fat yogurt

250 g (8.8 oz/1 cup plus 1 Tbsp plus ¾ tsp) heavy cream, whipped

1. In a saucepan, combine the peach purée, sugar, and peach liqueur and bring to a boil over medium-high heat. Add the drained gelatin and stir until dissolved. Cool completely.

2. Fold in the yogurt and whipped cream. Spread the mousse into a hotel pan to a thickness of ½ in (1.27 cm) and freeze.

3. When firm, cut out twelve 4-in- (10-cm-) long barquette shapes from the mousse. Freeze, covered, until ready to assemble the dessert.

Infused Red Peaches

300 g (10.58 oz/1¼ cups plus 1 tsp) water

150 g (5.3 oz/½ cup) grenadine syrup

150 g (5.3 oz/⅔ cup) peach schnapps

100 g (3.5 oz/½ cup) granulated sugar

6 g (0.21 oz/2 Tbsp) dried hibiscus flowers

2 g (0.07 oz/1 tsp) ascorbic acid

1 vanilla bean, split lengthwise and seeds scraped

1 star anise

500 g (17.6 oz/4 cups) Parisienne balls scooped from fresh peaches

1. In a saucepan, combine all of the ingredients except the peach balls and bring to a boil over high heat. Reduce the heat and simmer for 5 minutes. Cool completely.

2. Place the syrup and peach balls in vacuum-pack bags and seal. Cook the bags in hot water for 12 minutes. Cool, then chill.

Coconut Dacquoise

300 g (10.58 oz/10 large) egg whites

100 g (3.5 oz/½ cup) granulated sugar

5 g (0.17 oz/scant 1 Tbsp) egg white powder

120 g (4.23 oz/1 cup plus 2 tsp) confectioners' sugar

120 g (4.23 oz/1¼ cups plus 1 Tbsp plus 2½ tsp) almond flour

100 g (3.5 oz/1¼ cups) unsweetened desiccated coconut

2 g (0.07 oz/1 tsp) finely grated lemon zest

1. In the bowl of a stand mixer, stir together the egg whites and granulated sugar and let stand at room temperature for 1 hour to dehydrate.

2. Preheat the oven to 320°F (160°C).

3. Place the bowl with the egg white–sugar mixture in a skillet of barely simmering water and whisk occasionally until warm. Whisk in the egg white powder. Transfer the bowl to the mixer stand and, using the whisk attachment, whip on high speed to firm peaks.

4. In a bowl, sift together the confectioners' sugar, almond flour, and coconut and gently fold into the meringue along with the lemon zest.

5. Draw twelve 4-in- (10-cm-) long barquette shapes on a piece of parchment paper. Turn the paper over and place on a sheet pan. Using the outlines as a guide, pipe out the meringue into barquette shapes and bake for 10 minutes. Cool completely.

Raspberry Tuiles

250 g (8.8 oz/¾ cup) fondant

100 g (3.5 oz/¼ cup plus 2 tsp) glucose syrup

50 g (1.76 oz/½ cup plus 1 tsp) raspberry powder

3 g (0.1 oz/1½ tsp) red powder coloring

1. In a saucepan, combine the fondant and glucose and cook over high heat to 302°F (150°C). Remove from the heat and stir in the raspberry powder and color. Spread the mixture onto a silicone baking mat–lined sheet pan and cool until hardened.

2. Preheat the oven to 320°F (160°C).

3. Break the tuile mixture into pieces and grind in a food processor fitted with the steel blade to a fine powder. Sift the powder over an 8-in- (20.3-cm-) long barquette-shaped stencil, placed on a silicone baking mat–lined sheet pan. Bake for 10 minutes. While still hot, curve the tuiles into a horseshoe shape. Repeat to make 12 tuiles.

Sour Cream Berry Sorbet

250 g (8.8 oz/1 cup plus 1 Tbsp plus 1 tsp) heavy cream
100 g (3.5 oz/½ cup) granulated sugar
60 g (2.1 oz/3 Tbsp) invert sugar
8 g (0.28 oz/2¾ tsp) sorbet stabilizer
600 g (21.16 oz/2½ cups) sour cream
300 g (10.58 oz/1⅓ cups) red berry purée
50 g (1.76 oz/3 Tbsp plus ¾ tsp) freshly squeezed lemon juice

1. In a saucepan, combine the cream, granulated sugar, invert sugar, and sorbet stabilizer and cook over low heat until warm. Remove from the heat and let stand at room temperature for 2 hours.

2. Stir in the sour cream, red berry purée, and lemon juice. Process the mixture in an ice cream machine according to the manufacturer's instructions.

3. Spoon into twelve 1¾-in (7-cm) ring molds and freeze until ready to serve.

Sautéed Peaches

500 g (17.6 oz/about 4 medium peaches) fresh peaches, peeled
500 g (17.6 oz/2½ cups) granulated sugar
2 vanilla beans, split lengthwise and seeds scraped
150 g (5.3 oz/⅔ cup) peach schnapps
100 g (3.5 oz/⅓ cup plus 1 Tbsp plus 2¼ tsp) water
20 g (0.7 oz/1 Tbsp plus 1 tsp) 20-year-old balsamic vinegar

1. Cut the peaches in half, remove the pits, then slice.

2. In a heavy-bottomed saucepan, cook the sugar with the vanilla bean seeds and pods over medium heat, stirring occasionally, until the sugar liquefies and turns a dark amber caramel. Deglaze the caramel with the peach schnapps and water, add the peaches, and sauté until golden. Remove the peach slices and add the balsamic vinegar to the liquid in the pan. Reduce until thickened and reserve to use as a sauce. Remove the vanilla beans and store the sauce and peaches in separate covered containers in the refrigerator until ready to use.

Raspberry Cubes

400 g (14.1 oz/3½ cups) fresh raspberries

100 g (3.5 oz/½ cup) granulated sugar

1 vanilla bean, split lengthwise

100 g (3.5 oz/⅓ cup plus 1 Tbsp plus 2¼ tsp) water

20 g (0.7 oz/1 Tbsp plus 1 tsp) freshly squeezed lemon juice

2 g (0.07 oz/1 tsp) agar agar

1. Combine all of the ingredients, except for the agar agar, in a medium bowl. Let sit at room temperature for at least 3 hours.

2. Place in a double boiler and cook for 15 minutes until all the liquid has seeped out of the berries. Remove the vanilla bean and scrape the seeds into the sauce; discard the pod. Cool the sauce.

3. Strain the cooled sauce into a saucepan. Stir in the agar agar, bring to a boil, and continue to boil for 1 minute. Pour onto a flat sheet pan and refrigerate until firm.

4. Cut into ½-in (1.27-cm) cubes. Refrigerate, covered, until ready to use.

ASSEMBLY

1. Place each Praline Sablé on a dessert plate. Top with a layer of Peach Yogurt Mousse, then a layer of Infused Red Peaches. Top the peaches with the Light Citrus Cake, then a Coconut Dacquoise. Arrange a Raspberry Tuile on top, open end up. Unmold the Sour Cream Berry Sorbets and lay a sorbet on its side on top of each tuile. Garnish each plate with 3 Sautéed Peaches, drizzled with some of the sauce, and garnish with 3 Raspberry Cubes.

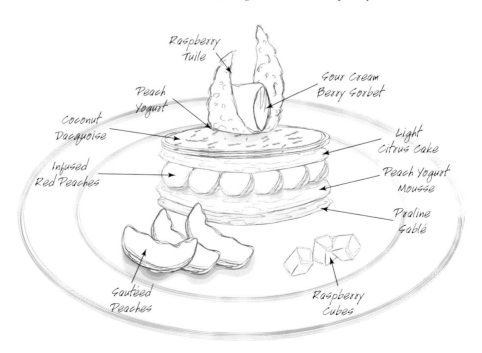

CHOCOLATE-PEAR MOUSSE AND CRÊPE SOUFFLÉ WITH PASSION FRUIT SAUCE

Team Trevethan's plated dessert earned second place at the 2009 National Pastry Team Championship. It artfully combined hot and cold elements, contrasting textures, and several different flavors, including chocolate, pear, raspberry, caramel, coconut, and passion fruit.

MAKES 12 SERVINGS

Chocolate Biscuit

31 g (1.09 oz) bittersweet chocolate (72%)

31 g (1.09 oz/2 Tbsp plus ¾ tsp) unsalted butter

90 g (3.17 oz/1 cup plus 1 tsp) almond flour

30 g (1.05 oz/¼ cup) all-purpose flour

20 g (0.7 oz/1 Tbsp) invert sugar

7 g (0.24 oz/1 Tbsp plus ¾ tsp) cocoa powder

74 g (2.62 oz/4 large) egg yolks

50 g (1.76 oz/1 large) whole egg

40 g (1.4 oz/⅓ cup plus 1½ tsp) confectioners' sugar

120 g (4.23 oz/4 large) egg whites

40 g (1.41 oz/3 Tbsp plus ¾ tsp) granulated sugar

1. Preheat the oven to 390°F (200°C).

2. Melt the chocolate with the butter in a bowl set over a saucepan of barely simmering water.

3. In a separate bowl, combine the almond flour, all-purpose flour, invert sugar, and cocoa powder.

4. In a third bowl, whisk together the egg yolks, whole egg, and confectioners' sugar. Whisk into the dry ingredients, then whisk in the melted chocolate and butter mixture.

5. In the bowl of a stand mixer fitted with the whisk attachment, whip the egg whites on high speed to soft peaks. Gradually add the granulated sugar and whip until stiff and glossy. Fold the beaten egg whites into the chocolate mixture. Spread out the batter in a silicone baking mat–lined sheet pan and bake until set. Unmold and cool completely.

6. Cut out twelve 2-in (5-cm) rounds from the biscuit.

Pear Mousse

112 g (3.9 oz/6 large) egg yolks

90 g (3.16 oz/⅓ cup plus 2 Tbsp plus 1 tsp) granulated sugar

340 g (12 oz/1½ cups) pear purée

30 g (1.06 oz/⅓ cup) nonfat dry milk

1 vanilla bean, split lengthwise and seeds scraped

10 g (0.35 oz/5 sheets) gelatin (silver grade), bloomed and melted

50 g (1.76 oz/¾ cup plus 1½ tsp) pear brandy

80 g (2.8 oz/2⅔ large) egg whites

30 g (1.06 oz/2 Tbsp) water

420 g (14.8 oz/scant 2 cups) heavy cream, whipped to medium peaks

1. In a bowl, whisk together the egg yolks and 30 g (1.06 oz/2 Tbsp plus ½ tsp) of the sugar over simmering water until it reaches 185°F (85°C). Remove from the heat.

2. In a saucepan, combine the pear purée, dry milk, and vanilla bean seeds and pod and bring just to a boil over medium heat. Remove from the heat and fold into the egg yolk–sugar mixture. Fold in the melted gelatin and pear brandy. Remove the vanilla pod.

3. In the bowl of a stand mixer fitted with the whisk attachment, begin whipping the egg whites on medium speed. In a saucepan, combine the water and remaining 60 g (2.1 oz/⅓ cup plus ½ tsp) of the sugar and cook to 245°F (173°C). Add the hot syrup to the beating egg whites in a thin stream and whip on high speed until a cool, stiff, and glossy meringue.

4. Fold the whipped cream into the pear mixture, then fold in the meringue. Refrigerate, covered, until ready to use.

Pâte à Bombe

60 g (2.1 oz/¼ cup plus 2½ tsp) granulated sugar

30 g (1.05 oz/1 Tbsp) water

125 g (4.4 oz/6¾ large) egg yolks

50 g (1.75 oz/1 large) whole egg

1. In a small saucepan, combine the sugar and water and place over medium heat.

2. Meanwhile, in the bowl of a stand mixer fitted with the whisk attachment, begin beating the egg yolks and whole egg on medium speed. When the sugar syrup reaches 248°F (120°C), add it in a slow stream to the beating eggs. Whip on high speed until tripled in volume, about 7 minutes. Prepare the Chocolate-Raspberry Mousse immediately, using the amount of Pâte à Bombe indicated below.

Chocolate-Raspberry Mousse

125 g (4.4 oz) bittersweet chocolate, chopped
270 g (9.5 oz/1 cup plus 2 Tbsp plus 2 tsp) heavy cream, whipped to medium peaks
115 g (4 oz/1 cups plus 2 Tbsp) Pâte à Bombe
5 g (0.17 oz/2½ sheets) gelatin (silver grade), bloomed and drained
50 g (1.76 oz/3 Tbsp plus 1½ tsp) raspberry purée

1. In a bowl set over a pot of barely simmering water (the bottom of the bowl should not touch the water), melt the chocolate. Cool to tepid.

2. Fold one-third of the whipped cream into the Pâte à Bombe. Fold another third of the cream into the melted chocolate. Place the drained gelatin in a small cup and place the cup in hot water, stirring until the gelatin is completely melted. Fold the melted gelatin into the Pâte à Bombe along with the raspberry purée, then fold the mixture into the melted chocolate along with the remaining third of the whipped cream. Refrigerate, covered, until ready to serve.

Caramel Pear Sauce

100 g (3.5 oz/½ cup) granulated sugar
2 pears, peeled, cored, and chopped
Pinch of salt

1. In a heavy-bottomed saucepan, cook the sugar over medium heat, stirring occasionally, until the sugar liquefies and turns a dark amber caramel. Remove from the heat and stir in the chopped pears and salt. Cool, then cover and refrigerate until ready to use.

Pear Gelée

150 g (5.3 oz/½ cup) simple syrup (made with equal parts sugar and water)
Finely grated zest of ½ orange
75 g (2.64 oz/⅓ cup) pear brandy
7 g (0.25 oz/3½ sheets) gelatin (silver grade), bloomed and drained

1. In a saucepan, combine the simple syrup with the orange zest and bring just to a boil over medium-high heat. Remove from the heat and stir in the pear brandy and drained gelatin. Pour the gelée into a hotel pan and chill until set.

2. Cut into small cubes and refrigerate until ready to serve.

Anise Fondant Crunch

120 g (4.2 oz/⅓ cup plus 1 Tbsp) fondant

70 g (2.46 oz/3 Tbsp plus 1 tsp) glucose syrup

0.050 g (0.0016 oz/small pinch) salt

10 g (0.34 oz/2 tsp) unsalted butter

10 g (0.34 oz/2 Tbsp plus 1½ tsp) anise seeds

1. In a saucepan, combine the fondant, glucose, and salt. Bring to a boil over high heat and cook to 315°F (157°C). Remove from the heat, add the butter, and stir until melted. Pour onto a silicone baking mat–lined sheet pan and cool completely.

2. Preheat the oven to 300°F (150°C).

3. When hard, break the fondant into pieces and process in a food processor fitted with the steel blade until finely ground. Sprinkle over a 2 x 1¼-in (5 x 3-cm) rectangular stencil, placed on a silicone baking mat–lined sheet pan, to form 12 shapes and sprinkle the powder with the anise seeds. Bake until melted, about 5 minutes. Cool.

Pear Glaze

430 g (15.16 oz/2 cups plus 2 Tbsp plus 1¼ tsp) granulated sugar

360 g (12.7 oz/1½ cups plus 1 Tbsp) pear purée

1 vanilla bean, split lengthwise and seeds scraped

180 g (6.34 oz/¾ cup) water

25 g (0.88 oz/3 Tbsp plus 1 tsp) cornstarch

13 g (0.47 oz/6 ½ sheets) gelatin (silver grade), bloomed and drained

1. In a heavy-bottomed saucepan, cook the sugar over high heat to 305°F (152°C) the hard-crack stage (see page 10). Deglaze with the pear purée, and add the vanilla bean seeds and pod. In a small bowl, combine the water and cornstarch and stir into the sugar mixture. Cook over medium heat until shiny. Remove from the heat, add the drained gelatin, and stir until dissolved. Remove the vanilla pod and store, covered, in the refrigerator until ready to use.

Crumb Cake

100 g (3.5 oz/¾ stick plus 1 Tbsp) unsalted butter

75 g (2.6 oz/⅓ cup plus 1 Tbsp) granulated sugar

75 g (2.6 oz/¾ cup plus 1 Tbsp plus 2 tsp) almond flour

20 g (0.7 oz/2 Tbsp) cornmeal

0.75 g (0.026 oz/¼ tsp) dry instant yeast

18.6 g (0.65 oz/1 large) egg yolk

½ vanilla bean, split lengthwise and seeds scraped

1 g (0.03 oz/scant ⅛ tsp) salt

100 g (3.5 oz/¾ cup plus 1 Tbsp plus 1 tsp) all-purpose flour

1. In the bowl of a stand mixer fitted with the paddle attachment, blend together the butter, sugar, almond flour, cornmeal, yeast, egg yolk, vanilla bean seeds, and salt on medium speed until combined. Change to the dough hook attachment. Add the all-purpose flour and mix on medium speed until a dough forms. Transfer to a work surface and knead to a smooth dough. Roll into a log, wrap in plastic wrap, and freeze.

2. Preheat the oven to 355°F (180°C).

3. Using the large holes of a box grater, grate the dough evenly onto a silicone baking mat–lined sheet pan. Bake until slightly brown. While still hot, cut into 2-in (5-cm) squares. Cool.

Passion Fruit Sauce

250 g (8.8 oz/1 cup plus 1 Tbsp) water

200 g (7 oz/1 cup) granulated sugar

0.25 g (0.008 oz/small pinch) cream of tartar

240 g (8.46 oz/1 cup) passion fruit purée

90 g (3.17 oz/¾ stick plus 1 tsp) unsalted butter

Seeds and pulp of 2 passion fruits

1. In a saucepan, combine the water, sugar, and cream of tartar and cook over high heat to a light amber caramel. Deglaze with the passion fruit purée and reduce slightly. Whisk in the butter, a tablespoon at a time. Stir in the passion fruit seeds and pulp. Refrigerate, covered, until ready to use.

Coconut and Yogurt Ice Cream

600 g (21.16 oz/2½ cups) cream of coconut

450 g (15.87 oz/2 cups) coconut milk

300 g (10.58 oz/1¼ cups plus 2 tsp) heavy cream

100 g (3.5 oz/¼ cup plus 2¾ tsp) light corn syrup

100 g (3.5 oz/1 cup) nonfat dry milk

100 g (3.5 oz/⅓ cup) invert sugar

10 g (0.35 oz/1 Tbsp plus 1½ tsp) ice cream stabilizer

1.3 kg (45.8 oz/5⅓ cups plus 1 Tbsp) plain nonfat yogurt

30 g (1.05 oz/2 Tbsp) freshly squeezed lemon juice

1. In a saucepan over medium-high heat, combine the cream of coconut, coconut milk, heavy cream, corn syrup, dry milk, invert sugar, and ice cream stabilizer, stirring until hot. Cool completely.

2. Stir in the yogurt and lemon juice. Process the mixture in an ice cream machine according to the manufacturer's instructions. Freeze in an airtight container until ready to serve.

Pastry Cream

500 g (17.6 oz/2 cups plus 1 Tbsp plus 1½ tsp) whole milk

1 vanilla bean, split lengthwise and seeds scraped

111 g (3.93 oz/6 large) egg yolks

100 g (3.5 oz/½ cup) granulated sugar

45 g (1.58 oz/⅓ cup plus 1 Tbsp) cornstarch

20 g (0.7 oz/1 Tbsp plus 2¼ tsp) unsalted butter

1. In a saucepan, combine the milk and vanilla bean seeds and pod and bring to a boil over medium-high heat.

2. In a bowl, whisk together the egg yolks, sugar, and cornstarch. Whisk the hot milk into the egg yolk–sugar mixture to temper the eggs, then return the entire mixture to the saucepan and cook over medium heat, whisking constantly, until the mixture thickens and boils. Remove from the heat and whisk in the butter. Remove the vanilla pod and refrigerate until completely cold.

Chocolate Cacao Nib Garnish

Dark chocolate (64%), tempered

Cacao nibs

1. Using a small plain tip, pipe the tempered chocolate into a 2½-in- (6.3-cm-) long leaf shape on a piece of acetate. Sprinkle with some cacao nibs and allow to set in the bottom of a terrine mold to give it a curved shape. Repeat to make 12 garnishes.

Crêpe Soufflé

756 g (26.67 oz/3 cups plus 2 Tbsp) whole milk

120 g (4.23 oz/1 stick plus 1½ tsp) unsalted butter

223 g (7.86 oz/12 large) egg yolks

120 g (4.2 oz/⅓ cup plus 2 tsp) granulated sugar

120 g (4.23 oz/1 cup) all-purpose flour

360 g (12.7 oz/12 large) egg whites

1 g (0.03 oz/scant ⅛ tsp) salt

1. Preheat the oven to 390°F (200°C).

2. In a saucepan, bring the milk and butter to a boil over medium-high heat, stirring until the butter is melted. Remove from the heat.

3. In a bowl, whisk the egg yolks and 60 g (2.1 oz/¼ cup plus 2½ tsp) of the sugar together until light. Whisk in the flour. Whisk in the milk mixture until well combined.

4. In the bowl of a stand mixer fitted with the whisk attachment, beat the egg whites and salt together on high speed until soft peaks form. Gradually add the remaining 60 g (2.1 oz/¼ cup plus 2½ tsp) sugar and whip to a cool, stiff, and glossy meringue. Fold the meringue into the egg yolk mixture. Spoon the batter into a 3-in (7.6-cm) nonstick crêpe pan and bake until lightly browned on top and puffed, about 5 minutes. Repeat to make 24 Crêpes Soufflés. Serve immediately.

ASSEMBLY

1. Place a Crêpe Soufflé in each small serving dish and pipe a layer of Pastry Cream on top. Top with another Crêpe Soufflé. Spoon some of the Passion Fruit Sauce around each of the crêpes and on top, and place each dish on a dessert plate.

2. Place a Crumb Cake square next to each of the dishes with the crêpes, and top with a quenelle of Coconut and Yogurt Ice Cream. Garnish with one of the Chocolate Cacao Nib leaves.

3. Place a few cubes of Pear Gelée in the bottom of each martini glass. Spoon on some Caramel Pear Sauce and top with a Chocolate Biscuit round. Using a pastry bag fitted with a medium, plain tip, pipe a layer of Chocolate-Raspberry Mousse on top. Fill each glass with the Pear Mousse, then finish with a thin layer of Pear Glaze. Garnish with a few cubes of Pear Gelée and an Anise Fondant Crunch.

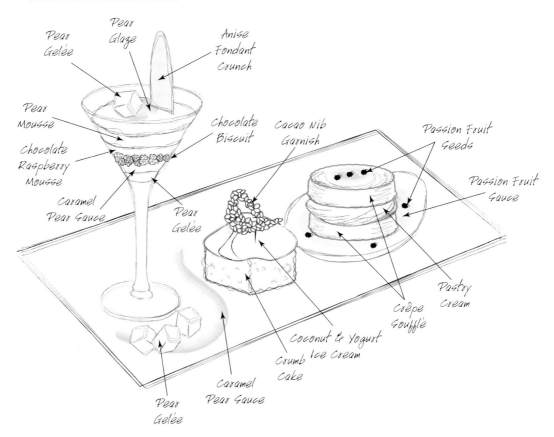

| Kathrine Velin Hansen |
| Nichlas Jamie Frese |
| Mads Kilstrup Kristiansen |

CHILDHOOD BUBBLES

Childhood was the theme for the 2010 WPTC, and Team Denmark's plated dessert that year represented the adolescent fascination with bubble making. The team crafted a bar of soap using a custom-made silicone mold filled with layers of Lemon Panna Cotta, Mango and Passion Fruit Gelée, and Almond Banana Cake. They formed "soap bubbles" out of a Passion Fruit Foam, and made clear Isomalt domes to emulate large blown bubbles. The problem the team faced was that it took 45 minutes just to make the blown bubbles, which didn't leave them much time for the rest of the dessert. But in the heat of the competition, Team Denmark pulled through, coming up with a "clean" favorite.

MAKES 12 SERVINGS

Almond Banana Cake

100 g (3.5 oz/3⅓ large) egg whites

130 g (4.58 oz/⅔ cup) granulated sugar

100 g (3.5 oz/1 cup plus 2 Tbsp plus ½ tsp) almond flour, sifted

30 g (1.05 oz/¼ cup) all-purpose flour

100 g (3.5 oz/1 medium) peeled and sliced bananas

1. Preheat the oven to 390°F (200°C).

2. In the bowl of a stand mixer fitted with the whisk attachment, beat the egg whites on high speed to soft peaks. Gradually add 30 g (1.05 oz/2 Tbsp plus 1¼ tsp) of the sugar and beat on high speed until stiff and glossy. Fold in the remaining 100 g (3.5 oz/½ cup) sugar, almond flour, and all-purpose flour.

3. Spread half of the batter into a 10-in- (25.4-cm-) square x ½-in- (1.27-cm-) high stainless steel frame that is set on a silicone baking mat–lined sheet pan. Top with sliced bananas, then cover with more batter. Bake for about 13 minutes, until set. Unmold and cool.

4. Cut the cake into 3 x 1½-in (7.6 x 3.8-cm) rectangles. Store, covered, at room temperature until ready to use.

Lemon Panna Cotta

240 g (8.46 oz/1 cup plus 1½ tsp) heavy cream

36 g (1.26 oz/2 Tbsp plus 2¾ tsp) granulated sugar

4 g (0.14 oz/2 tsp) finely grated lemon zest

½ vanilla bean, split lengthwise and seeds scraped

2 g (0.07 oz/1 sheet) gelatin (gold grade), bloomed and drained

4 g (0.14 oz/¾ tsp) Grand Marnier

1. In a saucepan, combine the cream, sugar, lemon zest, and vanilla bean seeds and pod. Bring to a boil over high heat, then lower the heat to medium and reduce for 5 minutes. Remove from the heat, add the drained gelatin, and stir until dissolved. Stir in the Grand Marnier. Pass the mixture through a fine-mesh sieve and pour into a squeeze bottle. Pour a 1/6-in (4-mm) layer of panna cotta from the squeeze bottle into each of 12 custom-made 3 x 1½-in (7.6 x 3.8-cm) silicone molds with the word soap imprinted in the bottom. Place in a blast freezer until firm. Reserve the remaining panna cotta in the bottle to use with the Mango and Passion Fruit Gelées.

Mango Gelée

100 g (3.5 oz/⅓ cup plus 2 Tbsp) mango purée

1.3 g (0.04 oz/⅔ sheet) gelatin (gold grade), bloomed and drained

1. In a saucepan, heat the mango purée until hot. Add the drained gelatin and stir until dissolved. Pour the mixture into a squeeze bottle. Pour a ⅛-in (3-mm) layer of gelée on top of the frozen panna cotta layer in each of the molds. Place in the blast freezer until firm.

2. Top this layer with a ⅛-in (3-mm) layer of panna cotta and freeze until firm.

Passion Fruit Gelée

100 g (3.5 oz/⅓ cup plus 2 Tbsp) passion fruit purée

17 g (0.59 oz/1 Tbsp plus 1 tsp) granulated sugar

1.67 g (0.05 oz/¾ sheet) gelatin (gold grade), bloomed and drained

1. In a saucepan, combine the passion fruit purée and sugar and bring to a boil over medium-high heat, stirring to dissolve the sugar. Remove from the heat, add the drained gelatin, and stir until dissolved. Pour the mixture into a squeeze bottle and pour a ⅛-in (3-mm) layer of Passion Fruit Gelée on top of the panna cotta layer in each of the molds. Place in the blast freezer until firm.

2. Top with another ⅛-in (3-mm) layer of panna cotta and freeze until firm.

3. Place a rectangle of Almond Banana Cake on top of each mold and freeze again until firm.

Tuile

155 g (5.46 oz/1¼ cups plus 2 tsp) all-purpose flour

75 g (2.64 oz/⅔ cup) confectioners' sugar

180 g (6.3 oz/6 large) egg whites

125 g (4.4 oz/1 stick plus 2¾ tsp) unsalted butter, melted

1. Sift the flour and sugar into a bowl. Add the egg whites and then the melted butter and whisk just until combined. Cover the bowl and refrigerate for at least 1 hour before using.

2. Preheat the oven to 355°F (180°C).

3. Spread the tuile batter over a bubble-maker, ring-shaped stencil and a 3 x 1-in (7.6 x 2.5-cm) rectangular stencil, placed on a silicone baking mat–lined sheet pan, to make 12 of each shape. Bake until lightly browned around the edges, 7 to 8 minutes. Cool.

Pistachio Dacquoise

70 g (2.46 oz/2⅓ large) egg whites

1.5 g (0.05 oz/¾ tsp) powdered egg whites

26 g (0.91 oz/2 Tbsp) granulated sugar

86 g (3 oz/1 cup) pistachio flour

26 g (0.91 oz/3 Tbsp plus 2 tsp) confectioners' sugar

1. Preheat the oven to 355°F (180°C).

2. In the bowl of a stand mixer fitted with the whisk attachment, beat the egg whites with the powdered egg whites on high speed to soft peaks. Gradually add the granulated sugar and beat on high speed until a stiff and glossy meringue forms.

3. Sift together the pistachio flour and confectioners' sugar and gently fold into the meringue. Transfer the batter to a pastry bag fitted with a medium, plain tip.

4. Pipe the batter into twelve 2½-in (6.3-cm) round, flexible silicone molds and bake until set, 10 to 12 minutes. Cool and unmold.

Lemon and Lime Ice Cream

342 g (12 oz/1¼ cups plus 3 Tbsp plus 1½ tsp) heavy cream (35% butterfat)

230 g (8.1 oz/¾ cup plus 3 Tbsp plus 1 tsp) skim milk

18 g (0.63 oz/1 Tbsp) Trimoline (invert sugar)

83 g (2.92 oz/¾ cup plus 1 Tbsp plus 2½ tsp) nonfat dry milk

35 g (1.23 oz/⅓ cup plus 2½ tsp) glucose powder

138 g (4.86 oz/⅔ cup plus 1 Tbsp) granulated sugar

2.2 g (0.07 oz/1 tsp) ice cream stabilizer

Finely grated zest of 3 lemons

Finely grated zest of 3 limes

75 g (2.6 oz/⅓ cup) freshly squeezed lemon juice

75 g (2.6 oz/⅓ cup) freshly squeezed lime juice

1. In a saucepan, combine the cream, milk, Trimoline, dry milk, and glucose and place over medium heat until the mixture registers 113°F (45°C) on a thermometer. Stir in the sugar and ice cream stabilizer and heat to 185°F (85°C). Remove the pan from the heat and stir in the lemon and lime zests. Chill the mixture in an ice bath. Cover the bowl and let mature in the refrigerator for at least 4 hours.

2. Strain the base through a fine-mesh sieve and stir in the lemon and lime juices. Process in an ice cream machine according to the manufacturer's instructions.

3. Place a dacquoise round in the bottom of each of twelve 2½-in (6.3-cm) ring molds and fill the molds with ice cream. Freeze until set.

4. Unmold and place in the freezer until ready to plate.

Passion Fruit Foam

200 g (7 oz/¾ cup plus 2 Tbsp) passion fruit purée

75 g (2.6 oz/⅓ cup plus 1 Tbsp) granulated sugar

30 g (1.05 oz/2 Tbsp) water

3 g (0.1 oz/1½ tsp) lecithin

1. Combine all of the ingredients and, just before plating, mix with an immersion blender until foamy.

Isomalt Bubbles

1 kg (35.27 oz/5 cups) Isomalt

100 g (3.5 oz/⅓ cup plus 1 Tbsp plus 2¼ tsp) water

1. In a saucepan, combine the Isomalt and water over high heat and cook to 333°F (168°C). Pour onto a silicone baking mat, and let stand until cool enough to handle with gloves.

2. Using a bulb pump, form blown sugar domes from the sugar. The domes should be about 4 in (10 cm) in diameter. Remove each bubble from the tube and seal the hole.

ASSEMBLY

1. Unmold each frozen soap bar onto a piece of Plexiglas and allow to thaw in the refrigerator.

2. Arrange each Lemon Panna Cotta dessert on a plate and place a rectangular Tuile against each of the long sides of the rectangle. Spoon some Passion Fruit Foam next to each bar.

3. Arrange a Lemon and Lime Ice Cream dessert next to each bar. Place an Isomalt Bubble over it. Spoon some of the Passion Fruit Foam around each bubble, and lean the bubble-maker ring tuile on top.

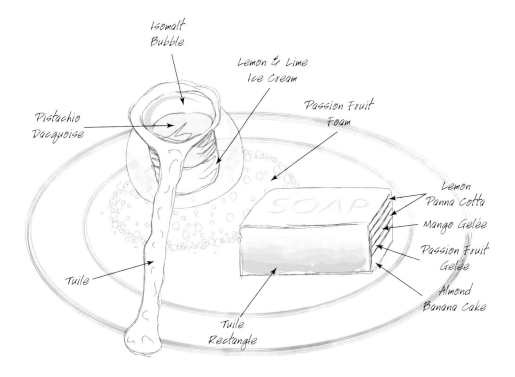

| Takao Yamamoto |
| Yoshiaki Miyake |
| Hiroshi Igarashi |

ADVENTURE

Molten chocolate cake, ubiquitous on menus in restaurants across America, was considered by many to be a risky choice for a plated dessert at the 2010 WPTC, but Team Japan's multicomponent rendition turned out to be a real winner. Set on a round of Flourless Chocolate Biscuit, the cake was poised above a layered dessert made of Hazelnut Dacquoise, Raspberry Semi-Confit, and Hazelnut Milk Chocolate Cream. It was placed so that the liquid chocolate interior of the chocolate cake would converge with the other elements when the diner spooned into it. With this show-stopping dessert, Team Japan proved that with creativity and skill, even an old favorite can be remade into something truly special. **MAKES 12 SERVINGS**

Cristaline

438 g (15.44 oz/1⅓ cups plus 1 Tbsp) fondant

85 g (3 oz/¼ cup) glucose syrup

85 g (3 oz/⅓ cup plus 2 Tbsp) Isomalt

1. In a saucepan, combine all of the ingredients and cook over high heat to 310°F (155°C). Pour onto a silicone baking mat and cool completely.

2. Preheat the oven to 320°F (160°C).

3. Grind the Cristaline into a powder in a food processor and spread over a 5 x 3-in (12.7 x 7.6-cm) rectangular stencil, placed on a silicone baking mat–lined sheet pan, to form 12 rectangles.

4. Heat the Cristaline in the oven until melted, 3 to 5 minutes. While warm, form each rectangle into a tube shape by bringing the long sides together.

Raspberry Espuma

480 g (16.93 oz/1½ cups plus 1 Tbsp) raspberry purée

36 g (1.26 oz/2 Tbsp plus 1½ tsp) water

36 g (1.26 oz/2 Tbsp plus 1 tsp) freshly squeezed lime juice

10 g (0.35 oz/2¾ tsp) granulated sugar

8 g (0.28 oz/1½ tsp) kirsch

55 g (1.94 oz/⅓ cup) stabilizer

1. Mix all of the ingredients together except for the stabilizer.

2. Add the stabilizer and emulsify with an immersion blender.

3. Pour the raspberry mixture into a siphon and charge with a N_2O cartridge.

Hazelnut Dacquoise

162 g (5.7 oz/5½ large) egg whites

72 g (2.53 oz/⅓ cup plus 2¼ tsp) granulated sugar

116 g (4 oz/1 cup) confectioners' sugar

94 g (3.31 oz/1 cup plus 1 Tbsp) hazelnut flour

27 g (0.95 oz/3 Tbsp plus 2 tsp) all-purpose flour

1. Preheat the oven to 355°F (180°C).

2. In the bowl of an electric mixer fitted with the whisk attachment, beat the egg whites at high speed, gradually adding the granulated sugar, beating until medium peaks form. Sift together the confectioners' sugar, hazelnut flour, and all-purpose flour and gently fold into the meringue.

3. Spread out the batter in a silicone baking mat–lined sheet pan and bake for 14 minutes. Cool completely.

Hazelnut Milk Chocolate Cream

142 g (5 oz) milk chocolate, chopped

47 g (1.65 oz/2 Tbsp plus 1½ tsp) hazelnut paste

64 g (2.25 oz/¼ cup plus 1¼ tsp) heavy cream (35% butterfat)

4 g (0.14 oz/2 sheets) gelatin (silver grade), bloomed and drained

295 g (10.4 oz/1¼ cups plus 1 tsp) heavy cream (35% butterfat), whipped

1. Place the chopped milk chocolate in a large bowl; add the hazelnut paste.

2. In a saucepan over medium-high heat, bring the cream to a gentle boil. Pour the hot cream over the milk chocolate and hazelnut paste in the bowl and whisk until smooth.

3. Add the drained gelatin and whisk until dissolved. Cool until tepid, then gently fold in the whipped cream.

4. Pour the Hazelnut Milk Chocolate Cream over the dacquoise and freeze until firm.

Raspberry Semi-Confit

90 g (3.17 oz/⅓ cup plus 2 Tbsp plus ¾ tsp) granulated sugar

2.5 g (0.08 oz/¾ tsp) powdered pectin

300 g (10.58 oz/2⅔ cups) IQF raspberries

5 g (0.17 oz/1 tsp) kirsch

1. Mix a small quantity of the sugar with the pectin.

2. In a saucepan, combine the raspberries with the remaining sugar and place the pan over medium heat. Stir in the pectin mixture and bring to a boil, stirring. Remove from the heat and stir in the kirsch. Set aside, covered, at cool room temperature until ready to use.

Flourless Chocolate Biscuit

69 g (2.43 oz/¾ cup plus 1½ tsp) almond flour

69 g (2.43 oz/½ cup plus 1 Tbsp plus 2 tsp) confectioners' sugar

62 g (2.18 oz/⅔ cup) cocoa powder

150 g (5.3 oz/8 large) egg yolks

450 g (15.87 oz/15 large) egg whites

225 g (7.9 oz/1 cup plus 2 Tbsp) granulated sugar

1. Preheat the oven to 395°F (202°C).

2. In a bowl, whisk together the almond flour, confectioners' sugar, cocoa powder, egg yolks, and 225 g (7.93 oz/7½ large) of the egg whites.

3. In the bowl of a stand mixer fitted with the whisk attachment, whip the remaining 225 g (7.93 oz/7½ large) of the egg whites on high speed to soft peaks. Gradually add the granulated sugar and whip on high speed until it forms a stiff and glossy meringue. Fold the meringue into the egg yolk–sugar mixture.

4. Spread out the batter in a silicone baking mat–lined sheet pan and bake for 12 minutes, or until set. Unmold and cool completely.

Milk Chocolate Ganache

441 g (15.5 oz) milk chocolate, chopped

168 g (5.9 oz/⅔ cup plus 1 Tbsp plus 1 tsp) water

105 g (3.7 oz/⅓ cup plus 2 Tbsp plus ¾ tsp) heavy cream (35% butterfat)

63 g (2.22 oz/½ stick plus 1½ tsp) unsalted butter, softened

1. Place the chopped milk chocolate in a large bowl and set aside.

2. In a saucepan, combine the water and cream over high heat and bring to a boil. Pour it over the chopped chocolate in the bowl and whisk to emulsify.

3. Whisk in the butter. Pour into twelve 1-in (2.5-cm) round, flexible silicone molds and freeze.

Moelleux Chocolat

297 g (10.47 oz) bittersweet chocolate (70%)

135 g (4.76 oz/1 stick plus 1 Tbsp plus 1½ tsp) unsalted butter

108 g (3.8 oz/5¾ large) egg yolks

243 g (8.57 oz/1 cup plus 3 Tbsp plus 1½ tsp) granulated sugar

108 g (3.8 oz/1¼ cups) almond flour

162 g (5.7 oz/5½ large) egg whites

113 g (3.98 oz/¾ cup plus 3 Tbsp) rice flour

1. Preheat the oven to 330°F (166°C).

2. Melt the chocolate and butter together in a bowl set over a saucepan of barely simmering water.

3. Whisk together the egg yolks and 27 g (0.95 oz/2 Tbsp plus ½ tsp) of the sugar. Whisk the egg yolk–sugar mixture and the almond flour into the melted chocolate.

4. In the bowl of a stand mixer fitted with the whisk attachment, beat the egg whites on high speed to soft peaks. Gradually add the remaining 216 g (7.6 oz/1 cup plus 1 Tbsp plus 1 tsp) sugar and beat on high speed until a stiff and glossy meringue forms. Fold the meringue into the chocolate mixture. Fold in the rice flour.

5. Transfer the mixture to a pastry bag fitted with a medium, plain tip. Pipe the Moelleux Chocolat into twelve 3-in (7.6-cm) cake rings to half the height of the ring. Place a frozen milk chocolate ganache round in the center, then fill each mold with the batter. Bake for about 20 minutes, until set.

Vanilla Ice Cream

500 g (17.63 oz/2 cups plus 1 Tbsp) whole milk

100 g (3.5 oz/⅓ cup plus 2 Tbsp) heavy cream (35% butterfat)

2 Bourbon vanilla beans, split lengthwise and seeds scraped

100 g (3.5 oz/5⅓ large) egg yolks

80 g (2.82 oz/⅓ cup plus 1 Tbsp plus 1¼ tsp) granulated sugar

30 g (1.05 oz/2 Tbsp plus 1¼ tsp) invert sugar

3 g (0.1 oz/1 tsp) ice cream stabilizer

21 g (0.74 oz/1 Tbsp plus 1½ tsp) kirsch

1. In a saucepan, combine the milk, cream, and vanilla bean pods and seeds over medium-high heat and bring to a gentle boil. Remove from heat, cover, and allow to infuse for 20 minutes.

2. In a bowl, whisk together the egg yolks, granulated sugar, invert sugar, and ice cream stabilizer. Reheat the milk until hot. Whisk half of the hot milk mixture into the yolk mixture, then return the entire mixture to the saucepan and cook, stirring constantly with a wooden spoon, until the mixture thickens and reaches 175°F (80°C). Strain the mixture into a bowl, then cool in an ice bath.

3. Stir in the kirsch and process the mixture in an ice cream machine according to the manufacturer's instructions.

4. Spread a layer of the ice cream over the Hazelnut Milk Chocolate Cream and freeze until firm.

ASSEMBLY

Bittersweet chocolate plaquettes
Chopped pistachios

1. Top the Vanilla Ice Cream layer with a layer of Raspberry Semi-Confit and freeze until firm.

2. Cut the layered Hazelnut Dacquoise into 5 x 1-in (12.7 x 2.5-cm) rectangles. Cut the layered Hazelnut Milk Chocolate Cream component into rectangles of the same size. Fill each Cristaline tube with Raspberry Espuma. Place each of the dacquoise rectangles on a serving plate and top with a rectangle and a Cristaline tube. Sprinkle with chopped pistachios. Place a chocolate plaquette at each short end of the rectangle.

3. Cut out 3-in (7.6-cm) rounds from the Flourless Chocolate Biscuit. Set one next to each dessert rectangle on the plate and top with a Moelleux Chocolat.

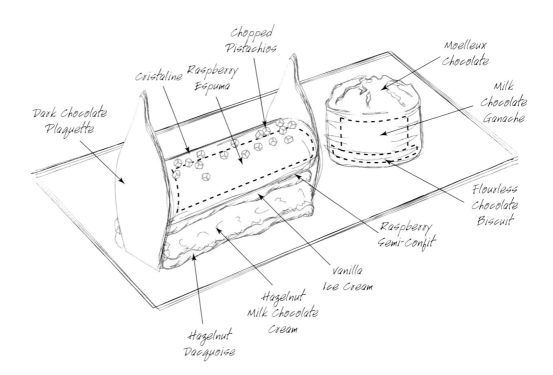

Oscar Ortega

Mirko Bucci

Alejandro Lechuga

SPICED COCO

Mexicans were the first to combine chili with chocolate, so it's no surprise that Team Mexico's plated dessert for the 2010 WPTC features a flourless chocolate cake enlivened with Pasilla chile powder. A creamy vanilla and chocolate flavored pudding tops the cake, along with a tube of Hazelnut Praline Chocolate Mousse, which has been sprayed with red-tinted cocoa butter. A scoop of spicy-sweet Strawberry and Green Peppercorn Gelato accompanies this lively dessert.

MAKES 12 SERVINGS

Spiced Cocoa Flourless Cake

600 g (21.16 oz/2½ cups) pasteurized egg whites

200 g (7 oz/1 cup) granulated sugar

700 g (24.69 oz) bittersweet chocolate (64%), melted

240 g (8.46 oz/2 sticks plus 1 Tbsp) unsalted butter

280 g (9.87 oz/1 cup plus 1 Tbsp plus 1½ tsp) pasteurized egg yolks

20 g (0.7 oz/2 Tbsp) Pasilla chile powder

1. Preheat the oven to 355°F (180°C).

2. In the bowl of a stand mixer fitted with the whisk attachment, whip the egg whites on high speed to soft peaks. Gradually add the sugar and whip on high speed until a stiff and glossy meringue forms.

3. In a bowl set over a saucepan of barely simmering water, melt the chocolate and butter together, stirring to blend. In a bowl, stir together the egg yolks and chili powder. Gently stir the yolks into the chocolate mixture. Fold in the meringue.

4. Spread out the batter in a parchment paper–lined sheet pan and bake until set, about 15 minutes. Cool.

Hazelnut Praline Chocolate Mousse

75 g (2.64 oz/⅓ cup plus 1 Tbsp) granulated sugar

50 g (1.76 oz/3 Tbsp plus 1 tsp) water

115 g (4 oz/about 6 large) egg yolks

100 g (3.5 oz) Mexique chocolate (66%), chopped

100 g (3.5 oz) Tanzania bittersweet chocolate, chopped

280 g (9.87 oz/1 cup plus 2 Tbsp plus 1½ tsp) heavy cream

60 g (2.1 oz/3 Tbsp) hazelnut praline paste

8 g (0.28 oz/4 sheets) gelatin (gold grade), bloomed and drained

280 g (9.8 oz/1 cup plus 2 Tbsp plus 1½ tsp) heavy cream, whipped

Red tinted cocoa butter, as needed

1. In a saucepan, combine the sugar and water over high heat and bring to a boil. Continue to boil until the mixture reaches 248°F (120°C).

2. Meanwhile, in the bowl of a stand mixer fitted with the whisk attachment, begin beating the egg yolks on medium speed. When the sugar syrup reaches 248°F (120°C), drizzle it onto the egg yolks and beat on high speed for 3 to 5 minutes, until it forms a firm, yellow foam, to form a pâte à bombe.

3. In a large bowl, combine the chocolates.

4. In a saucepan, bring the heavy cream and hazelnut praline paste to a gentle boil over medium-high heat. Remove from the heat and pour over the chocolates in the bowl, add the drained gelatin, and whisk to emulsify. Fold the pâte à bombe into the chocolate mixture, then gently fold in the whipped cream.

5. Transfer the mousse to a pastry bag fitted with a medium, plain tip. Pipe into twelve 1-in (2.5-cm) diameter x 7-in- (17.8-cm-) long PVC tubes that have been lined with acetate and freeze.

6. Unmold the mousses and spray with red cocoa butter. Store in the freezer until ready to serve.

Vanilla-Chocolate Pudding

80 g (2.8 oz/4 large) egg yolks

100 g (3.5 oz/½ cup) granulated sugar

500 g (17.63 oz/2 cups) heavy cream

7 Mexican vanilla beans, split lengthwise

160 g (5.64 oz) dark chocolate (60%), chopped

1. In a bowl, whisk together the egg yolks with the sugar until light.

2. In a saucepan, combine half of the cream with the vanilla beans and bring to a boil over medium-high heat. Whisk about half of the cream into the yolks and then return the entire mixture to the saucepan and cook over medium-high heat, stirring constantly, until thickened. Remove from the heat.

3. Place the chocolate in a bowl and pour the cream mixture through a fine-mesh sieve over the chocolate. Whisk until the chocolate is melted and the mixture is emulsified. Cool until tepid.

4. In the bowl of a stand mixer fitted with the whisk attachment, whip the remaining cream on high speed to medium peaks. Gently fold into the cooled chocolate mixture. Cover and refrigerate until ready to use.

Strawberry and Green Peppercorn Gelato

330 g (11.64 oz/2 cups plus 1 Tbsp) glucose powder

125 g (4.4 oz/1 cup plus 1 Tbsp plus 1¼ tsp) confectioners' sugar

12 g (0.42 oz/1 Tbsp plus 2¼ tsp) ice cream stabilizer

750 g (26.45 oz/3 cups plus 1 Tbsp plus 1½ tsp) whole milk

75 g (2.64 oz/¾ cup) nonfat dry milk

330 g (11.64 oz/1⅓ cups plus 1 Tbsp plus 2¼ tsp) heavy cream

600 g (21.16 oz/2⅔ cups) strawberry purée

15 g (0.53 oz/1 Tbsp) wild strawberry compound

8 g (0.28 oz/1 Tbsp) whole fresh green peppercorns, ground

1. In a bowl, combine the glucose powder, sugar, and ice cream stabilizer.

2. Place the milk in a saucepan and place over low heat until it registers 80°F (26°C) on a thermometer. Stir in the dry milk. Heat to 95°F (34°C), then add the cream and stabilizer mixture. Bring the mixture to 185°F (85°C) and cook for 2 minutes. Cool the mixture down rapidly. Add the strawberry purée, wild strawberry compound, and ground green peppercorns and mix with an immersion blender.

3. Process the mixture in an ice cream machine according to the manufacturer's instructions.

4. Press the ice cream into twelve 2¼-in (5.7-cm) full-sphere, flexible, silicone molds and freeze until ready to serve.

Orange Tuile

100 g (3.5 oz/¾ cup plus 2 Tbsp) confectioners' sugar, sifted

40 g (1.41 oz/2 Tbsp plus 2 tsp) freshly squeezed orange juice

35 g (1.23 oz/2 Tbsp 1½ tsp) unsalted butter, at room temperature

55 g (1.94 oz/⅓ cup plus 2 Tbsp plus 1 tsp) all-purpose flour

1. Preheat the oven to 180°F (82°C).

2. In a bowl, stir together the sugar and orange juice. Add the butter and mix until blended. Stir in the flour.

3. Spread out the batter in a silicone baking mat–lined sheet pan and bake until just beginning to turn golden around the edges. Cool and then break into irregular 3-in (7.6-cm) pieces.

Raspberry Fluid Gel

250 g (8.8 oz/1 cup plus 1 Tbsp plus 1 tsp) raspberry purée

200 g (7 oz/¾ cup plus 2 Tbsp) apricot purée

4 g (0.14 oz/1¼ tsp) xanthan gum

75 g (2.6 oz/3 Tbsp plus 1½ tsp) glucose syrup

25 g (0.88 oz/2 Tbsp) granulated sugar

3 g (0.1 oz/1½ sheets) gelatin (gold grade), bloomed and melted

1. Make this element just before plating. In a saucepan, stir together the raspberry and apricot purées. Add the xanthan gum and stir to dissolve. Stir in the glucose and sugar and place the pan over high heat until the mixture comes to a boil. Remove from the heat and cool to 100°F (38°C). Stir in the melted gelatin. Emulsify with an immersion blender. Use immediately to garnish the plates.

ASSEMBLY

Chocolate cups for serving ice cream
Chocolate loop for garnish
Candied kiwi

1. Cut the Spiced Cocoa Flourless Cake into 5 x 2-in (12.7 x 5-cm) rectangles. Arrange each of the cakes on a serving plate. Using a pastry bag fitted with a medium, plain tip, pipe dollops of the Vanilla-Chocolate Pudding over each rectangle, covering it completely. Cut a tube of Hazelnut Praline Chocolate Mousse to fit the cake rectangle and place on top of the pudding.

2. Place a sphere of the Strawberry and Green Peppercorn Gelato in each chocolate cup and arrange one on each plate. Top with an Orange Tuile. Pipe a few dots of the Raspberry Fluid Gel onto each plate and garnish with a chocolate loop and a piece of candied kiwi.

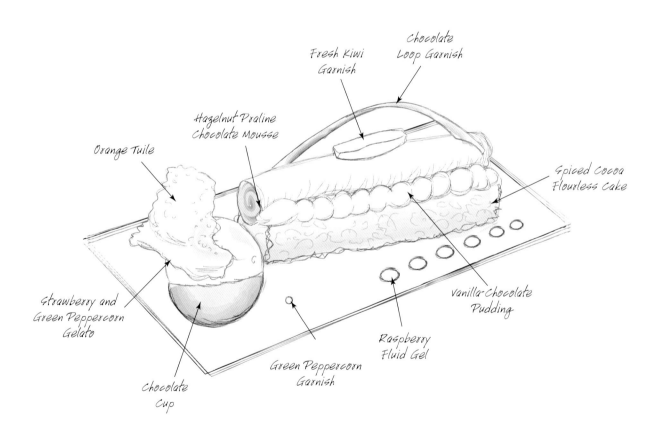

Jaycent Lau Tse Kwang

Alex Chong Chi Hung

Tai Chien Lin

ROSEBUD CRÈME BRÛLÉE

WITH STRAWBERRY JELLY AND CHAMPAGNE ROSÉ SORBET

The minimalist presentation of Team Singapore's plated dessert for the 2010 World Championship belies a sophisticated blend of flavors. Layers of Strawberry Jelly and a Champagne Rosé Sorbet top a delicate, rose-infused crème brûlée, all wrapped up in a pretty band of pink-tinted white chocolate. The difficulty in presenting this dessert is its tricky timing; it's important that the sorbet does not melt and collapse before the dessert is encased in its white chocolate cylinder. The team had some problems with this during run-throughs, but, happily, got it just right the day of the competition.

MAKES 12 SERVINGS

Brown Sugar Sablé

75 g (2.64 oz/½ stick plus 1⅓ Tbsp plus 1 tsp) unsalted butter

38 g (1.34 oz/2 Tbsp plus 2¾ tsp packed) brown sugar

0.2 g (0.007 oz/pinch) salt

6 g (0.21 oz/⅓ large) egg yolk

75 g (2.64 oz/⅔ cup) all-purpose flour

1. In the bowl of a stand mixer fitted with the paddle attachment, cream the butter and sugar together on high speed until pale. Add the salt and egg yolk and beat until combined. Add the flour and mix until blended. Shape the dough into a disk, wrap in plastic wrap, and let rest in the refrigerator for 2 hours.

2. Preheat the oven to 355°F (180°C).

3. Roll the dough out to a thickness of 0.08 in (2 mm) and cut out 3-in (7.6-cm) rounds. Place on a silicone baking mat–lined sheet pan and bake until golden. Cool completely.

Rosebud Crème Brûlée

370 g (13 oz/1½ cups plus 1 Tbsp 1½ tsp) heavy cream

246 g (8.67 oz/1 cup plus 2 Tbsp) whole milk

20 g (0.7 oz/½ cup) organic rosebuds

246 g (8.67 oz/13 large) egg yolks

124 g (4.37 oz/⅔ cup) granulated sugar

20 g (0.7 oz/1 Tbsp) rose syrup

1. In a saucepan over low heat, heat the cream and milk to 140°F (60°C). Add the rosebuds, cover, and allow to infuse for 30 minutes.

2. Preheat the oven to 250°F (122°C).

3. In the bowl of a stand mixer fitted with the whisk attachment, beat the egg yolks and sugar on high speed until pale and light. Strain the cream mixture and whisk into the egg yolk–sugar mixture along with the rose syrup. Pour into twelve 3-in (7.6-cm) round, flexible silicone molds and bake in a water bath for about 1 hour, until set. Cool, then chill.

Champagne Rosé Sorbet

260 g (9.17 oz/1⅔ cups) glucose powder

210 g (7.4 oz/1 cup plus 2¾ tsp) granulated sugar

6 g (0.21 oz/2 tsp) sorbet stabilizer

380 g (13.4 oz/1½ cups plus 1 Tbsp plus 2¼ tsp) water

630 g (22.22 oz/2¾ cups) rosé Champagne

120 g (4.23 oz/½ cup) Mara des Bois strawberry purée

1. In a saucepan, combine the glucose powder, sugar, and sorbet stabilizer. Add the water and bring to a boil over high heat. Remove from the heat and blend with an immersion blender. Cool.

2. Stir in the Champagne and purée. Allow to mature in the refrigerator for 2 hours.

3. Blend with an immersion blender and process in an ice cream machine according to the manufacturer's instructions.

Caramelized Rice Krispies

70 g (2.46 oz/⅓ cup plus 2 tsp) granulated sugar

24 g (0.84 oz/1 Tbsp plus 2 tsp) mineral water

50 g (1.76 oz/¾ cup) Rice Krispies cereal

4 g (0.14 oz/1 tsp) unsalted butter

1. In a saucepan over high heat, cook the sugar and water to 220°F (104°C). Add the Rice Krispies and stir until the mixture is caramelized.

2. Remove from the stove, add the butter, and pour onto a silicone mat placed on a cold marble table. Cool completely.

3. Store in an airtight plastic container with silica gel.

Strawberry Jelly

220 g (7.7 oz/¾ cup) strawberry juice

30 g (1.05 oz/2 Tbsp plus 1¼ tsp) granulated sugar

4 g (0.14 oz/2 sheets) gelatin (silver grade), bloomed and drained

1. In a saucepan over low heat, warm the strawberry juice with the sugar. Add the drained gelatin and stir to dissolve. Pour into a shallow pan and refrigerate until set.

Strawberry Foam

280 g (9.87 oz/1¼ cups) Mara des Bois strawberry purée

5 g (0.17 oz/2 Tbsp) organic rosebuds

70 g (2.47 oz/¾ cup) chewy strawberry candy (preferably Haribo Tagada brand)

30 g (1.05 oz/2 Tbsp plus 1¼ tsp) granulated sugar

6 g (0.21 oz/3 sheets) gelatin (silver grade), bloomed and drained

1. In a saucepan, combine the strawberry purée and rosebuds and bring to a boil over medium-high heat. Remove from the heat, cover, and allow to infuse for 20 minutes.

2. Add the strawberry candy and sugar to the purée and heat until both are dissolved. Remove from the heat, add the drained gelatin, and stir until dissolved. Strain the mixture through a fine-mesh sieve and pour into the bowl of a stand mixer fitted with the whisk attachment. Just before serving, beat on high speed for 20 minutes, until foamy.

ASSEMBLY

Twelve 3¼-in (8.2-cm) pink-tinted white chocolate cylinders
Gold leaf for garnish

1. Arrange each Brown Sugar Sablé on a plate. Top with a Rosebud Crème Brûlée.

2. Top each crème brûlée layer with 12 pieces of the Caramelized Rice Krispies, pressing gently to stick the Rice Krispies into the crème brûlée. Top each crème brûlée layer with a 3-in (7.6-cm) round of Strawberry Jelly. Top with a layer of Champagne Rosé Sorbet.

3. Slide a prepared pink-tinted white chocolate cylinder over each stack of layers.

4. Add 12 more pieces of Caramelized Rice Krispies and another round of Strawberry Jelly to each dessert. Top with Strawberry Foam, and garnish with gold leaf.

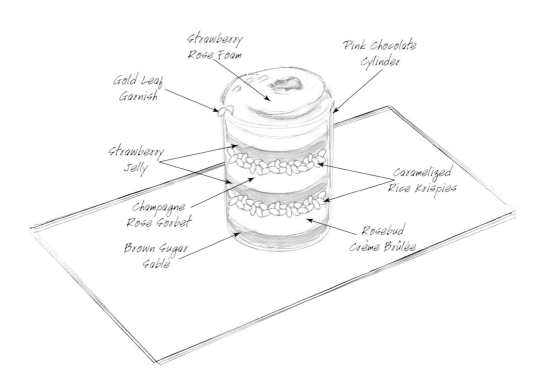

Strawberry Rose Foam

Pink Chocolate Cylinder

Gold Leaf Garnish

Strawberry Jelly

Caramelized Rice Krispies

Champagne Rose Sorbet

Rosebud Crème Brûlée

Brown Sugar Sablé

| Kim, Deok-Kyu |
| Oh, Byung-Ho |
| Ryoo, Jae-Eun |

LE BLANC

A bright yellow orb of caramel-filled, lemon-orange pudding is the focal point of Team South Korea's plated dessert for the 2010 WPTC. Sitting on a honey and walnut base, the simple pudding is accompanied by a red wine and berry compote and a lacy cookie garnish.

MAKES 12 SERVINGS

Honey-Walnut Base

75 g (2.64 oz/½ stick plus 1⅓ Tbsp plus 1 tsp) unsalted butter, softened

75 g (2.64 oz/3 Tbsp plus 1½ tsp) honey

62 g (2.18 oz/½ cup plus 1 tsp) all-purpose flour

170 g (6 oz/1¾ cups) walnuts, finely chopped

1. Preheat the oven to 350°F (175°C).

2. In a bowl, mix together the butter and honey until blended. Stir in the flour and walnuts and mix until blended.

3. Spread out the batter thinly in a silicone baking mat–lined sheet pan. Bake until set, about 7 minutes. While warm, cut into rough 3-in (7.6-cm) rounds and cool completely.

Berry Compote

150 g (5.3 oz/⅔ cup) red wine

100 g (3.5 oz/½ cup) granulated sugar

1 cinnamon stick

1 lemon, halved

15 g (0.53 oz/2 Tbsp) cornstarch

50 g (1.76 oz/3 Tbsp plus 1 tsp) water

358 g (12.62 oz/2½ cups) fresh blueberries

150 g (5.3 oz/1⅓ cups) fresh raspberries

60 g (2.11 oz/½ cup) fresh blackberries

50 g (1.76 oz/scant ½ cup) fresh strawberries, hulled

1. In a saucepan, combine the red wine with the sugar, cinnamon stick, and lemon over high heat and bring to a boil.

2. In a small bowl, stir together the cornstarch and water, add to the red wine mixture, and stir to dissolve; let boil for 1 minute. Add the blueberries, raspberries, blackberries, and strawberries and boil for 2 minutes longer. Taste and adjust the sweetness, if necessary. Cool, then refrigerate, covered, until ready to serve.

Le Blanc

150 g (5.3 oz/1 stick plus 2 Tbsp plus 1½ tsp) unsalted butter

150 g (5.3 oz/⅔ cup) freshly squeezed orange juice

50 g (1.76 oz/3 Tbsp plus ¾ tsp) freshly squeezed lemon juice

150 g (5.3 oz/¾ cup) granulated sugar

74 g (2.61 oz/4 large) egg yolks

6 g (0.21 oz/3 sheets) gelatin (silver grade), bloomed and drained

350 g (12.34 oz/1½ cups) heavy cream

30 g (1.05 oz/2 Tbsp) Cointreau

1. In a saucepan, combine the butter, orange juice, and lemon juice and bring to a boil over medium-high heat, stirring until the butter is melted.

2. In a bowl, whisk together the sugar and egg yolks until pale. Whisk half of the hot citrus juice into the mixture, then return the entire mixture to the saucepan. Cook, stirring constantly, until the mixture is thickened and reaches 175°F (80°C) on a thermometer. Remove from the heat, add the drained gelatin, and stir until dissolved. Strain the mixture through a fine-mesh sieve into a bowl and cool in an ice bath.

3. In the bowl of a stand mixer fitted with the whisk attachment, beat the cream with the Cointreau on high speed to medium peaks. Gently fold the whipped cream into the cooled orange mixture.

4. Spread the mixture into twelve 2¾-in (7-cm) flexible, silicone demisphere molds, leaving an indentation in the center. Freeze until set.

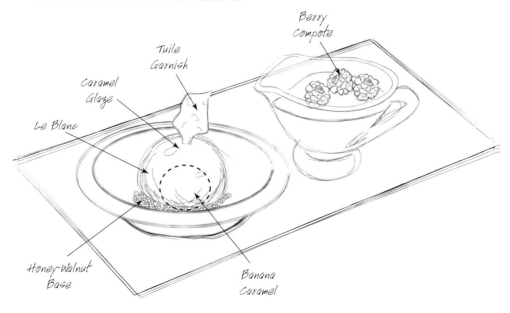

Banana Caramel

100 g (3.5 oz/½ cup) granulated sugar

1 g (0.03 oz/pinch) salt

200 g (7 oz/¾ cup plus 2 Tbsp) passion fruit purée, warm

450 g (15.87 oz/4½ medium) bananas, cut into ¼-in (6.3-mm) cubes

6 g (0.21 oz/3 sheets) gelatin (silver grade), bloomed and drained

1. In a saucepan, combine the sugar and salt and cook over high heat to the caramel stage (see page 10). Add the warm passion fruit purée and cubed bananas and stir to combine. Add the drained gelatin and stir to dissolve.

2. Pour the caramel into the demisphere molds with the Le Blanc mixture in them, filling them completely. Freeze until set.

Caramel Glaze

140 g (4.93 oz/⅔ cup plus 1 Tbsp plus ¾ tsp) granulated sugar

250 g (8.81 oz/1 cup plus 1 Tbsp) mango purée

175 g (6.17 oz/¾ cup) water

70 g (2.46 oz/3 Tbsp plus 1½ tsp) starch syrup

4 g (0.14 oz/2 sheets) gelatin (silver grade), bloomed and drained

1. In a saucepan, combine the sugar, mango purée, water, and starch syrup and bring to a boil over medium-high heat. Add the drained gelatin and stir until dissolved. Set aside, covered, at room temperature, until ready to use. Rewarm in the microwave, if necessary, before using.

Tuile Garnish

10 g (0.35 oz/1 Tbsp plus 1 tsp) all-purpose flour

100 g (3.5 oz/⅓ cup plus 2 Tbsp plus 1½ tsp) extra-virgin olive oil

90 g (3.17 oz/⅓ cup plus 1 Tbsp) water

1. In a bowl, stir together the flour, olive oil, and water.

2. Heat a nonstick skillet over medium-high heat and drizzle the batter in a free-form lace pattern onto the hot skillet. Cook until light golden brown and remove with a spatula to a wire rack to cool. Repeat to make 12 garnishes.

ASSEMBLY

1. Unmold the Le Blanc demispheres and place on a wire rack, placed on a sheet pan. Glaze with the Caramel Glaze. Place each Honey-Walnut Base on a plate and top with a glazed dessert. Top with the Tuile Garnish.

2. Serve the Berry Compote in a small bowl alongside each dessert.

TEAM UNITED KINGDOM 2010

Javier Mercado

John Costello

Chris Loder

CHEESECAKE WITH CHERRY AND PISTACHIO

Team United Kingdom's dessert for the 2010 WPTC had an unusual presentation—it was assembled in a rounded glass that was set on top of a Petri dish (yes, the kind where bacteria usually flourish) containing dry ice. The dessert itself was made of layers of Cheesecake Mousse, Pistachio Sponge, white chocolate and Cherry Jelly, tucked into the bowl in a C shape. A tart Lemon Curd and cylinder of Raspberry Ice Cream cut through the richness of the mousse. On the first day of the competition, Team U.K. had an unpleasant surprise, which left them in catch-up mode: all the ingredients for their plated dessert had somehow been stored in the freezer instead of the refrigerator. They were forced to defrost each ingredient before they could begin.

MAKES 12 SERVINGS

Pistachio Sponge

110 g (3.88 oz/3⅔ large) egg whites

70 g (2.46 oz/⅓ cup plus 2 tsp) superfine granulated sugar

60 g (2.1 oz/3¼ large) egg yolks

25 g (0.88 oz/1 Tbsp plus 1 tsp) pistachio paste

38 g (1.34 oz/3 Tbsp) cornstarch

38 g (1.34 oz/¼ cup plus 2 tsp) bread flour

1. Preheat the oven to 355°F (180°C).

2. In the bowl of a stand mixer fitted with the whisk attachment, beat the egg whites with half of the sugar on high speed to stiff peaks to form a meringue.

3. In a separate bowl, set over a saucepan of simmering water, whip the egg yolks with the remaining sugar and pistachio paste until airy and thick, as for a sabayon. Fold into the meringue.

4. Sift together the cornstarch and bread flour and fold into the meringue mixture. Spread out the batter in a silicone baking mat–lined sheet pan. Bake for 10 minutes, until set. Cool completely.

Cheesecake Mousse

720 g (25.39 oz/3⅓ cups) cream cheese, softened

4 vanilla beans, split lengthwise and seeds scraped

150 g (5.3 oz/8 large) egg yolks

210 g (7.4 oz/1 cup plus 2½ tsp) granulated sugar

18 g (0.63 oz/9 sheets) gelatin (gold grade), bloomed and melted

360 g (12.69 oz/1½ cups plus 2½ tsp) heavy cream

1. In the bowl of a stand mixer fitted with the paddle attachment, mix the cream cheese with the vanilla bean seeds on medium speed.

2. In a large bowl set over a saucepan of simmering water, whisk together the egg yolks and sugar to a stiff sabayon. Whisk in the melted gelatin. Continue to whisk until the mixture is cool. Fold the sabayon into the cream cheese mixture.

3. In the bowl of a stand mixer fitted with the whisk attachment, whip the heavy cream on high speed to soft peaks. Gently fold the whipped cream into the cream cheese mixture.

4. Scrape the mousse into twelve 7-in- (17.8-cm-) long x 2¼-in- (5.7-cm-) wide *C* shape silicone molds and freeze until set.

Lemon Curd

Finely grated zest of 2 lemons

105 g (3.7 oz/⅓ cup plus 1 Tbsp plus 2¼ tsp) freshly squeezed lemon juice

180 g (6.35 oz/3½ large) eggs

120 g (4.23 oz/½ cup plus 1 Tbsp plus 2 tsp) superfine granulated sugar

75 g (2.64 oz/½ stick plus 1⅓ Tbsp plus 1 tsp) unsalted butter

1. In a saucepan, combine the lemon zest and juice over high heat and bring to a boil. Remove from the heat.

2. In a bowl, whisk together the eggs and sugar. Whisk this mixture into the lemon juice and cook over medium-low heat, stirring constantly, until thickened. Remove from the heat and add the butter, mixing it in with an immersion blender. Cool the lemon curd, then cover and refrigerate until ready to use.

Cherry Jelly

400 g (14 oz/3½ cups) frozen Bing cherries

200 g (7 oz/¾ cup plus 2 Tbsp) cherry purée

60 g (2.1 oz/¼ cup plus 2½ tsp) superfine granulated sugar

5 g (0.17 oz/1 tsp) freshly squeezed lemon juice

11 g (0.38 oz/5½ sheets) gelatin (gold grade), bloomed and drained

1. In a saucepan, combine the frozen cherries with the cherry purée over high heat and bring to a boil. Continue to boil for about 2 minutes. Stir in the sugar and lemon juice and return to a boil, stirring. Remove from the heat, add the drained gelatin, and stir until dissolved. Cool, then cover and set aside at cool room temperature until ready to use.

Raspberry Ice Cream

53 g (1.86 oz/¼ cup plus 1 tsp) superfine granulated sugar

5 g (0.17 oz/2¼ tsp) ice cream stabilizer

327 g (11.53 oz/1¼ cups plus 1 Tbsp plus 2 tsp) whole milk

33 g (1.16 oz/⅓ cup) nonfat dry milk

148 g (5.2 oz/⅔ cup plus ¾ tsp) heavy cream

36 g (1.26 oz/3 Tbsp plus 2 tsp) glucose powder

230 g (8.1 oz/1 cup) raspberry purée

4 g (0.14 oz/1 tsp) freshly squeezed lemon juice

1. In a small bowl, combine the sugar with the ice cream stabilizer.

2. Pour the milk into a saucepan and place over medium heat. When the mixture reaches 86°F (30°C), add the dry milk, then the sugar and stabilizer mixture. When the temperature reaches 105°F (40°C), add the cream and glucose powder and stir to combine. When the mixture reaches 185°F (85°C), cook for 2 minutes more, then cool down rapidly over an ice-water bath. Allow the base to mature for 2 hours in the refrigerator.

3. Stir the raspberry purée and lemon juice into the base and process with an immersion blender. Process the base in an ice cream machine according to the manufacturer's instructions.

4. Scrape the ice cream into twelve 7-in- (17.8-cm-) long x ¾-in- (2-cm-) wide acetate tubes. Freeze until ready to plate.

ASSEMBLY

White chocolate, tempered
Green food coloring

1. Tint the white chocolate a pale green color and spread thinly onto a 7 x 1¼-in (17.8 x 3.17-cm) acetate transfer sheet. Allow to set slightly, then place, chocolate side down, onto a strip of Pistachio Sponge of the same size. Set into a cup to form it into an open circle shape and allow to set completely. Repeat to form 11 more shapes.

2. Spoon some Lemon Curd into each of 12 serving glasses. Top with one of the chocolate-lined Pistachio Sponge shapes. Nestle a strip of the Cheesecake Mousse on top of each sponge, then a smaller strip of the Cherry Jelly. Lean a strip of the Raspberry Ice Cream against each dessert.

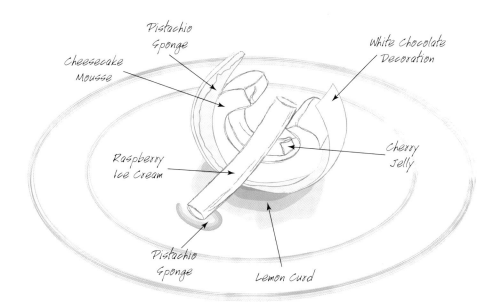

| Kaushik Chowdhury |
| Keith Taylor |
| Melynda Gilmore |

CITRUS OLIVE OIL CAKE

WITH VANILLA-MINT PANNA COTTA AND BERRY GELÉE

For the 2010 World Pastry Team Championship, Team USA topped off their plated dessert with a tuile shaped like a paper airplane that a child might make. The main components of the dessert included a Citrus Olive Oil Cake, paired with a Vanilla-Mint Panna Cotta filled with a red berry gelée and a citrus sauce. A pretty Raspberry Florentine filled with Citrus Jalapeño Sorbet lies just under the whimsical tuile.

MAKES 8 SERVINGS

Citrus Olive Oil Cake

200 g (7 oz/1 cup) granulated sugar

Finely grated zest of 4 lemons

1.67 g (0.06 oz/¼ tsp) salt

181 g (6.38 oz/¾ cup) plain full-fat yogurt

161 g (5.68 oz/¾ cup) extra-virgin olive oil

150 g (5.3 oz/3 large) eggs

182 g (6.4 oz/1½ cups) all-purpose flour

2.5 g (0.08 oz/½ tsp) baking soda

2.5 g (0.08 oz/½ tsp) baking powder

1. Preheat the oven to 350°F (175°C).

2. In a bowl, whisk together the sugar, lemon zest, and salt. Add the yogurt, olive oil, and eggs and whisk until well blended.

3. Sift together the flour, baking soda, and baking powder in a bowl, then stir into the wet mixture just until blended.

4. Spread out the batter in a silicone baking mat–lined sheet pan and bake for 12 minutes, until set. Cool completely.

Vanilla-Mint Panna Cotta

680 g (23.98 oz/2¾ cups plus 3 Tbsp) heavy cream

168 g (5.92 oz/¾ cup plus 1 Tbsp plus 1½ tsp) granulated sugar

1 vanilla bean, split lengthwise and seeds scraped

10 g (0.35 oz/3 Tbsp) fresh mint leaves

6 g (0.21 oz/3 sheets) gelatin (silver grade), bloomed and drained

1. In a saucepan, combine the cream, sugar, and vanilla bean seeds and pod over medium-high heat and bring to a gentle boil. Remove from the heat and add the mint. Cover and allow to infuse for 15 minutes.

2. Strain the mixture, return it to the stovetop, and reheat until hot. Add the drained gelatin and stir until dissolved. Pour the mixture into a ridged, 5 x 10-in (12.7 x 25.4-cm) rectangular mold to a depth of ¼ in (6.3 mm) and freeze until firm.

Berry Gelée

750 g (26.45 oz/6⅔ cups) fresh raspberries

600 g (21.16 oz/5⅓ cups) fresh strawberries, washed and hulled

125 g (4.4 oz/⅔ cup) granulated sugar

9 g (0.31 oz/4½ sheets) gelatin (silver grade), bloomed and drained

1. In the top of a double boiler, combine the raspberries, strawberries, and 100 g (3.5 oz/ ½ cup) of the sugar and cook, stirring occasionally, until the sugar is dissolved and the berries release their juices.

2. Strain the mixture, then add the drained gelatin and the remaining 25 g (0.88 oz/2 Tbsp) sugar into the juice, and stir until dissolved.

3. Unmold the set Vanilla-Mint Panna Cotta and fill the ridges with the gelée. Refrigerate until set.

Citrus Jalapeño Sorbet

453 g (15.97 oz/1¾ cups plus 2 Tbsp plus 2¼ tsp) water

453 g (15.97 oz/2¼ cups) granulated sugar

6 g (0.21 oz/2 tsp) sorbet stabilizer

1 whole jalapeño pepper

680 g (23.98 oz/2¾ cups plus 1 Tbsp) freshly squeezed orange juice

75 g (2.64 oz/¼ cup plus 2¼ tsp) freshly squeezed lemon juice

1. In a saucepan over high heat, bring the water to a boil and stir in the sugar and stabilizer. Remove from the heat, add the jalapeño, and allow to infuse for 5 minutes.

2. Remove the jalapeño from the mixture and stir in the orange and lemon juices. Process in an ice cream machine according to the manufacturer's instructions. Freeze.

Citrus Sauce with Zest

227 g (8 oz/¾ cup plus 3 Tbsp) freshly squeezed orange juice

28 g (1 oz/1 Tbsp plus 2¼ tsp) freshly squeezed lemon juice

57 g (2 oz/3 Tbsp plus 2¼ tsp) Grand Marnier

170 g (6 oz/¾ cup plus 1 Tbsp plus 2 tsp) granulated sugar

1.6 g (0.058 oz/½ tsp) powdered pectin

Finely grated zest of 1 orange

Finely grated zest of 1 lemon

Finely grated zest of 1 lime

1. Preheat the oven to 200°F (94°C).

2. In a saucepan, combine the orange juice, lemon juice, and Grand Marnier and bring to a boil over medium-high heat.

3. In a small bowl, combine the sugar and pectin, add to the juices, and cook, whisking, until thickened. Remove from the heat and cool. Cover and refrigerate until ready to use.

4. Sprinkle the orange, lemon, and lime zests onto a silicone baking mat–lined sheet pan and dry out in the oven for about 20 minutes. Process in a spice grinder and set aside until plating.

Raspberry Florentine

300 g (10.6 oz/2½ sticks plus 1 Tbsp plus 1 tsp) unsalted butter

150 g (5.3 oz/⅓ cup plus 2 Tbsp plus ½ tsp) glucose syrup

450 g (15.87 oz/2¼ cups) granulated sugar

7 g (0.24 oz/2¼ tsp) powdered pectin

30 g (1.05 oz/¼ cup) all-purpose flour

130 g (4.58 oz/½ cup plus 1 Tbsp) raspberry purée

20 g (0.7 oz/1 Tbsp plus 1 tsp) water

1. Preheat the oven to 325°F (163°C).

2. In a saucepan, combine the butter and glucose and cook over medium-high heat until the butter is melted, stirring frequently. Remove from the heat.

3. In a small bowl, combine the sugar with the pectin and add to the glucose mixture, stirring to combine. Add the flour, raspberry purée, and water and whisk to combine. Bring the mixture to a boil, whisking frequently.

4. Spread out the batter in a silicone baking mat–lined sheet pan and bake until bubbly. While still warm, cut into 4 x 1½-in (10 x 3.8-cm) rectangles and curve lengthwise.

Vanilla Tuile

156 g (5.5 oz/1⅓ cups plus 2¼ tsp) confectioners' sugar

85 g (3 oz/¾ stick) unsalted butter

100 g (3.5 oz/3⅓ large) egg whites

113 g (4 oz/¾ cup plus 3 Tbsp) all-purpose flour

4 g (0.14 oz/1 tsp) pure vanilla extract

1. In the bowl of a stand mixer fitted with the paddle attachment, cream together the sugar and butter on high speed. On low speed, gradually add the egg whites, flour, and vanilla, mixing just until blended. Let the batter rest in the refrigerator for at least 2 hours.

2. Preheat the oven to 350°F (175°C).

3. Spread the batter over a triangle-shaped stencil with two 3-in (7.6-cm) sides and one 2-in (5-cm) side, placed on a silicone baking mat–lined sheet pan, to make 12 tuiles. Bake for about 5 minutes, until set. While still warm, form each tuile into a paper airplane shape.

ASSEMBLY

1. Spread a thick line of the Citrus Sauce with Zest lengthwise down each of 12 rectangular plates. Sprinkle with the dried citrus zest. Cut the Citrus Olive Oil Cake into 5 x 1¼-in (13 x 3-cm) rectangles and arrange one of the cake rectangles on top of the sauce on each plate. Top each cake rectangle with the Vanilla-Mint Panna Cotta, cut to the same size. Top with a Raspberry Florentine, then a quenelle of the Citrus Jalapeño Sorbet. Garnish with a Vanilla Tuile.

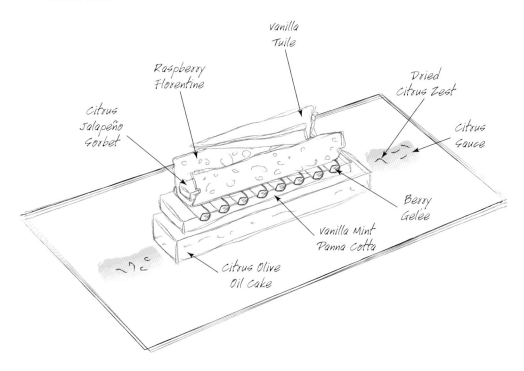

BASIC GARNISH RECIPES

Basic Sugar Syrup for Blowing and Pulling

MAKES 2.1 KG (74 OZ/6 ½ CUPS) SUGAR SYRUP FOR BLOWING AND PULLING

1.36 kg (3 lbs/6¾ cups) granulated sugar

454 g (1 lb/scant 2 cups) filtered water

284 g (10 oz/¾ cup) glucose syrup

10 drops tartaric acid

1. Place the sugar and water in a 3-quart nonreactive pot over high heat. Before the mixture boils, remove any scum that forms on the surface.

2. Once the mixture comes to a boil, scrape the glucose and tartaric acid into the mixture, stirring gently to combine. At this point, the ideal boiling time is 15 minutes per pound of sugar, although this will depend on the humidity and altitude of your cooking environment. Cook the syrup to 320°F (160°C) as fast as possible and with the heat concentrated directly under the center of the pan. Once the sugar reaches temperature, it is ready to use.

Ganache (Medium-bodied)

MAKES 833 G (29.38 OZ/3¼ CUPS) GANACHE

500 g (17.6 oz) bittersweet chocolate, finely chopped

333 g (11.76 oz/1⅓ cups plus 2 Tbsp) heavy cream

1. Place the finely chopped chocolate in a medium bowl.

2. In a saucepan, bring the cream just to a boil over medium-high heat. Immediately remove from the heat and pour over the chocolate in the bowl, covering it completely. Let stand for 2 minutes to melt the chocolate. Using a spatula, stir until smooth and emulsified. Cool completely before using.

Sablé Cookies

MAKES ABOUT 36 COOKIES

260 g (9.17 oz/2 cups) all-purpose flour

2.45 g (0.08 oz/½ tsp) baking powder

2 g (0.07 oz/¼ tsp) salt

140 g (4.9 oz/1 stick plus 2 Tbsp) unsalted butter, at room temperature

100 g (3.5 oz/½ cup) granulated sugar

50 g (1.76 oz/1 large) egg

4 g (0.14 oz/1 tsp) pure vanilla extract

50 g (1.76 oz/1 large) egg, whisked with 10 g (0.35 oz/2 tsp) water for egg wash

1. In a medium bowl, gently whisk together the flour, baking powder, and salt; set aside.

2. In the bowl of a stand mixer fitted with the paddle attachment, cream the butter and sugar on high speed until light, about 3 minutes. Add the egg and vanilla and beat until blended. While mixing on low speed, add the flour mixture and mix until combined.

3. Transfer the dough to a work surface and gently knead it a few times until smooth. Wrap in plastic wrap and refrigerate for at least 1 hour, or until firm.

4. Preheat the oven to 350°F (177°C). Line two baking sheets with silicone baking mats.

5. On a lightly floured work surface, roll out the dough to a thickness of ¼ in (1 cm). Using a 2-in (5-cm) round cutter, cut out cookies and arrange them on the prepared baking sheets. Refrigerate the cookies for 15 minutes.

6. Brush the cookies with the egg wash, then, using the back of a paring knife, draw a crisscross pattern on the tops of the cookies. Bake for 12 to 14 minutes until golden brown. Transfer to a wire rack and cool completely.

SOURCES

ALBERT USTER IMPORTS

Hundreds of chocolate and pastry products for the professional chef, from chocolate couvertures to fruit purées to decorative marshmallow sheets. They also carry Albert and Ferran Adrià's Texturas line of products for molecular gastronomy.

800-284-3663
www.auiswiss.com

AMADEUS VANILLA BEANS

Bulk vanilla beans and extracts from Madagascar, Tahiti, Indonesia, and other exotic locales.

310-670-9731
www.amadeusvanillabeans.com

AMORETTI

A large variety of pastry flavorings and ingredients including extracts, compounds, pastes, flavor sprays, pralines, and nut flours.

800-266-7388
www.amoretti.com

ATECO

Cake decorating supplies and an assortment of pastry tools, including pastry tips and the iconic Ateco cake turntable.

800-645-7170
www.atecousa.net

BOB'S RED MILL

A variety of grains and flours, including almond flour, hazelnut flour, and semolina.

13521 SE Pheasant Court
Milwaukie, OR 97222
800-349-2173
www.bobsredmill.com

CHICAGO SCHOOL OF MOLD MAKING

Food-grade silicone, sphere molds, ready-made pastry molds, silicone noodles, silicone mold making tool kits, mold knives, clink boards, and many other tools relating to casting chocolate and sugar.

46 Lake Street
Oak Park, IL 60302
708-660-9707
www.chicagomoldschool.com

GUITTARD CHOCOLATE COMPANY

This American-based chocolate maker produces chocolate in syrups, blocks, large chips, and powders for pastry chefs. The E. Guittard Collection vintage product line contains blends and single bean varietal chocolates, including the Quevedo, a varietal couverture chocolate from Ecuador, the Chucuri from northwest Colombia, the Sur del Lago couverture chocolate from western Venezuela, and the Ambanja from Madagascar.

10 Guittard Road
Burlingame, CA 94010
800-468-2462
www.guittard.com

JB PRINCE

Professional-grade bakeware, silicone molds, chocolate molds, tart pans, and other pastry equipment.

36 E. 31st Street, 11th Floor
New York, NY 10016
800-473-0577
www.jbprince.com

KEREKES

Full line of professional pastry, baking, and cake decorating supplies, including chocolate molds and supplies, silicone molds, and large and small bakery equipment.

6103 15th Avenue
Brooklyn, NY 11219
800-525-5556
www.bakedeco.com

LA TIENDA

Albert and Ferran Adrià's Texturas line of products for molecular gastronomy, including Calcic, Agar, Citras, Algin, and Gluco.

1325 Jamestown Road
Williamsburg, VA 23185
888-331-4362
www.tienda.com

NIELSEN-MASSEY VANILLAS

High-quality vanilla beans, vanilla paste, powder, and extract in Madagascar bourbon, Tahitian, Mexican, and organic varieties. They also have a line of pure extracts in a variety of flavors, including coffee, chocolate, almond, and rose.

1550 Shields Drive
Waukegan, IL 60085-8307
847-578-1550
www.nielsenmassey.com

PARIS GOURMET

A leading specialty food importer and distributor, Paris Gourmet carries a wide range of pastry ingredients including chocolate from Cacao Noel, Weiss, and Valrhona; pastry ingredients from Pastry 1; molecular gastronomy ingredients from Cuisine-Tech; Gahara vanilla beans and extracts; Ravifruit fruit purées; and Mec3 gelato and pastry ingredients.

800-727-8791
201-939-5656
www.parisgourmet.com

PASTRY CHEF CENTRAL

This Internet site offers a large line of professional-grade baking tools (i.e., molds and rings), small equipment (i.e., scales, knives, and cake decorating equipment), and pastry ingredients.

561-999-9483
www.pastrychef.com

PASTRYITEMS.COM

This Web site offers a variety of pastry equipment, including baking mats, sheet pans, pastry cutters, and molds.

1304 Beckett Court
Bel Air, MD 21014
443-417-8854
www.pastryitems.com

PFEIL & HOLING

Bakery equipment and supplies, including cake pans, cake rings, Flexipan molds, food colorings, gum paste, and fondant tools.

58-15 Northern Boulevard
Woodside, NY 11377-2297
718-545-4600
www.cakedeco.com

PREGEL

Ingredients for gelato, sorbetto, frozen yogurt, semifreddo, and pastries, including bases, fillings, toppings, nut pastes, and dextrose.

4450 Fortune Avenue NW
Concord, NC 28027
704-707-0300
www.pregelamerica.com

SWISS CHALET

Large selection of pastry ingredients, including Felchlin chocolate, fondant, marzipan, flavorings and extracts, fruit purées, gels, and glazes.

800-347-9477
www.scff.com

THE PERFECT PURÉE OF NAPA VALLEY

A large line of excellent-quality fruit purées and concentrates for use in pastry components, from sauces to mousses to ice creams and sorbets.

2700 Napa Valley Corporate Dr., Suite L
Napa, CA 94558
800-556-3707
707-261-5100
www.perfectpuree.com

TUILE TIME CULINARY TEMPLATES

A large selection of excellent-quality half-sheet pan–size tuile templates made of high-density polyethylene. The templates are stain-proof and meet FDA and USDA certification for food processing.

954-907-7292
www.culinarytemplates.com

VALRHONA

This French chocolate maker produces a line of premium chocolate favored by top pastry chefs around the world. Valrhona pioneered the production of high-quality chocolate from carefully controlled sources, and started the trend of featuring the percentage of cocoa solids in chocolate. They also have led the way towards chocolate from known origins and quality beans. The product line includes chocolate confectionery, flavored and plain chocolate bars, and bulk chocolate in bars or pellets.

888-682-5746
www.valrhona.com

WILLPOWDER

A variety of pastry products specializing in molecular gastronomy.

866-249-0400
www.willpowder.net

ACKNOWLEDGMENTS

Many thanks to Christine McKnight, my editor at John Wiley, for taking on this project and guiding me through it with such expertise and grace.

Thanks to Michael Schneider for creating the finest pastry competition in the world, and inviting me to write this book.

Thanks to sharp-eyed copy editor Leah Stewart and senior production editor Marina Padakis Lowry for making the production process go so smoothly.

Thanks to Alison Lew and Gary Philo of Vertigo Design NYC for designing such a beautiful book.

Thanks to the following pastry chefs for their input in the Plating for Points chapter:

Sébastien Canonne

Stephen Durfee

Robert Ellinger

Ewald Notter

Kathryn Gordon

En-Ming Hsu

Francisco Migoya

Gilles Renusson

Thanks to the following companies for their loyal support of the championship over the years:

Felchlin Chocolates

Swiss Chalet Fine Foods

Nielsen-Massey Vanillas

Guittard Chocolate

Godiva Chocolatier

Albert Uster Imports

Amoretti

Dobla

French Pastry School

Irinox

Taylor Freezers

Carpigiani

ABS Bakery Equipment

Spring Induction Cookware

Dessert Professional magazine

Thanks to Maia Cheslow for her dogged assistance in tracking down chefs and editing the recipes.

Thanks to Lisa Baron, Matt Stevens, Juanita Jeys, Tina Korting, and Zach Townsend for their generous and invaluable help with many aspects of this project.

Thanks also to Charlie Williams, Jeff Dryfoos, and Elizabeth Hall for their support and help at the event.

INDEX

Page numbers in *italics* indicate illustrations; Plated dessert titles are **boldfaced**

L

M

R

S

U

T

V